ENGLISH EAST INDIA COMPANY AND THE LOCAL RULERS IN KERALA

English East India Company and the Local Rulers in Kerala

A CASE STUDY OF ATTINGAL AND TRAVANCORE

LEENA MORE

MANOHAR
2026

Cover illustration: The North East View of Angengo Fort on the Coast of Malabar.
From: A Voyage to the East Indies. Containing Authentic Accounts of the Mogul Government in General, the Viceroyalties of the Decan and Bengal by John Henry Grose. Published by S. Hooper, London, England 1772.
Source: https://commons.wikimedia.org/wiki/File:The_north_east_view_of_Angengo_Fort_on_the_coast_of_Malabar_Wellcome_L0038350.jpg

First published by IRISH in 2003
Reprinted 2025, 2026

ISBN 978-93-6080-089-5

Published by
Ajay Kumar Jain *for*
Manohar Publishers & Distributors
4753/23 Ansari Road, Daryaganj
New Delhi 110 002

Cover design by Manoj Kumar

Printed and bound in India

Dedicated

To My Parents

CONTENTS

Foreword

Trade and commerce, especially maritime trade in the Indian Ocean Regions brought about considerable changes in the socio-political milieu in the pre-industrial era. Several groups of traders entered into the region and established their sway not only on trade but also on politics. The role played by pepper produced on the Malabar coast has a long story to tell. Pliny testifies that the use of pepper had become a fashion in Europe. Pepper from the Malabar coast was an important item in the Indo-Roman sea-borne trade. Alaric, the leader of Visigoths spared Rome in A.D. 408 by obtaining as part of the ransom 3,000 pounds of pepper.[1] It was in search of pepper that the undaunted admiral of the Indian ocean, Vasco da Gama came to Calicut in 1498 facing manifold difficulties. The Portuguese obtained a number of papal bulls to keep away other European traders and nationals from entering into the Indian Ocean Regions and posing a challenge to them in trade in pepper and other spices. The Portuguese declared pepper as an item of royal monopoly. Charles I of England, while marrying Princess Catherine of Braganza got a few quintals of pepper besides the Bombay islands as dowry from the Portuguese.

The English established the East India Company at the dawn of the seventeenth century and reached the Malabar coast for starting trade in the products of Malabar among which pepper occupied the prime of the place. Being aware of the importance of pepper trade on the Malabar Coast, the Dutch sent their spy to India, namely John Linschotten who succeeded in collecting detailed information about the various aspects of trade and sent the material to Holland. Allured by pepper and other spices of the Malabar coast the Dutch too established the Dutch East India Company (VOC). They captured some of the Portuguese vessels

---

[1] Gibbon, chap. xxxi

and employed a Jurist to justify their claims.It was in this respect that Hugo Grotius brought out, in the first decade of the seventeenth century, his famous tract on the *Freedom of Sea* challenging the monopoly established by the Portuguese. In course of time they ousted the Portuguese from the Malabar coast by 1663 and occupied all the former Portuguese factories and fortresses there besides establishing a few more counters for trade. The Danes too wanted a share in the trade in pepper and so they reached the Malabar coast and started exporting it to Denmark. Subsequently the French came to the Western coast of India and opened counters in Calicut and other places. Finally they settled in Mahe with a view to collecting pepper from the neighbouring areas of production. Most of the foreign merchants and companies contacted the local rulers for signing contracts for large volume of pepper and also to establish their settlements in strategically important places. The local rulers used the opportunity to get arms and ammunitions to fight against their enemies. Just as the foreign merchants and companies tried to fish in the troubled waters, the local rulers too shifted their allegiances from one to the other looking for profit.

The present work of Dr. Leena More dwells on the way in which the local rulers of Attingal and Travancore reacted to the overtures made by the English East India Company and how they dealt with other powers like the Dutch and the French. The study also deals with the relations among the local rulers. The Queen of Attingal invited the English to her realm and extended necessary facilities for trade. But the nobility under her did not permit the English to continue amicably for long time. The author discusses the Attingal revolt in detail and throws considerable light on the various aspects of the relations of the Queen with the English East India Company. The rise of Travancore under Martanda Varma dealt a fatal blow to the realm of Attingal, which was annexed, to Travancore in due course of time. The feudatories like the *Pillas* and the *Madambees* were taught a lesson by the ruler of Travancore. He himself set up a commercial department for conducting trade and commerce and found necessary funds to raise a standing army to destroy the power of the *Pillas* and *Madambees*. He made use of the military expertise of the English, the Dutch and the French in realizing his target. The author underlines the fact that MartandaVarma expiated for the atrocities committed by him through extraordinary demonstration of devotion to Sri Padmanabha of whom he became a vassal and *dasan*. The attacks of Hyder Ali and Tippu from the North disturbed the expansion of Travancore . But the English managed at times to divert their attention by attacking the areas under Hyder Ali and Tippu. The period covered by the study is a crucial one in the history of Travancore in particular and history of South India in general.

The author has very carefully collected the relevant original sources for the work from various repositories in India and abroad and analyzed them systematically. The editorial board of IRISH took keen interest in assessing the work, which sheds great light on the history of foreign contacts of Malabar in the wider sense and appreciated the work since it breaks new grounds for the researchers. Those who are fed up with the interpretations of interpretations will find it a welcome work useful to widen the scope of future research. Therefore the IRISH has great pleasure in placing the book before the readers for their constructive comments and objective evaluation.

Pondicherry
12 March 2003

Professor K.S.Mathew
Director
IRISH

Preface

We have many interesting studies done on the history of Kerala and the interaction of the Malabaris with the West Europeans. Yet, much remains to be done. In this work, I intend to shed some light on certain aspects of the activities of the English East India Company in the kingdoms of Attingal and Travancore during the late seventeenth and eighteenth centuries when the Europeans gained a foothold in this region.

In order to attain the preceding objective, I have mainly relied on the original records, documents and old Books, available at the various Archives and Libraries located in India, France and England. I must acknowledge most gratefully the prompt assistance rendered by the Directors and Staff of Tamil Nadu Archives, Chennai, Connemara Library, Chennai; Adayar Theosophical Library, Chennai; Secretariat Library, Chennai; Madras University Library, Chennai; Maharashtra State Archives, Mumbai; Bombay University Library, Mumbai; Royal Asiatic Society, Mumbai; National Archives, Delhi; Nehru Memorial Museum Library, Delhi; India Office Library Records, London; Bibliotheque Nationale, Paris; Centre d'etudes de l'Inde, Paris; and the History Department Library, University of Calicut.

This work would not have seen the light without the solid support and guidance of Professor Dr. Sreekumaran Nair, of Calicut University . I profusely thank Professor M.G.S Narayanan, present Chairman of the Indian Council of Historical Research, Delhi and former Head of the Department of Calicut University for his useful advice, Dr. K.K.N. Kurup, Vice Chancellor of Calicut University, and Dr. Kunjhali, Head of the Department of the Calicut University. I express my profound gratitude to Professor K.S.Mathew former head of the history department of Pondicherry University and Honorary Director of the Institute of Research in

Social Sciences and Humanities of Thallessary (Kerala) for his constant encouragement and advice.

I owe a lot to my father and mother and other family members, who were a great source of encouragement in the accomplishment of this work. My husband Dr.J.B.P More, historian and social scientist, living in Paris and Deputy Director of Institute for Research in Social Sciences and Humanities (IRISH) based at Tellicherry, went through the whole manuscript and offered many valuable suggestions, apart from editing it. I thank him for that. Also I thank my little boy Rahul who wanted me to complete this work quickly, so that he can find more time to talk and play with me.

Leena More

Introduction

The reconstruction of the history of Kerala or Malabar has never been an easy task. This seems to be largely due to the fact that systematic compilation of historical information was not available. As a result one is left with no other alternative but to rely on various other sources like epigraphy, archaeology and literary works. One has to also look for references on Kerala in the literatures of other languages like Sanskrit and Tamil and also Chinese, Arabic and Persian. But from the sixteenth century onwards, we have ample references to Kerala and valuable accounts on its history and society in the Portuguese, Dutch, Danish, English and French language records.

Our intention in this book is to concentrate on the west European records, especially those in English, taking also into account the other sources whenever they are relevant and reconstruct the history of south Malabar, with a special focus on the Attingal and Travancore kingdoms, during the latter part of the seventeenth century and the whole of the eighteenth century, upto the period when Travancore was subordinated to the British as a Princely State. It is not our intention to deal with the history of north Malabar in this book for the simple reason that it seems to have a somewhat distinct historical evolution and its own traditions, quite distinct from south Malabar in many ways though united by a common language, Malayalam. It is not also our intention in this book to go into the ancient history of Kerala, which is still not unravelled to the fullest extent and where there seems to exist a lot of controversies and debates. Nevertheless it will be useful to have a peep into it, and also into the period leading to the modern era, before tackling our prime objectives.

Pre-Modern Kerala and the arrival of west Europeans :

Tradition holds that the land of Kerala as it exists today was retrieved from the sea by some miracle or superhuman activity. Though the truth or untruth of this contention remains to be settled, yet it is now an almost established fact that a sizeable portion of Kerala as we know it today was part of the ancient Chera kingdom of the Sangam age, which lasted until about 500 A.D.[1] In fact the Chera kingdom was part of what was then known as *Tamilagam.*[2] Though much work from the historical and sociological point of view has been done and is being done on the Pandya and Chola kingdoms of Tamilagam, yet scholars have shown hitherto less interest on the Chera kingdom or empire that existed during the Sangam age.

The Ramayana and the Mahabharata mention Kerala, though incidentally. Alexander's invasion of India in 327 B.C. seems to have led to a more accurate knowledge of the sea route and trade between the western coast of India and west Asia. The Greek ambassador, Megasthenes, who came to India in the fourth century B.C. speaks of Kerala and also of its king. The edicts of Emperor Ashoka emphasizes its status as a premier kingdom of the peninsula.[3] Clearer indications emerge from the 'Periplus' written about 80 A.D., that ships from the west coast of India actually traded with Arabia. In A.D.414, the Chinese pilgrim, Fa-Hien mentions about his meeting with the people of 'Po-lo-mon' in a ship bound from Java to Canton. Po-lo-mon was a name used in those days by the Chinese to designate the west coast of India from Quilon or Kollam to the mouth of the Indus. This would imply that the Chera kingdom which flourished on the south-west coast of India upto about 500 A.D. with its capital at Tiruvanchikulam (probably Cranganore) would have had direct trade relations with west Asia and south-east and east Asia. This seems to give the lie to the contention that Indians did not travel across the seas to foreign countries for purposes of trade during this period.[4]

In the sixth century A.D., Cosmas Indicopleustes mentions various regions of the Indian continent from Ceylon to Sind. He refers to Malé or Malabar where pepper was grown. Huan-Tsang who travelled to India in 629 A.D., characterises the Malabar country as Mo-la-loi-ts'a. In the seventh century, Jesujabius of Adiabene, who died in 660 A.D., had mentioned Colon (Quilon) in a letter written to Simon Metropolitan of Fars. He contends that India extended from the coast of the kingdom of Fars to Colon. In the itineraries compiled by the Chinese geographer, Kia Tam between 785 and 805 A.D., we find that the Chinese had trade relations as far as Kulam (Quilon) on the Malabar coast. So it appears probable that Quilon had come into existence in the seventh century itself or even before, contrary to the popular notion that Quilon was founded only in 825 A.D.[5] It also appears probable that there must be some etymological connection between Tiruvanchikulam of the Sangam age and Kulam or Kollam or Quilon of the subsequent period. So it will not be unreasonable to suppose that Kollam must have been derived from Tiruvanchikulam, though we cannot confirm it for sure at present.

In the ninth century, we have the Arab accounts of Souleyman and Masudi and a commentary on Souleyman's accounts by Abu Zeydul Hassan of Siraf, which identifies Kulam Malé (Quilon) as the calling place for Chinese and Arab ships and as the most considerable port of southern India. Abu Zeyed Hassan also mentions the country of Komari, which he says was situated on the continent of India on that side which faces the country of the Arabs. Ibn Khurdadbha also mentions Komari and Mali, ie., Malabar. It also appears that the Arabic work, Sindbad the Sailor' belonged to the ninth century, in which reference has been made to Malabar, where pepper was found, and to Comorin.[6]

Closely following Masudi, the Arab, Ibn Haukal also visited Malabar. Al-Idrissi of Morocco refers to Kulam Mali (Quilon) and Manibar (Malabar) during the first half of the twelfth century. A Spanish Jew, Benjamin of Tudela reached Malabar in the early part of the twelfth century and visited Chulam (Quilon), which he describes as a well organised port, where pepper, cinnamon, ginger and other spices were grown. Al-Kazwini writing during the second half of the same century, describes Kulam (Quilon) as a large city in India. We know from the Chinese Chu-K'u-fei that until the end of the twelfth century at least, Chinese junks never ventured beyond Ku-lin (Quilon). Chau Ju Kua also mentions 'Ku-lin'(Quilon). He had also noted the insatiable demand for presents in foreign lands, which must have included Malabar.[7]

Rashiddudin of Persia refers to Malibar (Malabar) and Kulam (Quilon) in the early part of the thirteenth century. Abul Feda of Damascus situates Quilon at the extreme end of the pepper country of Malabar in the thirteenth century. During the latter part of the thirteenth century, the Venetian traveller Marco Polo who visited Malabar had mentioned in his accounts about the kingdom of Coilum (Quilon), where he met some Christians and Jews, besides Hindus. He asserts that the king of Quilon was independent and was not a tributary to anyone.[8]

Friar Odoric Di Poderone who travelled in the East and India between 1316 and 1330 mentions about Malabar and its pepper forest towards the south. Friar Jordanus was at Quilon as a missionary sometime before 1328, in which year he was nominated as Bishop of the See of Kaulam (Quilon), latinised as Columbum. Friar John de Marignolli also arrived at Quilon probably between 1339 and 1347.[9]

Ibn Batuta of Tangiers in Morocco visited Mulaybar (Malabar) and Calicut where he found Chinese junks bound to China during the fourteenth century. He not only mentions the products of Malabar like pepper, ginger and spices, but also asserts that the country was sub-divided into numerous principalities. He says that Malabar extends from Sandapur to Kawlum (Quilon). Ibn Batuta also notes that in Malabar, except in Calicut, whenever a ship is destroyed, whatever is saved it goes to the treasury.Ibn Batuta also visits Quilon which he holds to be one of the most beautiful places in Malabar with magnificent bazars. He asserts that of the whole country of Malabar, Quilon lies nearest to China and to it travel the Chinese for the most part. He adds that the Muslims were honoured and respected in Quilon and that the king of Quilon resided in Quilon itself.[10]

Though some interesting studies have been done on what is claimed to be the second Chera kingdom or more exactly the kingdom of the Perumals, that existed between 800 A.D. and 1300 A.D., yet much remains to be done. However, this kingdom would have certainly developed in the course of time its own characteristics. It appears that the confrontation with the Cholas in the eleventh and twelfth centuries had brought about the dislocation of the Chera kingdom, which resulted in the splitting up of the Chera kingdom into several independent principalities during the subsequent centuries. As a result the power of these principalities and kingdoms and their kings and chiefs grew. Many of these principalities traded independently with merchants hailing from China, the Arab heartlands and Persia.[11]

It appears that generally the Chera kings were never absolute monarchs in the strict sense of the term. They never seem to have attempted to concentrate all powers in their hands. In fact, institutions like the *nattukuttam* or the village assemblies, were playing such a pivotal role in the collective life of the people, that no ruler Chera or otherwise could dispense with them and their role in the society. In fact, they seem to have exercised a restraining influence on the ruler or king and the latter never really seems to have tried to curtail or eliminate their power and influence, until at least the modern period.[12]

It is also generally admitted that in Kerala there were always several chieftains and princes in control of their respective regions, very much restricted in area, subject only to the Chera monarch. But when this monarchy collapsed due to Chola onslaught, the various chieftains and princes assumed full control of their dominions. This had given birth to the emergence of several independent kingdoms and rulers, not answerable to any higher authority.[13]

The contribution of the Cheras to classical Tamil literature is truly remarkable. But the examination of many west coast inscriptions seems to have revealed that it was only from the ninth century A.D. that speech-forms which could be described as Malayalam begin to appear in the inscriptions. A fourteenth century Sanskrit tract known as *Lilatilakam* seems to distinguish Malayalam from Tamil. In the thirteenth century, Marco Polo had noted that the inhabitants in the kingdom of Quilon spoke their own language, which was different from that of the Pandyan country.[14]

In the works of Cherusseri Nambuttiri, the fifteenth century poet, we have the first symptoms of a new style. But it was Tunjattu Ramanuja alias Raman Eluthachan, who invented the modern Malayali alphabet, most probably in seventeenth century. He seems to have also been the author of *Keralolpatti*, which deals with the origin and evolution of Kerala, a largely legendary and mythological piece of literature.[15]

Duarte Barbosa writing about 1510 refers to the tradition of the conversion of Cheraman Perumal to Islam and the division of his kingdom. Joao de Barros, Diogo Di Couto and Camoens had given a slightly different version of this legend in the 16th century. Shaikh Zainuddin writing during the second half of the sixteenth century also differs somewhat in his version of the conversion of Cheraman Perumal to Islam and the division of his kingdom.[16]

Pachu Moothathu in his *Kerala Vishesha Mahatmaya* has stated that a certain Bana Perumal, who is identified as a Chera, had converted to Buddhism and gone to China, after dividing the Malayalam country into 18 divisions.[17] However, there are several other versions regarding the exile of the Chera king and the division of his kingdom before his departure.

Mandelso visiting Malabar during the first half of the seventeenth century records that sometime back the whole of Malabar was under one king, called Sarama Perimal (Cheraman Peurmal). He became a Muslim and divided his kingdom into three, Cannanore, Cochin and Chaul, subject to the sovereignty of Calicut. Alexander Hamilton relates another version according to which the Zamorin of Calicut went to Mecca only after the Portuguese arrived, after dividing his country into four between his four nephews as Callifree, Calicut, Attinga and Coil, extending from Decully to the river of Nagapatam. Later during the last quarter of the 18th century, Fra Paolina San Bartolomeo gives another version of the Cheraman Perumal legend. According to this version, in the tenth century, Cheraman Perumal had several sons and nephews that he decided to distribute the land of Kerala between them. He however divided Kerala into three categories of kingdoms and principalities. The first category which was the most important consisted of Calicut and Quilon. The second category consisted of 14 principalities which included Tanore, Kodungaloor and Kayamkulam, while the third category of 12 principalities was allotted to the local chiefs. More recently, MG.S.Narayanan had attributed the partition of Kerala and the conversion of the last Cheraman Perumal to 1122-24 A.D. He puts forward the view that the partition of Kerala was nothing but the transformation of districts of the Perumal kingdom into independent principalities.[18]

However from the preceding versions, it become quite clear that Cheraman Perumal's abdication and the division of his kingdom do not rest on any sound historical foundation. As a result it will only be judicious to accept Sewell's conclusion with regard to *Keralolpatti*, which is as follows:

> '---The Keralopatti is a very fair specimen of a native attempt at history. It may contain germs of truth, and it certainly embodies a number of scattered traditions, but in the attempt to weave them into a connected story the author is signally unsuccessful.'[19]

As a result, the traditions related to the conversion of Bana Perumal to Buddhism or Cheraman Perumal to Islam still needs to be elucidated.

Nicolo Conti, a Venetian of noble origin, was in Malabar in the early part of the fifteenth century. He visited Coloen (Quilon), which he describes as a noble city with a circumference of 12 miles. He calls the country Melibaria (Malabar), where ginger, pepper, brazil wood, cinnamon and jack fruit were found. He then arrives at Cochym (Cochin). After visiting Colungaria (Cranganore) and a few other places, he reaches Calicut, which he describes as a noble emporium for all India.[20]

During the 1440s Abd-er-Razzak of Herat arrives at Calicut port where he met the Zamorin. He calls Malabar as Melibar. Like Chau Ju Kua and Ibn Batuta, he draws our attention to the practice on the Malabar coast (except at Calicut) where when a vessel sets sail for a certain point, and suddenly is driven into another roadstead, the inhabitants under the pretext that the wind has driven it there, plunder the ship.[21]

The Russian, Athanius Nikitine, also known as Khoza Issuf Khorassan arrives at Calicut during the 1470s after passing through Gujarat. He describes Calicut as the port for the whole Indian sea, where pepper, ginger, cloves, spices, etc., were found in cheap rate. He does not visit Quilon, but goes straight to Ceylon. The Genoese traveller, Hieronimo Di Santo Stefano arrives at Calicut at the close of the fifteenth century. This shows the great importance of Calicut on the western coast of India during this period. Like Nikitine, Hieronimo travels straight to Ceylon, without visiting Quilon. This only shows that Quilon was fast losing its importance during this period.[22]

The historic landing of Vasco da Gama, hailing from Portugal, a small and upcoming maritime nation of western Europe, in May 1498 at Kappad or Kappakadavu near Calicut in north Malabar heralded a new era in the history of the entire Malabar region and also the Indian continent.[23] Vasco da Gama's arrival at Calicut was not an accident. He seems to have had the intention to arrive at Calicut and not anywhere else on the western coast because Calicut by the close of the fifteenth century had become the greatest trading centre on the western coast of India, outstripping Quilon, which as we know from the preceding was the principal port and trading centre, known especially for its pepper in the merchant world. This was a time when Muslims of Turkish-Mongol origin were the rulers in northern India. They seem to have made no attempt to confront the Portuguese. In fact Malabar was far away from the territories under their control. The Portuguese had actually established a factory in Calicut in 1500 itself.[24]

Instead it was left to the Mappila Muslims of Malabar, who were of Indo-Arab breed or local converts to Islam and allies of Malabar kings like the Zamorin of Calicut, to confront the Portuguese military might. When Ludovio Di Varthema arrived at Malabar during the first decade of the sixteenth century, he still found Quilon bristling with merchants trading especially in pepper.[25] As early as 1501, the rulers of Quilon and Cannanore had contacted Cabral to strike an alliance with the Portuguese king. As a result Cabral visited Cannanore, but not Quilon. At Cannanore he took aboard his ship the ambassador of the king of Cannanore, along with those of Quilon and Cochin and sailed to Lisbon to meet the King of Portugal, Emmanuel I. The Zamorin of Calicut perceived this alliance of Cochin, Quilon and Cannanore with the Portuguese as a threat to his sovereignty and superiority in the region.[26]

At this time the heir to the throne of Quilon was a minor, and the Queen Dowager governed the country as Regent. In 1502, the Queen sent a message to the Portuguese Captain-major at Cochin to buy pepper in her place. This she did with the concurrence of her headmen and principal merchants. She apprised the Portuguese that her kingdom had enough pepper to load twenty ships each year. She contended that the merchants of Cochin actually came to Quilon to buy pepper and carry it through the inland waterways upto Cochin. She was therefore prepared to sell the pepper straightaway to the Portuguese at Quilon, instead of selling it to the merchants of Cochin, under the same conditions that prevailed in the latter place. Though the Portuguese saw the advantage in buying pepper directly from Quilon, they hesitated because they thought that this might offend their faithful ally, the King of Cochin. So they asked the Queen to contact the King of Cochin directly, who in fact was related to her. This the Queen did. As the King of Cochin derived some duties levied on the transport of pepper through the waterways, he was at first hesitant because he stood to lose these duties, if the pepper was loaded directly at Quilon. But the Queen of Quilon managed to obtain permission from the King of Cochin to load pepper at Quilon under certain conditions. Thus the Portuguese established themselves at Quilon. They gave the Queen a present of a handsome mirror, and corals and a large bottle of orange-flower water and for her headmen thirty scarlet baret-caps, and thirty dozen of knives with sheathes. The Queen in her turn sent a present to the Portuguese captain-major of several silk stuffs of various colours, which were made in the country and very fine white stuffs of very great width.[27]

The Queen generally lived in the interior of the country. She appointed a Council of leading men to manage the affairs of the Quilon State. It appears that these men were bribed by the Zamorin of Calicut to oppose the establishment of the Portuguese in that place. But fearing Afonso d'Albuquerque, neither the Queen nor her headmen dared to offer any resistance. Instead, Afonso was given a hearty reception in the name of the Queen and was permitted to establish a factory there towards the end of the year 1503 or in January 1504.[28]

It also appears that the Rajah of Cochin was subject to the Rajah of Calicut, until sometime after the arrival of the Portuguese. The Rajah of Cochin had actually befriended the Portuguese with the intention of extricating himself from Calicut's influence. As a result the Portuguese had established a factory there in 1500 itself. The Portuguese finding a precious ally in the Rajah of Cochin, vanquished the Zamorin of Calicut and his Mappilla allies and annihilated their immense trade interests in the region to their own benefit. As a result the Portuguese obtained permission to build a fort and church at Cochin and became virtually the masters of that place. Muslim accounts claim that this church was built on the site of a mosque which was destroyed earlier by the Portuguese on the seashore. Albuquerque approached the Rajah of Cochin with even a request to convert to Christianity. Barbosa in his turn asserts that the King of Cochin had a very small country and was not really a king before the Portuguese arrival. It is interesting to note however, as pointed out by K.S.Mathew, that many Mappillas had trade relations with the Portuguese at Cochin. In 1510, the Portuguese acquired Goa and by this conquest established their naval supremacy along the Malabar coast.[29]

In 1505, the Portuguese factor at Quilon, Antonio de Sa, Padre Fr.Rodrigo along with 26 other Portuguese were killed in an uprising by the Mappillas of Quilon. The Portuguese church known as 'Our Lady of Mary' church or the San Thomé church, was destroyed. On coming to know of this, three Portuguese ships and three caravels were sent to Quilon, with order to procure lading and not avenge the killings.[30]

In 1515, Lopo Soares succeeded Afonso d'Albuquerque as Governor of the Portuguese territories in India. He concluded a treaty with the King of Quilon and with the headmen on 25th september 1515, by which the latter agreed to rebuild at his own expense, in the same style and in the same place where it had formerly stood, the church of San Thome, and to endow it with the same revenues as it originally possessed. He also promised to favour and protect the Christians as previously; to pay 500 *bahars* of pepper in three years instalments; to let the Portuguese have all the pepper and other spices they might require at the same price as they paid for them in Cochin, and to export no drugs or spices without their consent. In case of war with a common enemy each party even agreed to assist each other. Besides no ships from Quilon were to enter the Sraits of Aden beyond Cape Guardafui, unless in the service of the Portuguese; and any of the King's subjects, whether Hindu or Muslim who might desire to become Christians were to be at full liberty to do so.[31]

During the year 1517, once again we hear from Portuguese accounts that there was a Queen at Quilon and that she was at war with the King of Traunzor (Travancore), a neighbour of Quilon. In the meantime, the Queen seems to have given permission to the Portuguese to build a citadel in Quilon, to the great displeasure of the Mappillas. While the Queen was absent from Quilon due to her personal engagement in the war with the Rajah of Travancore, the Mappillas seem to have tried to stop the building of the citadel. But on the return of the Queen, the Portuguese were able to complete the construction of the citadel.[32] Thus peace seems to have returned to Quilon for a short while.

However very soon in 1519, the Queen of Quilon changed her mind. Along with a neighbouring Queen whose territory bordered Comorin in the south, the Queen of Quilon tried to drive the Portuguse away. This Queen seems to be none other than the Queen of Attingal. These two Queens having combined their forces of more than 20000 men under the command of three brothers, reputed among the Nayars, declared war against the Portuguese in the month of June 1519. They got the wells poisoned to deprive the Portuguese of sweet water, attacked the citadel from all sides and killed some converted Christians who inhabited the town. It appears that there were only thirty Portuguese within the citadel, of which five were invalid, under Hector Roderie. But very soon reinforcements arrived from Cochin and many assailants were killed in the battle. The Queens realising the difficulty in storming the citadel decided to put an end to the war and sue for peace. The Portuguese immediately agreed, on condition that a fine was paid by both the Queens for not honouring the precious treaty.[33] The preceding account proves that neither the Queen of Quilon nor the Queen of Attingal were tributaries to the King of Travancore. In fact, they ruled their kingdoms independently and even joined forces whenever in need as in 1519. It is quite probable that the Queen of Quilon had sought the assistance of the Queen of Attingal in her war with the Travancore king in 1517, though we do not have records in the present state of our knowledge to prove this probable fact.

Another treaty on much the same lines as the one of 1515, was subsequently concluded on 17 November 1520 with the Queen of Quilon by Diogo Lopes de Sequeira, after an attack on the Portuguese fortress had been made. The treaty stipulated chiefly that all the pepper in the land was to be sold to the King of Portugal and nobody else.[34]

As references to Travancore, Attingal and Quilon in the early Portuguese accounts is beyond question, it is only logical to infer that these kingdoms pre-existed the Portuguese arrival, though we do not know the exact period of their origin. Quilon as we know has been referred to by foreign travellers and writers since at least the seventh century. These very same foreign travellers have failed to take note of Travancore and Attingal, probably because they did not exist or if at all they existed they were only petty states. Recently some evidence of the existence of the Venad (Travancore) kings had come to the light in the form of a literary piece known as the 'Unnilisandesam', which is believed to belong to the 14th century.[35]

In the beginning of the 16th century, Barbosa writes that the king of Quilon was called Benate-deri (Venattiri). From the French sinologist, Pauthier we learn that in the Chinese annals, the king of Koulam (Quilon) was styled as 'Pinati'. Yule concludes on the basis of information from Caldwell that 'Pinati' or 'Benate' represented 'Venadam', 'the land of Venadu', that being the name of the district to which belonged the family of the old king of Quilon, and Venadan being their regular dynastic name.[36]

At the beginning of the Portuguese era in India we hear of a small kingdom of Comori, the prince of which had succeeded to the kingdom of Kaulam (Quilon). This as Dr.Caldwell has pointed out must have been the Travancore state. But Tomé Pirès who was in the Malabar in 1511 refers to the kingdom of Travancore. He wrote that the kingdom of Travancore was bounded on one side by Quilon and on the other it ends at Cape Comorin. It is quite possible that Travancore might have emerged as a small independent kingdom from the kingdom of Comori (Cape Comorin), which Tomé Pirès has identified as a separate kingdom, bounded on one side by Travancore and on the other extending upto Kayal. He even asserts that the prince of Comori became King of Quilon on the death of the king of Quilon and that the king of Quilon had the most land and most people and his domains ended in the King of Vijayanagar's land in the east.[37]

In 1514, Afonso d'Albuquerque makes a reference to the Rajah of Travancore. It appears from his accounts that Travancore was originally the name of a village, south of Trivandrum, from which the ruling dynasty of the kingdom which is known by that name has been called. The true name is said to be Tiruvithenkodu, shortened to Tiruvankodu. It is also known as Tiruvithamkur.[38]

Barbosa writing around 1515 says that the Moors of Mecca went to Quilon in search of pepper. Passing southwards from the city of Quilon, Barbosa attracts our attention to a small town calld Tiramgoto (Tiruvankodu). It was originally the capital of a small state, as described by Barbosa.[39] Sewell derives Travancore from Tiruvarankodu. But Barbosa equally claims that the kingdom of Quilon extended upto Kayal and Kilakarai on the eastern coast. This practically reduces Travancore to a small peripheral state. It appears that the rulers of Quilon successfully defended thier territories upto Kayal against the Vijayanagar kings upto at least 1532. As a result, throughout the Tinnevely district inscriptions of these rulers were found. Barbosa even situates the residence of the king of Quilon at or near Kayal. Even Vasco da Gama had reported earlier that Kayal was under the rule of the Rajah of Quilon. Varthema had also affirmed that the kingdom of Quilon extended upto Kayal. So Sathyanatha Aiyer seems to have claimed with reason that during the first half of the 16th century, the Tiruvadi (Travancore) rajah, who was not to be equated with the ruler of Quilon, was a feudatory of Vijayanagar.[40]

But Barbose admits that the lord of Tiramgoto or Travancore was a kindred of the king of Quilon, but neither he nor any other Portuguese or other European, Chinese or Muslim writers of the period state that the kingdom of Quilon derived its power from Travancore, like the more recent historians like Shungoony Menon or Sreedhara Menon. As for the name Venad which is identified with Travancore, we still do not have a satisfactory explanation either of this identification or of the derivation or the meaning of the word 'Venad' But 'Venattiri' had somehow became the title of the Travancore rajas.[41]

Sreedhara Menon attempts to derive a continuity for the Travancore rajas from the second Chera or Perumal dynasty. But there is no supporting evidence from the Chinese, Arabian, Persian and European accounts.[42] Sreedhara Menon following Shungoony Menon in this respect, who more than a century earlier on the basis of tradition, not corroborated by any authentic literature, had tried to trace the origin of the Travancore rajas to the Chera Perumals and to attribute a certain degree of pre-eminence to the Travancore rajas during the fifteenth and sixteenth centuries, perhaps equal or even exceeding in power and prestige the Rajahs of Calicut. In fact Shungoony Menon himself had admitted that from 1458 to 1680, a period of about two and a quarter centuries, no detailed accounts of the sovereigns can be found except a list of their names, the dates of their accession to the throne and the period of their reign, in some inscriptions. But these names and dates even have been dismissed as unhistorical and legendary by both Caldwell and Sewell.[43]

However there seems to be no doubt in the fact that the Travancore Rajah was related to the king of Cochin. But Barbosa along with other Portuguese writers have dismissed Travancore as a small principality and accorded greater importance to Quilon. This only seems to confirm the assertions of S.Ayyangar that the rajas of Travancore were the off-springs of minor dynasties which ruled on the coast during the fifteenth century and therefore cannot claim a more ancient origin.[44]

In 1553, Barros apprises us that the kingdom of Quilon terminates at a place called Travancore.[45] All this only confirms the observations of Caldwell and Yule that the kings of Quilon, Comori and Travancore were related to one another and independent of one another at the same time. But there is nothing to prove that Travancore had any precedence over Comori or Quilon or even Cochin and the other kingdoms. If that was the case, the Portuguese would have definitely taken note of it. In fact, if we take into account the early Portuguese accounts it was the ruler of Quilon who wielded the greatest power in the region, for his domains extended upto Kayal in the east.

Merely on the basis of a few inscriptions, Venadu (from which modern Travancore is supposed to have emerged) has been identified as a district during the reign of the Chera Perumals from 800 A.D. to 1124 A.D. But these are not corroborated again by any literary evidence. Anyhow it appears certain that Venadu if at all it existed was not an independent kingdom during this period. Besides there is no mention of Attingal at all during this period. M.J.Koshy asserts again without any literary evidence that Venad rose to independent status in the 12th century. He even claims that the sovereign of this tiny principality administered the state from Quilon as his headquarters. But this again is a mere supposition.[46]

Subsequently, we find Shungoony Menon claiming independent status to the Travancore kingdom, on the basis of five inscriptions, dating from 1469 to 1532. Though inscriptional evidences is an indispensable aid to the reconstruction of history, it has been reasonably claimed that it can only give us the dry bones of history and it is the function of literary accounts to make them real and living. As a result in the absence of literary evidences, much caution needs to be exercised in dealing with materials that epigraphy affords.[47]

Besides we find Sreedhara Menon asserting that the original seat of Venad (Travancore) rulers was Quilon. M.J.Koshy in his turn supposes that Venad as an independent kingdom began its career with Rama Varma Kulasekhara, who shifted the Chera capital from Mahodayapuram to Quilon. He has thus tried in his turn to find a continuity between the Cheras and Venad. Further regarding the origin of Attingal, Sreedhara Menon asserts that Attingal estate had its origin in the fourteenth century from two princesses adopted by the Venad family from the family of Koloattiri Raja of northern Malabar. He attributes a certain independence to the territories that came under their control, but insinuated that they were ultimately subject to the Raja of Venad. As we have seen, M.G.S.Narayanan, had claimed to have identified the district of Venad under the Chera Perumals and had noted the hereditary nature of the governors of Venad. But he has not mentioned about the Ranis of Attingal during that period. It will be appropriate to quote a Dutch record here in order to understand the various claims put forward time and again by the various kings of Malabar about the extent of their territory. The record states that the different Malabar princes 'always had claims, often of great obscurity, to places in one another's territories.'[48]

However from the preceding we know for sure that there was a Queen at Quilon in 1517 who had waged war against the Raja of Travancore, probably because he was a tributary of the Vijayanagar kings. We also know that the Queen of Quilon along with the Queen of Attingal had waged war against the Portuguese in 1519. There is a great possibility that both were related to one another. Anyhow all this only shows that the various kingdoms of south Malabar were independent of one another during this period and the Queen of Quilon was certainly a much greater force to be reckoned with than the Rajah of Travancore.

However it has been elucidated on the basis of some epigraphical and also literary evidences that during the 16th and 17th centuries, the Nayakas of Madura, who were subordinate to Vijayanagar until the time of Tirumala Nayaka, launched raids into Tinnevelly and Travancore (Tiruvadidesa) and conquered territory. It appears on the basis of epigraphical evidences that the Travancore Rajas became a tributary to Viswanatha Nayaka (1526-1564) of Madura.[49] However Quilon continued to exist independently all throughout the sixteenth century. Some time during the last two decades of the 16th century, the Dutch traveller, Linschoten was in Malabar. He asserts that Malabar was divided into several kingdoms and that at Coulon (Quilon) was a Portuguese fort, where every year they lade a ship with pepper.[50]

In the course of the 16th century, the Portuguese established settlements at Goa, Daman, Salsette, Bassein, Bombay, Santhome and Hughli.[51] They also established settlements at Cochin, Quilon, Cranganore and Cannanore.[52] They had garrisoned and fortified Fort Manuel at Cochin and Fort St. Angelo at Cannanore. In Attinga or Attingal in the south of Malabar they possessed a college of Jesuits and a number of Christian churches.[53] They even imposed a monopoly over the spice trade of the Malabar coast.[54]

Along with the Portuguese colonisers came also the missionaries. The famous missionary, Saint Francis Xavier was operating in Travancore during the latter half of the 16th century. On account of his efforts, 10000 *mukkuwas* (fishermen) were converted to Christianity. Even during the lifetime of Francis Xavier, a Portuguese royal decree forbade the practice of Hinduism in Portuguese domains and commanded the destruction of Hindu idols.[55]

But the Portuguese were not merely peaceful and passive proselytisers. Their encounters with Muslims in and around their homelands in Europe, had rendered them staunchly anti-Muslim. So on the Malabar coast, whenever it was possible, they put the Muslims who were reputed to be inconvertible, to death or destroyed or secularised their mosques. As for the Hindus they baptised them forcibly by giving them Portuguese names or compelled them to eat beef or wear leather slippers.[56]

The Portuguese were generally reported to have been guilty of unspeakable acts of cruelty and barbarism, debauchery and vice. It appears that in Quilon alone, the Portuguese had forcibly converted about 12000 Muslims to Christianity. Actually in 1562, a number of Muslim traders were also forcibly converted to Christianity.[57]

The practice of forcible conversions seems to have been introduced into south-west India by the Portuguese. They were the pioneers in the art of fanaticism on the Malabar coast. The missionary, Roland Miller, a renowned specialist of Mappilla Muslims, maintains that while Islam permitted the use of force, however interpreted, there is no record of the Mappillas having engaged in any militant activity defensive or offensive, prior to the Portuguese period.[58]

We find a reference to the King of Travancore in 1609 in a letter written by the king of Spain. Later in 1662, Schouten had reported that there was an old Queen ruling at Quilon. The French traveller, François Pyrard de Laval was in Malabar during the second half of the seventeenth century. He had identified several major kings like that of Cannanore, of Badagara, of Calicut, of Tannanore, of Cochin and of Quilon and several other small kingdoms. He has also identified the king of Calicut as the greatest among them. Cochin was next in importance to him, while the other small kings controlled only small territories. They generally held the King of Calicut in respect. As for the King of Quilon who was far away from Calicut near Cape Comorin, Pyrard de Laval tells us that he maintains himself more sovereignly than others. It is strange to note anyhow that Pyrard de Laval mentions neither Travancore nor Attinga during this period, not because they did not exist, but probably because he would have considered them as relatively small kingdoms.[59]

About the same time, the Englishman John Fryer visited Malabar. He also mentions the existence of the kingdom of Quilon, Calicut, Cochin, Porcad and Cannanore. During the same period, the French traveller Thevenot writes that before Calicut shot into prominence, all the commerce was at Quilon, which had then become a little kingdom.[60]

By the dawn of the 17th century the Dutch and the English merchant adventurers had organised themselves as East India

Companies and found their way to India.[61] They soon established factories at Pulicat (1610), Surat (1616), Chinsura (1653), Cassimbazar, Baranagore, Patna, Balasore, Negapatam (1659) and Cochin (1663).[62] The Dutch East India Company actually sent its fleet under Steven Vander Hagen to Calicut.[63] The Zamorin or King of Calicut who did not very much relish the monopolistic tendencies of the Portuguese and the latter's alliance with his rival, the Rajah of Cochin, welcomed the Dutch to his territory with open arms.[64] He entered into a treaty with the Dutch to expel the Portuguese from his territories and the rest of Malabar.[65]

The Dutch however had to wait for over a century to outwit the Portuguese. In 1653, they captured Cochin.[66] They founded settlements in the southern Malabar region such as Porcad, Eddawa, Calliquilone, Quilon, Karunagapally and Tengapatanam.[67] The princes of these states did not offer any resistance to the Dutch. Instead they entered into exclusive contracts with them by which all strangers were denied trade in pepper, cinnamon, spice, timber and teak which the Dutch called 'prohibited goods'.[68] The Dutch concluded a treaty with the Kolattiri Rajah in north Malabar that gave them the monopoly of exporting pepper and cinnamon and importing opium. Thus the Dutch, supplanting the Portuguese practically maintained a monopoly of the spice trade in the East throughout the seventeenth century.

The English did not lag behind. Frustrated in their attempts to get a share of the spice trade of the Eastern Archipelago by the Dutch a few decades earlier, the English were inclined to secure the upper hand in the pepper trade of 'Malabar'. This inaugurated an era of severe competition between the Dutch and the English in south India.

Actually the pioneer English man to visit the coast of Malabar was Ralph Fitch who arrived at Cochin as early as 1588. It was in fact from Ralph Fitch, that the London merchants received first hand account of the resources of Kerala and the possibilities and prospects of trade with her.[69] But the real contact of the English with this coast began with the arrival of Captain Keeling at Calicut, with three ships on his way from Surat.[70] The English then established factories on the Malabar coast, first in Calicut and then in Tellicherry in 1684.Both were located in north Malabar.

With the defeat of the Portuguese squadron in 1612 near Surat on the west coast, at the hands of the English, the prestige of the English East India Company rose in the eyes of the Indian rulers. In January 1613, Captain Best received an imperial charter from the Mughal Emperor, granting the English Company permission to open trade at Surat, Ahmedabad, Cambaya and Goga.[71] By February 1619 the English East India Company had established factories at Agra, Ahmedabad and Broach.[72] All these were placed under the control of the President and Council of the Surat factory.

Meanwhile the Danes also founded their East India Company at Tranquebar on the Cholamandalam (Coromandel) coast and extended to Bengal.[73] In the year 1623, the Dutch overthrew the English from the spice archipelago.[74] Therefore the rivalry between these two powers in India became very intense. On the other hand, the treaty of Madrid terminated hostilities between the English and the Portuguese. Finally by the treaty of July 1654, Portugal fully accepted the rights of the English to the Eastern trade and later the treaty of 1661 enjoined the English to support the Portuguese in their actions against the Dutch in India.[75]

The English were thus on the road towards expansion. In the year 1633, a factory was opened at Balasore and another at Hariharapur, near Cuttack.[76] In the year 1639, they obtained the lease of Madras from the ruler of Chandragiri. There they built a fortified factory which came to be later called Fort St.George.This settlement was eventually raised to the rank of a Presidency in 1653.[77] In the year 1651, they opened their first commercial house in Bengal at Hughli, 25 miles north of Calcutta. Soon others were opened at Patna, Bihar and Cassimbazar in Bengal.[78] In 1661, the English settlements in India were re-organised. As a result two independent governments (President and Council) were set up at Surat and Madras. All the settlements in Bengal, Bihar were made subordinate to the Presidency of Madras.[79]

In the latter half of the seventeenth century, the English East India Company acquired the island of Bombay.[80] Bombay became so important and prosperous that in 1687 it superseded Surat as the chief settlement of the English on the west coast of India. Headquarters of the English were shifted from Surat to Bombay during the residency of John child in the year 1687.[81] On the eastern coast with the destruction of the Portuguese and Arakanese pirates in the Bengal waters, the English were able to found a settlement on the Hughli in Calcutta. In 1696, a fort was built there which was named Fort William. It was raised to the rank of a Presidency in 1709.[82] Thus by the end of the seventeenth century, the English Company had laid the foundation of the three presidencies, Madras, Bombay and Calcutta. In these settlements they were bestowed with the political responsibility of defence, maintenance of law and order and municipal administration.

Another important west European power, the French, established a factory at Surat in 1668.[83] In 1674, the French acquired Pondicherry on the Cholamandalam coast, which later on became the headquarters of the French in India.[84] They also founded trading posts at Chandernagore in 1690, Mahe on the Malabar coast in 1721 and Karaikal on the Cholamandalam coast in 1739.[85] India thus became a theatre of conflict between the west European powers. Of these powers, it was the English who eventually managed to embark upon an era of political expansion in the Indian continent. This was facilitated primarily by the decline of the Mughal empire.

Political and Socio-economic conditions :

While the west Europeans were thus establishing factories at various points of the Indian continent including its western coast, Malabar was politically fragmented into small principalities. The principal rulers in the 17th century were the Queen of Attinga, the Prince of Chenganatta, the Queen of Martinga, the King of Calliquilone, the King of Porcad, the King of Cochin, the Zamorin of Calicut, the Prince of Tellicherry, the King of Peritally, the King of Tekkenkur and the king of Badakkenkur.[86] All these principal kingdoms together with other minor principalities constituted what was known as 'Malabar'. It is strange to note that there is no mention of Travancore or Venad in the preceding list of the principal kingdoms. This implies that it was only a minor principality during this period.

Duarte Barbosa, the Portuguese writer who was at Cannanore during the early part of the 16th century used the term 'Malabar' to denote the geographical region inhabited by the Malayalam-speaking people.[87] The land of Malabar says Duarte Barbosa began from Cumbola near the mountain Dely and ends at Cape Commery (Comorin).[88] The traditional bounds of Malabar were Gokarnam in the north and Kanyakumari or Cape Comorin in the south.[89] The Ghats were its eastern boundary and the ocean its western.[90]

The Malabar people had always been heterogenous in character.The society itself was sharply divided on the basis of caste and also religion. During the period of European penetration into Malabar, the various strands of indigenous beliefs and customs collectively known to the Europeans as 'Hinduism' was the principal faith of the majority of the people. They were divided on a hierarchical caste basis.

The highest place in the hierarchy was occupied by the Nambudiris (Malabar Brahmins). Tradition holds that they did not belong to Kerala originally and that they migrated to Kerala from somewhere in the north. The Malabar Rajahs though they wielded power, were but subordinate to the Nambudiri. They especially the Rajah of Travancore spent large amounts of money for the support and comfort of the Brahmins.[91] The next in the hierarchy were the Shudras. In Malabar they were the Nairs. They were originally the lowest of the four-fold caste system, but in Malabar as there were so many divisions below them and as they were numerous and influential they were regarded as the high caste people.[92] They were the militia of the state.[93] They were sub-divided into Menon, Menoki, Muppil Nayar, Pada Nayar, Kuruppu, Kaimal, Panikkar, Kiriyatta, Mullar Ore, Kidavu, Kartavu, Eradi, Nedungadi, Vallodi, Mannadiyar and Menavalom.[94] The Nair's strength lay in their being recognised as the martial class of Malabar.

The next caste in the social pyramid were the Tiyyas. They were known by different names in the different regions. In the far south they were known as *Shanars*, in Central Travancore as *Ilavars,* from Quilon to Paravoor as *Chogans*, in Malabar as far as Calicut as *Tiyars* and still farther north as *Billavars.*[95] Tradition holds that they did not belong to Kerala but they migrated to Malabar from Ceylon.[96] They were a class of people who cultivated coconut trees.[97] This caste was the most numerous of the section of the Hindu population. The lowest rung in the social scale was occupied by the *Parayas* and the *Pulayas* or *Cheruman.*[98] These people enjoyed no privilege and were generally at the service of other castes.

The notions of caste were stretched to the extreme in Travancore. Distance between man and man was rigidly measured. The distance a Nair had to keep from a Nambudiri was arms length. The artisan castes were untouchable to the Nairs and unapproachable by twenty five paces to the Nambudiris. The *Panchamas* were unapproachable by ten paces to the artisans and twenty to the Nairs.[99] English records maintain that if the poor wretch who till the soil and reaps the grains happened accidently and ignorantly to cross a Nair in his path, the master drew his sword and killed him on the spot with impunity.[100]

Chastity was never the hall mark of many Malabar women during this period. It was customary for a Nair girl to reside with her brother and take many lovers.[101] She also enjoyed a certain position in the society because of her amorous connection with the Brahmin. The English records state that 'in this country no one enquires who the father of the child may be, neither is it considered of any consequence, all that is looked to is the mother.'[102] The Nair custom with respect to marriage was licentious in character. A Nair woman married before the age of ten. Her husband never co-habited with her.But the marriage set her at liberty to cohabit with any person that she chose of equal or higher rank. The French traveller Dellon states that the plurality of husbands had virtually exempted the Malabar women to be burnt alive along with their dead husbands as in other parts of India where a woman could have only one husband.[103]

Besides generally the women were not allowed to cover their breasts. Those women who did not yield to the wishes of the same or superior castes were looked down upon.[104] However Mr.Philips had noted in 1717 that as in many other parts of India, a widow seems to have been looked down upon in the whole of Malabar. The society held that the widow who remarried was no better than a whore. But the woman who continued to mourn the death of her husband till her death was supposed to obtain eternal happiness.[105]

Apart from the various Hindu communities, there were in Malabar, the Christians, the Muslims and the Jews. The members of the Christian community in Malabar were known as the *Nazranis* denoting their religious affinity with Nazareth.[106] They were largely converts from the various Hindu castes. Large sections of the

Muslim population were also converts, especially from the lower castes. They were known in Malabar as *Mappilas.* There was a mixture of Arab blood in many of them due to the contacts that the Arab traders had with local women since at least the 9th century.They became a major power to be reckoned with in north Malabar.Many coastal Muslims took to trade as it was generally forbidden for Hindus to cross the seas.[107]

The economy of the entire Malabar region during this period had become more and more dependent on trade with the west Europeans. It had become the habit of the rulers of the various kingdoms and principalities of Malabar to grant trading facilities to foreigners in return for the payment of customs duties and the offering of presents.[108] As agricultural production seems to have been mainly intended for local consumption, trade had gradually become the main source of revenue for the rulers. However, the economic conditions of those people placed in the lower ranks of the social scale seem to have gradually become quite appalling, due mainly to the rigid caste system, which had given rise more or less to a form of slavery, though in a restricted manner.[109] James Forbes writing in the early part of the 19th century maintains that during famine parents used to sell their children into slavery. He even stated that even when there was no famine, numerous people came to Anjengo to sell themselves or dispose of their children. He was actually horrified at the cool way in which the peasants sold their children at a very cheap rate. Fort St.George Records maintain that as early as 1696, homeless children without owners seems to have been ordered to be sold at public outcry.[110]

The Kingdoms of Attingal and Travancore:

The Kingdom of Attinga or Attingal was situated in south Malabar. It was a small principality along 60 miles of coast.[111] It was bounded on the north by the territories of the Prince of Chenganatta or Quilon, on the south by those of the King of Travancore, on the east by those of the King of Peritally and the

Ghats and on the west by the sea. Its utmost length was about 80 or 90 miles and its breadth 15 or 20.[112]

In this kingdom no male members could become sovereigns. Therefore it was called *Sree Bhagam* or sacred portion where only the woman had the right to rule.[113] The kingdom itself was situated between the kingdoms of Travancore, Berriata and Peritally, whose rulers acknowledged the Queen of Attinga's supremacy.[114] In 1693, the adjoining kingdom of Peritally was incorporated temporarily into the Attingal kingdom for want of heirs.[115]

The Attingal kingdom was comprehended under the following cantons: Attinga, the chief residence of the Queen, Capi, Travendevarong (Trivandrum) and Vavendevarong.[116] Each of these four cantons had a Pilla or chief administrator in charge of it. These cantons were further subdivided into many districts. Each district was under a *Rejadore* (Rajadurai) or magistrate. They were Cherenga, Anjenga, Mompoly, Baccon, Capi, Irvor, Illure, Baccala, Betture, Travendevarong, Brinjohn, Ruttura, Permadura, Pullecoreach, Vavendevarong, Pallichal, Cunjerata and Tonnipondet besides numerous other villages.[117]

The *Rajadurais* who were the district magistrates were answerable to the poolas. They were chosen by the community as their representatives in all matters relating to state affairs. Besides the *Pillas* and the *Rajadurais*, there was another called *Annavy*, whose work was to carry messages to and from the pillas and the neighbouring foreign powers.[118]

The administration of the country was carried out by the Queen with the help of the Pillas, the Rajadurais and the Annavy. The four main Pillas were Vanjamutta Pilla, Cuddamon Pilla, Barreba Pilla and Mandacca Pilla. Generally the Queen conferred with these Pillas to arrive at any decision concering the State. The first two were known to be very close to the Queen and wielded considerable power and influence. They were the great Pillas. On account of their influence, one could say that the Queen's power was not absolute.[119]

Generally the Queen's orders were respected and carried out not only by the Pillas of Attingal, but also by the twelve *madembees* of Travancore and the two *potas* of Peritally. The madembees and potas were the administrators and noblemen of their respective kingdoms.[120] In fact, the Attingal kingdom was the maternal house of the Rajah of Travancore and therefore the Queen of Attingal was entitled to give heirs to the Travancore kingdom. It is said that the eldest son of the Queen of Attingal was the heir apparent to the throne of Travancore and her eldest daughter was supposed to succeed her to the throne of Attingal.[121] Any failure in the direct female descent required the selection and adoption of two or more females usually from Kolathanad to assure her succession.[122]

It was supposed to be against the law for the Queens of Attingal to marry in the real sense. However it appears that she could choose two men for amorous relationship. It was customory to take one husband from the Brahmins attending the temple and the other being one of the four Pillas.The eldest daughter of the Brahmin or adopted husband was the rightful heir to the throne of Attingal.[123]

John Henry Grose in his account on the Queens of Attingal stated that in order to have a successor to the throne, the Queen chooses 'whom and as many as she pleases to the honour of her bed. The handsomest young men about the court generally compose her firaglio.'[124] He also wrote that in Attingal, it was the tradition that females do not cover their breasts. But one woman who had spent sometime with the Europeans, adopted their tradition of covering the breasts. The Queen was highly irritated by this lack of respect and ordered her breasts to be cut off to punish her for defying the customs of the country.[125]

Alexander Hamilton had written the following regarding the amorous customs of the Queen :

> 'In Anno.1685, when the present was sent, a young beautiful English gentleman had the honour to present it to her black majesty, and as soon as the Queen saw him, she fell in love with him and the next day made proposals of marriage to him but he modestly refused so great an honour. However, to please her majesty he staid at court a month or two and it is reported treated her with the same civility as Soloman did the Amazonian Queen and satisfied her so well that when he left her court, she made him some presents.'[126]

Years later, after the amalgamation of the Attingal kingdom with Travancore in 1743, Colonel James Welsh wrote

> 'I observed near the throne several naked Brahmins. Two of whom only good men were clothed in chintz and stood directly behind the Queen. These proved to be the husband of one of the former taumbratee, the other of the present Rani. In this family the boys of the elder women are always heir ---- these men though fed and kindly treated in the palace have no authority nor are they permitted to sit in the Rani's presence in public. In addition to which she may change them whenever she is tired of one by sending him away and selecting another, but only from amongst the Brahmin which very clearly proves that women bear the sway in Travencore'.[127]

During the last quarter of the 17th century, the Queen of Attingal was Aswati Tirunal Umayamma Rani. It appears that during the 1670s, a certain Aditya Varma, who was an adopted ruler from another Malabar kingdom and not the son of the Queen of Attingal, ruled at Travancore. Umayamma Rani had no male children. The tradition according to which Umayamma Rani's five male children were killed, in what was known as the

'Kalippankulam incident', has been actually disproved convincingly by Ibrahim Kunju.[128]

However Van Rheede writing in 1677 when Aditya Varma was still alive had also held the following about Travancore :

> 'His (Travancore) subjects are not bound to observe any rules, commands or whims and Council decisions of the King which are not in conformity with their laws, warfare or privileges and havenot been approved in their own district and ratifies at the meeting of their district assembles.'[129]

At the death of Aditya Varma in 1677, Umayamma Rani took over direct control of Travancore according to the custom, as Ravi Varma, the succesor of Aditya Varma was still a minor. She thus acted as Regent of Travancore till 1684, when Ravi Varma attained majority. Van Rheede, the Dutch commander at Cochin had confirmed this aspect. He even wrote the following about Umayamma Rani : 'She was of manly conduct, who makes herself as much feared and respected that no one dares to oppose her'.[130]

In spite of the above observation, it appears that Umayamma Rani was a very practical Queen. She knew that she needed the friendship and help of the Nayak of Madura probably to ward off any challenge to her power in south Malabar or simply in order to be in the good books of the Nayak to ward off a threat of invasion from him. In fact during Tirumala Nayak's reign at Madura from 1623 to 1659, Travancore had been subjected to further attacks. John Nieuhoff remarks in 1664 that the king of Travancore

> 'constantly keeps a garnison of 10000 negros(Nayars) on his eastern frontiers to secure the capital against the Nayak of Madura. So during her regency at Travancore, Umayamma Rani personally went to Tinnevelly with many rich presents to render homage to the Nayak of Madura who was on a visit there.[131]

Rama Varma attaining majority in 1684 took over the reins of Travancore from Umayamma Rani, who continued to be the Queen of Attingal. It appears that during the reign of Ravi Varma, Travancore kingdom was gradually gaining in importance and strength at the expense of the neighbouring kingdoms including Attingal and Quilon. During the regency of Queen Mangammal (1677-1706) at Madura, the new Travancore Raja Ravi Varma (1684-1718) becoming bolder probably due to the problems faced by Mangammal from the Marathas and the Mughals in her territories, refused to pay the annual tribute to the Queen of Madura. This obliged Mangammal to invade Travancore every year for the purpose of collecting the tribute, even by pillaging the country.[132]

However as Ravi Varma's power was continuously challenged by his own headmen or ministers, he seems to have been obliged to strike a bargain with the ruler of Madura by conceding a part of his dominions including the famous citadel of Kalkulam to the Nayak in return for his assistance against his ministers, known as the *Ettu Vittil Pillamars*. With such help, Ravi Varma murdered some of the ministers while others escaped or ransomed their lives. But very soon in 1697 on account of the refractory attitude of Ravi Varma, Queen Mangammal sent an expedition to Travancore under Dalavay Narasappaiya and collected all the arrears of tribute, including some arms and ammunitions and valuable presents of jewellery.[133] It is surprising to note that neither the Queen of Attingal nor the King of Quilon or any other Malabar ruler had come to the aid of the Travancore raja in his tussle with the Nayak of Madura.

With the preceding account, we are in an apt position to delve deep into the history of Attingal and Travancore kingdoms and their relationship with the English East India Company during the seventeenth and eighteenth centuries.

Notes and References

1. M.J. Koshy., *Encyclopaedia of India, Kerala*, vol.xx, New Delhi, 1994, p.26
2. M.G.S. Narayanan, *Perumals of Kerala: Political and Social conditions of Kerala under the Cera Perumals of Makotai (A.D.800-1124)*, Calicut, 1996, p.vi; Veluthat, Kesavan, 'Into the 'Medieval'- and out of it: Early South India in transition', Presidential address, Indian History Congress, 58th session, Nov.14-16, 1997
3. P.K. Parameswaran Nair, *History of the Malayalam Literature*, New Delhi, 1967, p.1; Robert Sewell, (ed.), *A sketch of the dynasties of southern India*, Madras, 1883, pp.1, 13; Rockhill & Hirth, *Chau Ju Kua...*, St.Petersburg,1911, pp.2, 5
4. Colonel Yule, (tr.&ed.), *Cathay and the Way Thither*, vol.I, London, MDCCCLXVI, p.xvvii; Rockhill&Hirth, *op.cit.*, pp.2,5; Legge, James, *Fa Hien, A Record of Buddhistic Kingdoms*, New York, 1965, pp.111-115
5. Rockhill&Hirth, *op.cit.*, pp.3, 10; M.G.S. Narayanan, *op.cit.*, pp.ix, 113; F.C. Danvers, *The Portuguese in India*, vol..I, p.72 (footnote); Paulin de Saint Barthélémy, *Voyage aux Indes Orientales, I*, Paris, 1808, p.194; Colonel Yule, *The Book of Marco Polo*, II, London, 1875, p.365 (footnote)
6. See, Reinaud, *Relations des Voyages faite par les arabes et les persans*, Paris, 1845; Reinaud, *Mémoire Géographique, Historique et Scientifique sur l'Inde*, Paris, 1845; R.H. Major, (ed.), *India in the fifteenth Century*, New York, n.d., pp.xxv, xxxiii, xxxiv; John Dowson, (ed.), *The History of India as told by its own Historians, The Muhammadan Period*, I, pp.8, 13-15; George Birdwood, *Report on the Old Records of the India Office*, London, 1891, p.107
7. John Dowson,(ed.), *Ibid.*, pp.32, 85, 90, 95; Yule, Colonel, *op.cit.* ; R.H. Major, Ibid., pp.xiv, xlv-xlviii; George Birdwood, Ibid., 1891, pp.109-110; Rockhill&Hirth, *op.cit.*, pp.15, 31, 22, 89
8. John Dowson, *Ibid.*, pp.32, 68-69; Colonel Yule, *op.cit.*, 363-365;*R.H.* Major, *op.cit.*, p.xiv
9. Colonel Yule , *Cathay and the Way thither, op.cit*, I, pp.xvii-xviii, 74,75; II, p.342; George Birdwood, *op.cit.*, pp.532-535; Colonel Yule, *The Book of Marco Polo, op.cit.*, p.365 (footnote); F.C. Danvers, *op.cit.*.
10. R.H. Major, *op.cit.*, pp.liv, lvi; Mahdi Husain, (tr.&commentary), *The Rehla of Ibn Batuta*, Baroda, 1976, pp.181, 185, 192-194

11. M.G.S. Narayanan, *op.cit.*, pp.51-70; H. Kulke, D. Rothermund, *A History of India*, London, 1992, p.123
12. M.G.S. Narayanan, *Ibid.*, p.105; Parameswaran Nair, *op.cit.*, pp.1-2; M.J. Koshy, *op.cit.*, pp.34,39
13. Parameswaran Nair, *Ibid.*, p.203; Dellon, *Nouvelle Relation d'un Voyage fait aux Indes Orientales,* Amsterdam, MDCXCIX, pp.82-88
14. A.C. Sekhar, *Evolution of Malayalam*, Poona, 1953, pp.2-3; Parameswaran, Nair, Ibid., pp.14-15; Yule, Colonel, *op.cit.*, p.363
15. Robert Sewell, *op.cit.*, pp.55, 95; Parameswaran Nair, *Ibid.*, pp.49,113
16. M.G.S. Narayanan, *op.cit.*, p.2; M.J. Rowlandson, (tr.), *Tuhfat al Mujahideen,* London, 1833, pp.50-56
17. Robert Sewell, *op.cit.*, p.57
18. M.G.S. Narayanan, *op.cit.*, p.x; Paulin de Saint Barthélémy, *op.cit.*, pp.312-313; A. de Wicquefort(tr.), *Voyages Célèbres et remarquables fait de Perse aux Indes Orientales,* by Mandelso, Amsterdam, 1727, p.269
19. Robert Sewell, *op.cit.*, p.57
20. R.H. Major, *op.cit.*, pp.lxvii, 17-20
21. *Ibid.*, pp.lxviii-lxxiv, 13-14; John Dowson, (ed.), *op.cit.*, V, pp.98-99
22. R.H. Major, *Ibid.*, pp. 4, 5, 8-20
23. Kappad is a hamlet 18 kilometres north of Calicut
24. F.C. Danvers, *Report to the Secretary of State for India----*, London, 1892, p.2
25. M.J. Rowlandson, *op.cit.*; Roland Miller, *Mapilla Muslims of Kerala,* Madras, 1976; Badger, George Perry, (ed.), *The Travels of Ludovico Di Varthema...*, New York, n.d., p.180; Simon Goulard, (tr.), *Histoire de Portugal...*, Paris, 1587, p.79
26. Abbé Guyon, *Histoire des Indes Orientales, Anciennes et Modernes, vol.1,* Paris, 1699, pp.368-369
27. F.C. Danvers, *The Portuguese in India,* vol.1, London, 1894, p.101; Simon Goulard, (tr), *op.cit.*, p.79; Stanley J. Henry, *The Three Voyages of Vasco Da Gama...*, New York, MDCCCLXIX, pp.348-354
28. F.C. Danver, *op.cit.*, p.101; Simon Goulard, *Ibid.*, p.79
29. K.S. Mathew, *Portuguese Trade with India in the 16th century,* Delhi, 1983, pp.100-103, 175, 210-211; Badger(ed.), *op.cit.*, p.260(footnote); M.J. Rowlandson, *op.cit.*,; Roland Miller, *op.cit.*,; John Dowson, (ed.), *op.cit.*, VIII, p.385; M.L. Dames, (tr.&ed.), *The Book of Duarte Barbosa,*

I, London, 1989, pp.xliii-xliv; II, p.94; W.W. Hunter, *A History of British India,* I, London, 1899, pp.126-127

30. F.C. Danvers, *op.cit.,* p.121
31. *Ibid.,* p.336; F.C. Danvers, *Report to the Secretary of State for India...,* London, 1892, pp.8-10; Badger, *op.cit.,* p.271(footnote)
32. Simon Goulard, (tr.), *op.cit.,* p.315
33. *Ibid.,* pp.348-349
34. F.C. Danvers, *Report to the Secretary of State for India---, op.cit.,* p.10
35. M.J. Koshy, *op.cit.,* p.16
36. Colonel Yule, *op.cit.,* p.368 (footnote); M.L. Dames, *op.cit.,* II, p.262
37. Yule Colonel, *Ibid.*, p.372; Tomé Pirès, *The Sumo Oriental, 1512-1515,* London, 1967, pp.xviii, pp.66, 80-81
38. Colonel Yules, & Burnell, *Hobson-Jobson---,* London, 1903, p.938
39. M.L. Dames, *op.cit.,* II, p.3
40. *Ibid.,* pp.102, 120, 121, 123 (footnote), 124; Robert Sewell, *op.cit.,* p.97; Arthur Morelet, (tr.), *Journal du Voyage de Vasco Da Gama,* Lyon, MDCCCLXIV, p.126; Sathianada Aiyer & Krishnaswami Aiyangar, *History of the Nayaks of Madura,* Oxford, 1924, p.120
41. M.L. Dames, *op.cit.*, II, p.262
42. Sreedhara Menon *Kerala District Gazeteers,* Trivandrum, 1964, p.87; Geneviève Bouchon, *L'Asie du Sud à l'époque des Grandes Découvertes,* London, 1987, III, p.17
43. Robert Sewell, *op.cit.,* pp.55, 97-98; Bishop Caldwell, *A History of Tinnevely,* New Delhi, 1982, pp.251-252; see Menon Shungoony, *A History of Travancore, Delhi,* 1984
44. Srinivas Aiyangar, 'Tamil Studies', *Journal of ANNAMALAI Unversity,* 21, 1957, pp.153-154
45. Colonel Yule, *op.cit.,* p.930; João de Barros, *Decadas da Asia,* vol.I, Lisboa, 1778, pp.ix, 1
46. M.G.S. Narayanan, *op.cit.,* pp.102-103; M.J. Koshy, *op.cit.,* p.31 ?
47. Sathianada Aiyer, *op.cit.,* pp.38-39; Shungoony Menon, *op.cit.,* pp.34-35
48. Sreedhara Menon, *A Survey of Kerala History,* Kottayam, 1967, p.190; M.G.S. Narayanan, *op; cit.,* p.104; Mohibbul, Hasan, *History of Tipu Sultan,* Calcutta, 1951, p.156
49. Sathianada Aiyer, *op.cit.,* p.120

50. A.C. Burnell, *The voyage of John Huygen Van Linschoten to the East Indias,* I, London, MDCCCLXXXV, pp.71, 277
51. Ramakrishna Mukherjee, *The Rise and the Fall of the East India Company,* Berlin, 1957, p.59
52. James Forbes, *Oriental Memoirs,I,* London, 1834, p.187
53. Anjengo Factory Records, 1704-1749, Simon Cowse, Anjengo to the Court of Directors, June 1704, p.5; J.B. Aquarone, *João De Castro, Gouverneur et Vice-roi Des Indes Orientales (1500-1548), I,* Paris, 1968, p.231
54. J.B. Aquarone, *João De Castro, Ibid.,* pp.211-212
55. Pierre, *Robert De Nobili, Apôtre des Brames,* III, Paris, 1931, p.255; K.S. Latourette, *A History of the Expansion of Christianity,* III, New York, 1971
56. S. Delacroix, (ed.), *Histoires Universelles des Missions Catholiques- Les Missions Modernes,* II, Paris, 1957, p.44
57. Roland Miller, *op.cit.,* p.70; K.S. Latourette, *op.cit.,* p.25; Abbé Guyon, *Histoire des Indes Orientales---,* vol.I, Paris, 1699, pp.371-373
58. Roland Miller, Ibid., p.77
59. Colonel Yule, *op.cit.,* p.938; *Livros des Moncoëõs,* Lisboa, 1869, p.57; R.C. Reneville, *Revueil des Voyages de Schouten de la Compagnie des Indes Orientales,* vol.VII, Amsterdam, 1725, p.2; Du Val(ed.), *Voyage de François Pyrard de Laval,* Paris, 1679, pp.263-264
60. John Fryer, *A New Account of East Indies and Persia...,* I, London, MDCCCCIX, pp.132, 141, 144; S. Sen, *Indian Travels of Thevenot and Carreri,* p.124
61. Peter Auber, *An Analysis of the Constitution of the East India Company and of the Laws passed by Parliament,* London, p.ix
62. Ramakrishna Mukherjee, *op.cit.,* p.108
63. P.C. Alexander, *The Dutch in Malabar,* Annamalai, 1946, p.4
64. *Ibid.*
65. *Ibid.*
66. Nagam Aiya, *The Travancore State Manual,I,* Trivandrum, 1906, p.306
67. *Ibid.,* p.306; James, Forbes, *op.cit.,* p.212
68. Anjengo Factory Records, 1704-1749, Simon Cowse, Anjengo to the Court of Directors, June 1704, p.5
69. R.C. Prasad, *Early English Travellers in India,* Delhi, 1971, p.36

70. It was on this voyage that Sir Thomas Roe came as an Ambassador to the court of Emperor Jehangir. For details of his embassy see William, Forster, (ed.), *The Embassy of Sir Thomas Roe to Court of the Great Mogul 1615-1619,* Nandeln, 1899, 1967

71. Ramakrishna, Mukherjee, *op.cit.*, p.108; see also Maurice Collins, *British Merchant Adventurers,* London, 1942, p.16

72. See details in William Forster, (ed.), *op.cit.*, pp.93-100

73. John Bruce, *Annals of the Honourable East India Company,I,* London, 1810, p.136

74. Brian Gardner, *The East India Company,* London, 1971, p.39

75. Ramakrishna Mukherjee, *op.cit.*, p.99

76. Richard Burn, (ed.), *The Cambridge History of India, IV,* London, 1937, p.73

77. Edward Thornton, *History of British Empire in India,I,* London, 1841, p.73; Factory Records, G, India Office Library Records, p.49

78. Richard, Burn, *op.cit.*, p.306

79. *Ibid.*

80. A.B. Keith, *A Constitutional History of India, 1600-1935,I,* London, 1841, P.73; Bombay was initially a Portuguese settlement but it was ceded in the year 1661 to King Charles II of England as part of the dowry for marrying the Portuguese princess Catherine. In 1668, the King handed it over to the East India Company on payment of an annual rent of 10 pounds – Factory Records, G, India Office Library Records, London, p.5

81. George Forrest, (ed.), 'Selections from the despatches and other state papers preserved in Bombay Secretariat, Home Series',I, Bombay, 1887, p.xxii

82. Factory Records, G., India Office Library, London, p.ix

83. Ishwari, Prasad, *India in the Eighteenth Century,* Allahabad, 1973, p.65

84. *Ibid.*

85. *Ibid.*, pp.65-66

86. Anjengo Factory Records, 1704-1749, Simon cowse, anjengo to the Court of Directors, June 1704, p.3

87. Duarte Barbosa, *The Book of Duarte Barbosa* (tr.by M.L.Dames), II, London, 1621, pp.1,6. Barbosa was the secretary of the Portuguese factory in the Malabar port of Cannanore from 1500-1517

88. Duarte Barbosa, *A Description of the Coasts of East Africa and Malabar,* (tr. By Henry E.J.Stanley), London, 1767, p.101

89. R. Francis, Burton, *Goa and the Blue Mountains,* London, 1851, p.186

90. Fra Paolina da San, Bartolomeo, *A Voyage to the East Indies,* (tr.by Willima Johnstone), London, 1800, p.102

91. E.H. Nolan, *The Illustrated History of the British Empire in India and the East from the Earliest Times to the Suppression of the Sepoy Mutiny in 1859,* London, n.d., p.160; Shungoony Menon, *A History of Travancore,I,* Delhi, 1878, 1984, pp.55-57

92. Samuel Mateer, *Land of Charity,* London, 1871, pp.34-35

93. Anjengo Factory Records, 1704-1749, Simon Cowse, anjengo to the Court of Directors, June 1704, p.6

94. Willam Logan, *Malabar,I,* Trivandrum, 1887, 1981, p.12

95. Samuel Mateer, *Native Life in Travancore,* London, 1883, p.83

96. Francis Day, *The Land of Perumals,* Madras, 1863, p.319

97. Canter Jacob, Visscher, *Letters from Malabar,* Madras, 1862, p.57

98. Francis Buchanan, *A Journey from Madras through the countries of Mysore, Canara and Malabar,* Madras, 1870, p.67

99. P. Thomas, *Christians and Christianity in India and Pakistan,* London, 1954, p.9

100. Foreign Secret Department, 1804, Macaulay, Travancore to Bombay, 25 July 1800, p.336; Dellon, *op.cit.,* p.123

101. Ward and Conner, *Geographical and Statistical Memoir of the Survey of Travancore and Cochin States,* Travancore, 1863, pp.70-71

102. Foreign Secret Department, 12 December 1809, p.48

103. Francis Buchanan, *op.cit.,* p.411; Dellon, *op.cit.,* p.139

104. Elamkulam Kunjan, Pillai, *Kerala Charithrathile Iruladanja Edugal,* Kottayam, 1953, 1957, pp.160-161

105. Philips, *Account of the relgion, manners and learning of the people of Malabar in the East Indies,* London, 1717, p.28

106. P. Thomas, *op.cit.,* p.9

107. Roland, E., Millar *op.cit.,* p.30; Sreedhara, Menon, *A Survey of Kerala History,* Kottayam, 1967, p.100

108. Bombay leter copy books outwards, Bombay letter received, 1694, John Brabourne, Betture to John Gayer, Bombay, 29 July 1694, pp.6-7

109. James Forbes, *op.cit.*, II, pp.228-29; Francis, Buchanan, *op.cit.*, p.67; Samuel, Mateer, *op.cit.*, p.302; Francis, Day, *op.cit.*, p.183
110. Diary and Consultation Book of Fort St.George, 1696, 2 July 1696, p.85
111. John Biddulph, *The Pirates of Malabar and an English woman in India two hundred years ago,* London, 1907, p.271
112. Anjengo Factory Records, 1704-1749, Simon Cowse to court of Directors, June 1704, p.5. Prince of Chenganatta was also known as Prince of Desinganad or Quilon.
113. Samuel Mateer, *op.cit.*, p.123
114. Anjengo Factory Records, 1704-1749, Simon Cowse to court of Directors, June 1704, p.5
115. *Ibid.*, p.6
116. John Wallis, 'A short Treatise by way of essay of Attinga 1727', 7 September 1727, p.10. This treatise is not found in any of the Archives in India. The present author located it from India Office Library Records, London
117. *Ibid.*
118. *Ibid.*, p.12
119. *Ibid.*
120. Bombay letters received, 1697, John Brabourne, Anjengo to John Gayer, Bombay, 27 August 1697, p.8.
121. Edward Ives, *A Voyage from England to India,* London, 1773, p.192
122. *Maclean's Manual of Administration of the Madras Presidency,* Madras, 1938, p.36
123. John Grose, Henry, *A Voyage to East Indies,* London, 1757, p.386; John Wallis, *op.cit.*, p.10
124. Henry John, Grose, *op.cit.*, p.386
125. John Grose, Henry, *Voyage aux Indes Orientales,* London, MDCCCVIII, pp.350-351
126. Alexander Hamilton, *A New Account of the East Indies,* London, 1728, 1930, p.184
127. James Welsh, *Military Reminiscences,II,* London, 1830, pp.144-146
128. Ibrahim Kunju 'Umayamma Rani, First Woman ruler of Venad', *Journal of Kerala Studies,* 11 March 1975, II, Part I, p.12
129. Henrick Adriaan Van Rheede, *Memoir written in the year 1677 A.D.*, Madras, 1911, p.32

130. *Ibid.,* pp.17-18

131. Sathianad Aiyer, *op.cit.,* pp.44-45, 53-54, 62, 66, 80, 87, 93, 96, 120, 207-209, 314; Sreedhara, Menon, *op.cit.,* pp.239, 242, 243

132. Sathianada Aiyer, *Ibid.,* pp.207-209; Sreedhara Menon, *Ibid.,* pp.242, 243

133. *Ibid.*

Chapter 1

Attingal and the English

Initial Overtures to the English

The second half of the seventeenth century saw the west European powers in stiff competition with one another on the Malabar coast in order to obtain a monopoly or a greater share of the trade in the various kingdoms and principalities of the region. More than anything else this was due to the fact that the coast was known to be one of the largest, if not the largest producer and supplier of pepper in the world.

The kingdom of Attingal, located almost in the extreme south of Malabar, though it produced large quantities of pepper, yet was less productive than Peritally to its east and Quilon in the north and also Porca and Cochin. Attingal hardly yielded more than 500 or 1000 *candies* of pepper even in the most plentiful season.[1] The greatest quantity of pepper in the Attingal kingdom was produced in its southern parts, while the northern districts of Eddava, Baccala and Bettura yielded no pepper. Whatever pepper was found in the latter northern districts was the product of Peritally and Quilon. In fact, the king of Peritally and that of Quilon were responsible to a great extent for the availability of a large quantity of pepper in Attingal for purposes of trade.[2]

But the Dutch and the Danes had already established themselves at Paru and Eddawa respectively and commanded all pepper coming from the north to Attingal.[3] As early as 1659, they entered into a treaty with the ruler of Quilon, by which they obtained exclusive monopoly of spice trade at Quilon. In the year 1663, they had also concluded a treaty with the Rajah of Porca or

Purakad for the delivery of pepper and ginger and obtained permission to build a factory at Purakad.[4]

On the other hand the English, having earlier lost the spice trade of the Eastern Archipelago to the Dutch and wanting to find an alternative source of supply, sent explorative missions to ascertain the feasibility of establishing trade in various parts of the Malabar country. However, here too, the English had to contend with the Dutch to obtain a share in the pepper trade. Exclusive possession of pepper became a fixed target in the Dutch policy on the Malabar coast and they were extremely reluctant to allow the English any part of it. They tried their best to obstruct English trade wherever possible.[5]

The growing rivalry between the Dutch and the English threatened the state of comparative peace in Malabar. The English would have probably wanted to establish a settlement at a place abounding in pepper and out of the Dutch influence. This would have led them to choose the Attingal Queendom. During this period, Aswati Tirunal Umayamma was the Queen of Attingal. She was a monarch in her own right. Owing to the abundant supply of pepper in Attingal, its Queen was known as the 'pepper Queen'.[6]

Until the arrival of the English, the Queen had no other European power with whom she could trade other than the Dutch, who held a monopoly of Malabar spice trade. The arrival of the English provided her with a new opening to shake off her dependence on the Dutch. She was quick to seize the opportunity provided by the English to dispose off her pepper, knowing fully well that the English were at loggerheads with the Dutch. Consequently in the year 1678, the Queen of Attingal herself sent an invitation to the English(at Calicut)to open a factory in her territory.[7]

Following the Queen's invitation, the English factory broker, Verdaman Beca was sent to Attingal on a mission. But since the prospect was found to be precarious, the idea of settling in Attingal was abandoned. The English arrived at a similar decision in 1681 too.[8] According to a letter written to London in the same year, the reason for abandoning the project to settle in Attingal was that they had to contend with several mighty princes, who were the *Pillas* or *Pillaimars,* the administrators of the country, apart from the Queen of Attingal. This was thought to hamper their trade irreversibly. Then there was the constant opposition from the Dutch. As a result, the English refrained from settling in Attingal. But they did not completely cut off their contacts with Attingal.[9]

In 1684, John Child, the President at Surat and Governor-General of the Company's possessions in the East, ordered the Company to procure as much pepper from Attingal as the Queen could supply. The Queen was delighted by this development and welcomed the move.[10] The sudden interest of the English in the Queen of Attinga's country, and the Queen's positive attitude towards them were viewed with suspicion by the Dutch at Cochin. They warned the English to keep away from Attingal as they claimed to possess exclusive trade contracts with not only the Queen of Attingal, but also with the Rajah of Travancore and other Malabar princes.[11]

At that time the English were not prepared to back out of Attingal. As the Dutch, following the Portuguese, had restricted the movements of Malabar trading vessels without passes issued by them, the Dutch thought that by denying passes to the Queen's subjects ie., the Malabar merchants, who were mainly Muslims and depriving them thus of their commerce, they could turn the latter against the English and force them to leave the country. Later, they even went to the extent of seizing English ships going to the shore for pepper and declared that in four years time there would not be one Englishman in India.[12] But the Queen had other ideas in her mind which went against Dutch expectations. She renewed her invitation to the English to settle in her country. The English reported this invitation to the Surat Council.[13]

Though the offer was tempting, yet the English had to counter Dutch claims and their opposition had the possibility of compromising peace in the region and peace was essential to carry on trade profitably. Few months later, the Queen once again sent signals to the English factory at Calicut desiring a settlement.[14] At that two Englishmen, Daniel Acworth and Travers were sent to meet the Queen. She promised them protection and free trade.[15] They purchased pepper and decided to construct a warehouse in the Attingal territory, for the purpose of conservation of the pepper purchased. In 1687, the control of all the Company's possessions in India was transferred from Surat to Bombay. According to instructions from Bombay, they were ordered to keep in store 1000 or 1500 tons of pepper always in readiness to ship to England.[16] During the year, Thomas Mitchell, the Chief at Calicut shipped off to England 1200 *candies* of pepper. He spent 300 dollars as presents to the Queen of Attingal to gratify her, with a view to get maximum privilege from her.[17] The Queen in her turn was supposed to have given him permission through a written guarantee to build a factory or fort in her dominion. This guarantee however is not traceable.[18]

In 1688, two places Retorah and Brinjohn in the territory of the Queen were selected as factory sites.[19] Since both of them were situated near the sea coast incoming and outgoing ships could touch at these factories to collect pepper. Daniel Acworth was appointed chief of these factories. The English had two other small factories at Betture and Kalliquille or Mangatee in the Attingal kingdom.[20] These were the earliest factories of the English in Attingal kingdom. The English considered Brinjohn as the most impregnable for it was found to be the most ideal place for carrying on trade from Cochin to Cape Comorin.[21]

However, the Dutch who were determined to maintain their control on the coast prevented the English from erecting their flagstaff at both the factories. They were particularly against the settling of the English at Brinjohn. On account of the obstacles raised by the Dutch, the necessity for fortifying the settlements was felt more and more by the English. However, fortifications could not be carried out by the settlers themselves without the help and sanction of the Company's headquarters in Bombay or the Bombay Castle.[22] This involved a lot of time.

In fact, fortification could not be carried out immediately due to a number of reasons. The English had declared war against the Mughal empire under Emperor Aurangzeb at Surat and in Bengal in 1686. The war dragged on for three years at the end of which the English suffered a humiliating defeat. Bombay was captured by the Mughal forces. This war had drained much of the resources of the Company. But for the generosity and magnanimity of Emperor Aurangzeb and the commercial needs of his vast empire, the English would have never regained Bombay.[23] This would have naturally put the existence of the English settlements on the Malabar coast in jeopardy as they largely depended on Bombay Castle.

Actually, John Child himself had not sanctioned the fortification of Retorah due to the Company's then financial stringency. This was confirmed by the findings of the Court of directors in London, after the death of John Child.[24] Thus the wars against the Mughals and the ensuing financial constraints appears to have been the principal reasons for the delay in the fortification of the English factories in Attingal.

As time went by, Daniel Acworth became more and more desperate. He was afraid that any more delay on their part would make the Queen change sides and perhaps become inclined towards the Dutch. He insisted that in case they failed to settle the matters by November 1690, then the Dutch would gain the upper hand.[25] On the other hand, the Queen was assured by the English officials that the factories would be fortified soon and that she should not pay attention to the false reports and insinuations by the Dutch.[26]

Such a situation where important decisions were delayed by the head quarters in Bombay, not only created a climate of uncertainty among the English in Malabar and its princes and rulers, but also contributed to the unfavourable conditions in which the officials had to deal with the Queen of Attingal and the Dutch.

In 1691, money was sent from the English at Madras to various factories in Malabar. Ten thousand *pagodas* were sent to fortify Retorah.[27] But nothing came out of it. In 1693, Sir John Goldesborough was elevated to the post of Commisary General in India with residence at Fort St. George.[28] The very same year, the Company purchased Brinjohn from the Queen for 6000 *fanams* or 1400 rupees and Acworth bought all the coconut trees on the hill of Brinjohn.[29] Goldesborough arrived at Madras bringing with him positive orders to build a fort at Attingal. It was decided then to fortify Retorah as soon as season would permit.[30] Daniel Acworth who was all along complaining about the delay in fortification, suddenly sprang up by declaring that Retorah was not defendable and therefore there was no need for it to be fortified. Instead, he wanted to fortify Brinjohn for it had good drinking water.[31]

Fortification in Attingal needed not only the permission from Bombay Castle, but also permission from the Queen. Goldesborough tried to put across his argument in favour of fortification to the Queen by raising the point about Dutch threat not only to the English but also to her subjects and interests. In fact, the English wanted to ward off the Dutch menace at all costs for, of late, they had renewed harassment of the English Company servants without even the knowledge of the Queen.[32] Instead of approaching the Queen directly to conclude a trade treaty that would give them monopoly of spice trade by keeping out the Dutch, it seems that Goldesborough was convinced that he could attain the Company's objective of fortifying the factories and all that it implied to the English trade only by drawing the attention of the Queen to the Dutch threat to her and her country.

Brabourne's efforts in Attingal :

Unable to produce the agreement entered about nine years back by Thomas Mitchell, chief of Calicut factory with the Queen of Attingal for a settlement to be made in her country, Goldesborough decided to send John Brabourne under the title of Chief Captain or Commodor and Daniel Acworth, second-in-command to 'wait upon her majesty to enter into amicable treaty with her and conclude upon conditions to settle firmly in her country.'[33] As it was felt that the Queen's headmen, the *Pillas* had a share in the government of Attingal, Brabourne was also asked to confer with the two chief headmen, probably Vanjamutta Pilla and Cuddamon Pilla(also known as Couche Mauden Pilla), with a view to concluding a treaty enabling them to have full liberties of trade on all sorts of commodities in Attingal and to fortify on the hill called Brinjohn.[34] He was also asked to procure coolies and materials for construction and other privileges from the government of Attingal in favour of the Company.[35]

Under such a treaty the English demanded the right to trade in the Attingal country free from all duties, the right to travel in any part of Attingal for merchandize or buy provision for the Company servants without any molestation from any of the Queen's subjects, the power to impart justice in their factory sites and the power of coining any sort of money that existed in Attingal. Further, they insisted that the Queen's Rejadores should have no jurisdiction in the limits of their settlements nor in any part thereof so that they were absolutely free to be governed by themselves by their own laws without being accountable to the Queen or her governors in any manner whatsoever. They also wanted the people to sell all the pepper of their country only to the English company. Besides, they insisted that the Queen should come to their assistance with her powers to ward off any attack on them by anybody.[36] The treaty was supposed also to assure the Queen that the Company would buy all the pepper at a reasonable or stated price. Brabourne was also instructed to acquire any other privileges or liberties that might be necessary for the company from the Queen. However, the Company being unsure of the Queen's decision about the various clauses and conditions of the proposed treaty, considered it prudent to caution Brabourne to be content with whatever the Queen might grant them even if it might not mean a lot, so that they could embark upon fortification immediately.[37]

The intentions of the Company in their quest to conclude this treaty with the Queen and the government of Attingal were revealing in many ways. Though the Company's immediate objective was fortification by any means, yet it was not devoid of long-term objectives which had serious implications to the entire Malabar region. The Company's desire to govern their factory sites by their own laws without the interference of the Queen or her subordinates and their wish to have the power of coining and the power of imparting justice in their settlements proves beyond doubt that they wanted to establish themselves in the Attingal country in their own right independently of the Queen's jurisdiction. In fact, they were asking for independent political existence in the region through the proposed treaty.

Though the English Company offered some protection to the Queen and her subjects against the Dutch, yet their overall policy in their dealings with the Queen was not different from that of the Dutch. Both the English and the Dutch wanted the monopoly of the spice trade at the expense of the other and to achieve this objective they vied with each other to improve their political and military importance before the eyes of the Queen. However, the English were not still sure of their relative strength to impose a treaty on their terms upon the Queen which obliged them to caution Brabourne to accept whatever the Queen might agree to, in the belief that once the fortification was over, they could press for amendments in the treaty.[38] In any case, the fact that the Company ever devised such a treaty for the Queen's approval reveals the relative weakness of the latter in her dealings with the Europeans.

It is interesting to note that Brabourne was given 2000 *pagodas* to be spent on the Queen, her headmen and *Rejadores*, with the special purpose of obtaining the best terms from them and accomplish the company's mission.[39] But he was perplexed because he met with nothing that satisfied his expectations, for instead of finding the Queen an absolute ruler who was highly desirous of the English trade in her dominions, and who had sent invitations to the English several times to settle in her country, and with whom Daniel Acworth had prepared all matters, he found a powerless Queen who had hardly any power in the government but who was under the control of the *Pillas*.[40] This was the first impression that Brabourne seems to have got about the political situation in Attingal. Whether it was a correct impression is another matter.

That the Queen of Attingal was not an absolute ruler like Emperor Aurangzeb or the King of England, there was no doubt about it. She had a government where powers have been delegated to various administrators, among whom were the *Pillas*. It appears more probable that it was not in the traditions of south Malabar to take major decisions involving the country as a whole without the prior consultation and consent of the *Pillas* at least. The Queen might have contacted the English on her own accord previously, but when it was a question of settling the actual matter, she had to take into consideration the opinion of her administrators, especially the *Pillas*, who were probably more well-versed with the matters of the country than herself.

Unfortunately for the English, the *Pillas* were not in favour of any forts in their dominion. Their contention was that if trade was the motive for the English, then a factory rather than a fort would suffice.[41] As the Queen was no dictator, she could not overrule the opinions of the *Pillas*, which anyhow would have appeared reasonable in her eyes. She was probably a bit upset for it was she who invited the English.[42] But she could not take any decision against the larger interests of the country, as represented by the *Pillas*.

Brabourne got a further jolt when Cuddamon Pilla, one of the Queen's main headmen, sent word to Verdamon, the broker, that he desired a private meeting with Brabourne. Cuddamon informed Brabourne that the Queen would never consent to the Company fortifying Brinjohn for the simple reason that whoever was the master of that place commanded the only passage between the kingdom of Attingal and Travancore. Besides according to an understanding, probably with the King of Travancore, the Queen had a right only to one third of the customs of Brinjohn. This was in spite of the fact that Brinjohn was sold to the Company by the Queen earlier for 1400 rupees. Further Cuddamon advised Brabourne to accept any other place between Retorah and Eddawa where they might reside and fortify with the Queen's consent.[43] He himself suggested another convenient place known as Anjengo, saying that it was a better place than Brinjohn and the Dutch had formerly asked for it.[44]

The proposition of Anjengo was something that Brabourne never expected. Desperate in his desire to conclude a treaty with the Queen and not being in a position of sufficient strength to impose the Company's wishes on the Queen and the *Pillas*, Brabourne was obliged to accept the terms of the Queen. The very acceptance of the fortification of Anjengo by the Queen was a comforting point to Brabourne. Not wishing to delay any more and having no intention of going against the Queen's wishes, Brabourne visited Anjengo and found it to be conveniently situated on a small hill between the sea and the river.[45]

Brabourne decided to accept the Queen's proposition. He sent the broker Verdamon alone to Rettura to confer with Attinga Annavy, the Queen's chief *Rejadore* who seemed to have been one of the chief negotiators of the Queen. Brabourne conveyed through Verdamon his new terms of agreement to the Queen. He wanted for the company the hill of Iouges in Anjengo with a convenient extent of ground on each side of the hill to build warehouses and dwelling houses for the Company's officials and the right to fortify and govern the place according to their convenience. Secondly, Brabourne wanted the monopoly of pepper trade for the Company in Attingal with the right to prevent others from trading in the area. He further stipulated that the Queen's officers would receive the customs only after the pepper was weighed into the godowns to be shipped off wherever they chose to do so. Besides the Queen was expected never to enhance the customs and not to lay claim on an English ship-wreck. Moreover, under the terms of the agreement, the Queen's vessels would be issued with English passes which would guarantee them against robbery by the Dutch.[46]

Brabourne had to dilute and modify many of the points of Goldesborough's terms of agreement in order to suit the prevailing conditions. Consequently he did not insist upon having absolute territorial rights and the right to coin money. Instead, the primary aim of Brabourne seemed to have been to obtain the maximum trade rights and concessions. Subsequently Brabourne received a palm-leaf message from Verdamon, Cuddamon Pilla and Attinga Annavy that the Queen had promised to grant all the substantial part of the company's desires and that she desired to meet Brabourne in person at Manganatta(also known as Mangala)to confirm the articles.[47]

On 2 June 1694, Brabourne accompanied by 35 officers and soldiers arrived at Quilon. On 13 they arrived at Mangala where they met the messengers from the Queen, bringing word that Her Highness was still at Cottaracara. Two days later, Attinga Annavy and Verdamon met Brabourne apprising him that the Queen had already given orders to the *Pillas* to prepare the articles of agreement. Probably pleased with the message, Brabourne presented Attinga Annavy with 50 chequeens, some part of silk, sandalwood and rose water.[48]

The same day in the afternoon, Brabourne and the whole party visited the Queen. Brabourne presented to the Queen 250 chequeens, some velvet cloth, rich silk, lackered ware, arms and spices. The Queen in turn made some presentations to Brabourne which included a very handsome maneila and asked them to accompany them to Killequilee and Perenata where the *Pillas* would draw up and conclude the agreement.[49] The only explanation that could be given for the Queen's delayed meeting with Brabourne was the obvious fact that the Queen as a monarch in her own right preferred to deal with foreigners who were just representatives or paid servants of the Company, through intermediaries like the *Pillas* and the Annavys.

Unfortunately for the English, the differences of opinion between the Queen of Attingal and the King of Chenganatta or Quilon which led to an open war added to the delay in obtaining the grant from the Queen. The Queen sought help from the Rajah of Travancore. Though Brabourne tried to steer clear of the war, the Queen did not fail to approach the English for a loan of 10000 *fanams*, probably to meet the expenses of the war, knowing fully well that the Company could not refuse it to her for they, especially Brabourne were in dire need of coming to a settlement with regard to Anjengo.[50]

Anyhow it seems that the Queen had embarked upon a policy of extracting the maximum money from the English before signing the agreement, at least from the time she sold Brinjohn to the Company and then disallowed the Company from fortifying it This was obviously one of the reasons for which the Queen and the *Pillas* delayed to come to an agreement. On the other hand, Brabourne thinking that only financial inducements could obtain the assent of the Queen for his project lent her 350 chequeens amounting to 7350 *fanams*. He did not stop with that. He gratified the great Pilla, (probably Vanjamutta) with 20 chequeens, Couche Mauden Pilla with 50 chequeens, Curriche Pota with 50 chequeens, Cunje Mauden Pilla with 10 and Cujee Rambuttre with 10 chequeens. Servants were also sent to the Rajah of Travancore at Cottaricara with a present of 50 chequeens, arms, silk, cloth and 5 chequeens for his servants.[51] It is strange to note that the Rajah of Travancore was given just 50 chequeens like Couche Mauden Pilla. This demonstrates that the Rajah who was related to the Queen of Attingal was never a decisive or even an indispensable factor in the English dealings with Attingal.

Even at this juncture when an agreement was in sight, the Queen had dealings with the Dutch also. She informed Brabourne that she had refused 50000 *fanams* promised to her by the Dutch to break the agreement with the English. As a sort of compensation, she wanted the English to present her once every year with 250 chequeens. She also insisted that she should have half of the prize of pepper taken by the Company when anything was exported. Desperate to clinch the agreement, Brabourne agreed to present her with 100 chequeens ie., 75 chequeens for the Queen and 25 for the Annavy.[52]

On 2 July, the Queen, having patched up probably the differences with the King of Chenganatta in the meantime, went to Quilon. Brabourne followed her. After further expenses in presents, the Queen finally signed the palm-leaf grant on 9 July 1694. But she insisted on putting the date as 29 June as her priest(probably astrologer) had said it was a fortunate day. It was only on 27 July that the Company got possession of Anjengo and hoisted the King of England's flag.[53] Thus Brabourne managed at last to obtain the historical grant from the Queen of Attingal, after much delay and unceasing, tiresome efforts.

The Grant of Anjengo and its implications :

The translation of the grant reads as follows :[1]

Contract, concluded with the Queen of Attinga, dated 29 June An° : 1694

'Because the English, I called hither have allways bin obedient to mee, I do hereby grant unto them the following priveledges; I give unto them the hill of the Iouges that is at Anjengo, to fortefy with stone and to abide there for ever; And I will send thither my officers to set forth and appoint with stone Land-marks the limitts of Land that belong unto Mee, that on each side the said hill the Company may build warehouses for their goods, and houses for their people to dwell in, within which limitts, they shall rule, without any impediment, being obedient to me; I give unto the English Company all the pepper in my country that they may contract, and pay for it, at the price currant, And if any other do buy pepper, and carry it forth by sea; then shall the Company bye diligence, and take the vessels and goods, and one half that is taken they shall give unto mee; and the other half the Company shall have; For every candy of pepper that the Company buy, they shall pay me 5 Rajas; and for other goods that they embarque, or disembarque, they shall pay Custome to me 2 ½ percent; Once every year before they weigh pepper, they shall visitt me with 75 Chequeens; and they shall take my people to be present at the weighing of pepper; and for the pepper weighed, they shall pay custome to my officers; and the pepper that is weighed they may ship off, when they please. Any English vessells that shall be shipwrecked in my dominions shall be decided, half for me and half for the Company. They shall give passports to the Merchants of my dominions and if because of these passports the

[1] It was located for the first time by me at the National Archives of New Delhi and the India Office Library, London

Dutch take the vessells, the English shall satisfy for the boats and goods to the Merchants; and so I do ordered this Contract to be made in writing to the English Company at Quilon this 29th of June 1694.'[54]

Brabourne had achieved the Company's objective of finding a place to fortify in the Attingal country where they could rule themselves without any impediment on the condition that they were obedient to the Queen. He had also obtained the monopoly of the pepper trade. However, to conclude the agreement Brabourne incurred such a heavy expenditure, especially in the form of presents, that he was later criticised by his higher authorities.[55]

The Queen on her part managed to obtain considerable financial advantage in return for the trade and territorial concession. On the whole the wordings of the grant proves beyond doubt the unquestionable authority of the Queen in her dealings with the English East India Company. Actually the grant was a favour done to the English due to their obedience to the Queen, as pointed out in the grant itself. It is worth noting that she had not referred the contract to any neighbouring ruler, including the Rajah of Travancore, for advice or approval, before granting it.

However, the Court of Directors in London were not pleased with the grant, as, according to them it had a number of drawbacks. It was true that the English were conferred upon with the monopoly of pepper trade, yet they had to pay the Queen various custom duties and visit her with presents, before acquiring pepper. These clauses of the grant made pepper trade at Attingal very expensive to the English. It made tham realise that Malabaris were tough negotiatiors and were not cowards.[56]

Thus the historical grant of 1694 was instrumental in bringing out Anjengo, an obscure corner of the Attingal kingdom to the limelight of Malabar history. Anjengo was situated on a point of land at the mouth of a small river. This river flows rapidly between wooden banks forming islets, known for its feritility, greenery and beauty. The entire country was so thickly wooded, that a horseman can hardly pass through them.Anjengo was rounded on the north and south by Travancore kingdom, on the East by Anjengo backwaters and on the west by the Arabian sea. The name seems to have been derived from *Anju-Tengu*, which means ''five coconut trees' or *Anju Tangi*, literally meaning 'five porters' rest'.[57]

In spite of the beauty of Anjengo, it seems to have possesed a number of natural drawbacks. The water in Anjengo was blackish and unwholesome and not fit for drinking. The Attingal women had to go daily to the red cliffs of Boccoli about a league away to fetch the water which they sold to the English at Anjengo. Besides this serious drawback, the anchorage of Anjango under 10 fathoms was a foul rocky ground and outside that depth the bottom was sandy and full of shells. The river was also chocked up with sand during the greatest part of the year, preventing the ships from anchoring. To top this, the monsoon created havoc in Anjengo. It commenced with great severity and continued for six months from the month of May to October, provoking violent, noisy waves, making the shores the most inhospitable for vessels to approach.[58]

There is no indication in the records that Brabourne took into consideration all the foregoing drawbacks while obtaining the grant for the construction of a factory and fort in Attingal. Probably he was ignorant of it. Neither the Queen nor the *Pillas*, who were certainly aware of these drawbacks seemed to have thought it fit to inform Brabourne about them. Neither these drawbacks nor the unfavourable terms, especially regarding the trade clauses in the grant seemed to have deterred Brabourne from clinching the deal with the Queen. Instead, Brabourne tired of the delay and the perpetual demand for money from the Queen and the *Pillas* seemed to have clung to the first opportunity that presented itself to obtain a settlement.

Yet Anjengo had some advantages to its credit. Isolated and being surrounded by sea and back water on three sides, the protection of Anjengo in case of aggression was not a difficult task, because only the outlet to the mainland need to be protected. The fortified Anjengo could naturally offer the best security to carry on the pepper trade unhampered. Over and above the security that this place offered, the most important advantage that accrued from this place was that Anjengo backwater held water communication by the Vamanapura river with the neighbouring Peritally kingdom, which, with a production of about 1500 candy of pepper every year, was the largest producer of pepper in south Kerala. This neighbouring kingdom became part of Attingal temporarily from 1693, as noted earlier. Besides, there was a short cut route to the Madura country in the east, from where plenty of cloth could be procured.[59] It was also a vantage post from where sea traffic could be watched and regulated.[60]

Immediately after obtaining the grant, the English constructed a factory at Anjengo along with a warehouse and godowns made of cadjan leaf. The factory was at first placed under the English President at Surat, but it was subsequently made subordinate to Bombay Castle or Bombay Presidency. It was ranked as a very important trading centre and its officials were ranked second-in-council in Bombay.[61]

The Dutch were always watching with apprehension the attempts by the English to gain a foothold in Attingal. They were particularly alarmed when the English obtained the grant. In the year 1695, they brought about 1800 or 2000 soldiers to Quilon to put some pressure on the English. From Quilon they sent ambassadors to the Queen of Attingal and demanded the expulsion of the English.[62] Brabourne retaliated through a letter to the Dutch at Cochin stressing the point that they had obtained exclusive contract with the Queen of Attingal for all the pepper produced in the country, and the proprietory of trading in the commodity was wholly transferred to the English. He expressly asked the Dutch not to obstruct their rightful trade and to refrain from troubling the Queen of Attingal unnecessarily.[63]

The Dutch retorted by stating that by virtue of their previous conquest of the Malabar coast, they had the right to trade with Attingal. They contended that they had also obtained firm and authentic contracts from the Queen. But they were never in a position to produce the contracts for verification.[64] Fortunately for the peace of the Attingal country and the English, the Dutch did not press forward with their claim in a more strident manner and adopt a more hostile posture, for they had to respect the treaty of peace concluded at London in 1679 between the King of England, Scotland, France, Ireland and Netherlands.[65] At the most, it was just a war of words.

Further Observations :

The grant for the fortification of Anjengo in the Attingal country was accorded on 9 July 1694. However, many earlier authors had not subscribed to this date of origin of the factory and fort in Attingal. According to Walter Hamilton, Samuel Mateer, George Smith, William Logan and C.D.Maclean the year was 1684 when the East India Company received permission from the Queen of Attingal to settle or fortify at Anjengo.[66] Nagam Aiya and Velu Pillai have simply endorsed the date given by the preceding English authors.[67] According to the noted historian Sreedhara Menon, it was in the year 1690 that the English obtained permission to build a fort at Anjengo.[68] On the other hand, Ibrahim Kunju in his article '*Umayamma Rani*' held that the Anjengo factory records were destroyed by fire and that the English factory records so far published do not give any clue to the establisment of Anjengo factory.[69]

However, in the light of the documentary evidence collected it is quite obvious that the English factory in Attingal did not come into existence before 1694. It is baffling as to how such a serious error cropped up in regard to the year of the grant. In fact, the place Anjengo had never figured in the English Company's correspondence before the year 1694. It is true that in Retorah and Brinjohn, factories were constructed. But nowhere do we find the Queen giving permission to fortify Anjengo in the year 1684. The very idea of giving permission to the English to fortify at Anjengo occured only when John Brabourne visited her in the year 1693.

It is worth noting that the Queen and her headmen had considered the various implications while allowing the English to settle in their country. Their primary aim was of course to raise the revenue of the State through trade with the west Europeans. But at the same time they were bent upon finding a market to the products of their country, especially pepper, which constituted an essential part of the economy of the country. Besides, they extracted maximum money from the English by way of presents etc., before they accepted to grant Anjengo to them. This only shows that they were no push-overs in their dealings with the west Europeans. In fact, the economic and financial needs of their country and themselves seemed to have dictated largely their relationship with the west Europeans.

It is also worth noting that the Queen and her *Pillas* had taken into account the security of their dominions while dealing with the west Europeans. This is amply borne out by the fact that they had actually considered the strategic, security and also revenue implications when they refused to give permission to the English to fortify at Brinjohn and proposed Anjengo in its place. Couche Mauden Pilla's influence and role in the refusal of Brinjohn and the offer of Anjengo were of striking importance for it revealed the fact that though the Queen was the monarch yet her decisions were not entirely independent of the *Pillas* especially. In fact, Brabourne himself was unable to assess correctly the power of the Queen over the *Pillas* and vice versa. However the consent of the Queen for the fortification of Anjengo which was against the initial wishes of the *Pillas* proves that the Queen exercised a certain influence over the *Pillas*. Nevertheles such influence seemed to have been borne more out of negotiations and discussions between the Queen and the *Pillas* than her power alone.

All throughout the negotiations with the English, regarding the latter's settlement in Attingal, the Queen had consulted only her headmen and subordinates. There is no indication at all that she referred the matter to the rulers of the neighbouring kingdoms of Travancore or Chenganatta, who were actually closely related to her, for their advice or approval. She was acting all the time as a sovereign in her own right. The historical grant of 1694 was actually the consequence of protracted negotiations and consultations with her own headmen without any interference from the adjoining kingdoms. When the adjoining kingdom of Peritally fell short of heirs in 1693, it was annexed by the Queen of Attingal and not by the Rajah of Travancore. This demonstrates the power wielded by the Queen in the region.

In fact the Queen of Attingal was not answerable to the Rajah of Travancore during this period. The Dutch writer Galetti went one step forward when he stated that towards the end of the seventeenth century the Rajah of Travancore was the vassal of the Queen of Attingal.[70] Later Nagam Aiya upheld that the *tamburattis* (Queens) of Attingal possessed the sovereignty of Travancore from remote antiquity.[71] Jacob Canter Visscher had written that in all Malabar there was no Queen who possessed so much influence in public affairs as in Attingal.[72] In the light of what we have seen above, these authors had of course made a correct assessment of the position and status of Attingal and its Queens in south Malabar. As a result it is highly unreasonable and difficult to accept the contention of historians like Velu Pillai that the Queen of Attingal had no political power and whatever power she had was nothing more than powers delegated to her by the sovereign of Travancore.[73]

Notes and References

1. John Wallis, 'A Short Treatise by way of essay of Atinga, 1727, 7 September 1727, p.10. This treatise is not found in any of the archives in India. The present author located it from India Office Library, London
2. *Ibid.*, pp.67,70
3. *Ibid.*, p.71
4. Sreedhara Menon, *A Survey of Kerala History*, Kottayam, 1967, p.240; A. Galetti, *Dutch in Malabar*, Madras, 1911
5. John Bruce, *Annals of the Honourable East India Company, III*, London, 1810, p.194
6. Manohar Malgonkar, *Kanhoji Angrey*, Bombay, 1959, p.150
7. Surat Factory Records, 1678, Calicut to Surat, 6 February 1678, pp.64-65
8. Sir Charles Fawcett, *The English Factories in India, Bombay, Surat and Malabar coast, III*, p.xii
9. Collection of papers received from the India Office for Bombay Gazette work. Letter to London, 15 March 1681, p.10
10. *Ibid.*
11. Sir Charles Fawcett, *op.cit.*, p.xi
12. Collection of papers received from the India Office for Bombay Gazette work 1684-1685, p.41
13. Sir Charles Fawcett, *op.cit.*, p.365
14. *Ibid.* The Presidency at Surat had established two other factories at Calicut and Tellicherry in north Malabar lying outside Attingal kingdom. Tellicherry factory was established in the year 1683.
15. Anjengo Factory Records, 1704-1749, Simon Cowse to Court of directors, June 1704, p.5. Prince of Chenganatta was also known as Prince of Desingnad or Quilon.
16. Despatches from England, 1687, Public Department, Court of Directors, London to Bombay Castle, 3 August 1687, p.152
17. Anjengo Factory Records, 1704-1749, Simon Cowse to Court of directors, June 1704, p.7
18. Factory Records, Miscellaneous, 1693, John Goldesborough to Daniel Acworth, Retorah, 27 July 1693, p.38. On enquiry it was found that the treaty was carried from Retorah to Calicut and from there to Surat by a certain Mitchell and since his death, it was untraceable.

19. Despatches from England, 1687, Public Department, Court of Directors, London to Bombay Castle, 3 August 1687, p.152. Retorah was also referred to as Ruttera and Rettora by the English offcials. It is identified as 'Vettoor'. Brinjohn is identified as 'Vizhinjum'.

20. Bombay letter copy books outwards: Bombay letters received, 1694, John Brabourne, Anjengo to John Gayer, Bombay, 20 March 1694, p.31

21. Factory Records, Miscellaneous, 1693, John Goldesborough to Daniel Acworth, Attingqal, 29 July 1693, p.43

22. *Ibid.*, 26 July, 1693, p.31; Factory Records, General, India Office Library Records, London, p.129

23. J.B.P. More, 'West European and Mughal Interaction during the reign of Aurangzeb', Malekandethil Pius & Jamal Mohammed,T.(eds.), *The Portuguese, Indian Ocean and European Bridgeheads,* Tellicherry, 2001, pp.575-583

24. Anjengo Factory Records, 1704-1749, copy of a clause of the Rt.Honble. Company's general letter, London, 25 September 1691, p.11

25. Diary and Consultation Book of Fort St. George, 1690, January 1 to December 30, 1690, p.32

26. *Ibid.*, p.82

27. Diary and Consultation Book of Fort St. George, 1691, 16 July 1691, p.31. Pagoda is a name given to gold coins of about the value of seven or eight shillings

28. Anjengo Factory Records, 1704-1749, Simon Cowse to Court of Directors, June 1704, p.7; Bruce, John, *op.cit.*, p.138

29. Factory Records, Miscellaneous, 1693, Sir John Goldesborough to Daniel Acworth, Retorah, 29 July, 1693, p.42

30. Letters from Fort St. George, 1693, Sir John Goldesborough, Fort St. George to Daniel Acworth, 22 June 1693, p.31; Anjengo Factory Records, 1704-1749, Simon Cowse to Court of Directors, June 1704, p.6

31. Letters to Fort St. George, 1693, Daniel Acworth, Retorah to fort St. George, 31 May 1693, p.20; Anjengo Factory Records, 1704-1749, Dutch Governor, Cochin to Stephen Law, Bombay, 12 March 1740, p.180

32. Factory Records, Miscellaneous, 1693, John Goldesborough to Daniel Acworth, July 26, 1693, p.32

33. Factory Records, Miscellaneous, 1693, John Goldesborough to the Queen of Attingal, 26 July 1693, p.35

34. Diary and Consultation Book of fort St. George, 1693, 20 June 1693, pp.109-110; Factory Records, Miscellaneous, 1693, John Goldesborough to Daniel Aoworth, Retorah, 27 July 1693, pp.38-39

35. Factory Records , Miscellaneous, 1693, John Goldesborough to Daniel Acworth, Retorah, 27 July 1693, p.41

36. Factory Records, Miscellaneous 1693, John Goldesborough to John Brabourne, 27 July 1693, p.41

37. *Ibid.*

38. *Ibid.*

39. Anjengo Factory Records, 1704-1749, Simon Cowse to Court of Directors, June 1704, p.7

40. *Ibid.*

41. *Ibid.*

42. *Ibid.*

43. Bombay letter received, 1694, John Brabourne, Betture to John Gayer, Bombay, 29 July 1694, p.5

44. *Ibid.*

45. *Ibid.*

46. *Ibid.*, pp.5-6

47. *Ibid.*, p.6

48. *Ibid.*

49. *Ibid.*

50. *Ibid.*, pp.7-8

51. *Ibid.*, p.8

52. *Ibid.*

53. *Ibid.*, pp.8, 10

54. Bombay Letters Received, 1694, This grant is not referred to any book. It is surprising that even English factory records of later period does not mention about it, thinking it was lost – Anjengo Diaries 1808, A.W.Handley, Resident Anjengo to Francis Warden, Chief Secretary to government, Bombay, 10 May 1808, pp.304-309. The grant was located by the present author in India Office Libray Records, London, as well as in National Archives, Delhi, in micro-films.

55. Bombay letter received, 1694, John Brabourne, Betture to John Gayer, Bombay, 29 July 1694, p.5

56. Anjengo Factory Records, 1704-1749, Simon Cowse to Court of Directors, June 1704, p.4

57. *Ibid;* Maclean *Manual of Administration of the Madras Presidency*, Madras, 1938, p.33; Interview with Advocate Pereira in-charge of the dilapidated fort of Anjengo; James Forbes, *Oriental Memoirs, I,* London, 1813,1834, pp.216, 218; E.H. Nolan, *The Illustrated History of the British Empire in India and the East from the Earliest Times to the Suppression of the Sepoy Mutiny in 1859*, London, n.d., p.159

58. Alexander Hamilton, *A New Account of the East Indies*, London, 1728, 1930, 2 vols., p.332; James Forbes, *op.cit.*, pp.215-216

59. Anjengo Factory Records, 1704-1749, Simon Cowse to Court of Directors, June 1704, p.7

60. John Le Courtier, *Letters chiefly from India containing an account of the military transactions of the coast of Malabar during the late war together with a short description of the religion, manners and customs of the inhabitants of Hindustan*, London, 1790, p.104

61. Fort St. George Records, 1697, John Brabourne, Anjengo to John Gayer, Bombay, November 1697, p.23; Factory Records, G, India Office Library Records, London, p.1; C.D. Maclean, (ed.), *Glossary of the Madras Presidency*, Delhi, 1893, 1982, p.33; P.E. Robert, *History of British India*, London, 1938, p.75

62. Anjengo Factory Records, 1704-1749, Simon Cowse to Court of Directors, June 1704, p.7

63. Anjengo Factory Records, 1704-1749, John Brabourne, Anjengo to the Dutch, Retorah, 30 January 1695, p.14

64. Anjengo Factory Records, 1704-1749, Dutch, Quilon to John Brabourne, Anjengo, 12 February 1695, p.15

65. *Ibid.*

66. Walter Hamilton, *The East India Gazetteer, I,* London, 1828, p.54; Samuel Mateer, *Land of Charity*, London, 1871, p.11; George Smith, *The Student Geography of India*, London, 1882, p.393; William Logan, *Malabar, I,* Trivandrum, 1887,1981, p.389; Maclean's, *op.cit.*, p.35; C.D. Maclean, (ed.), *Glossary of the Madras Presidency*, Delhi, 1893,1982, p.33

67. Nagam Aiya, *Travancore State Manual, II,* Trivandrum, 1906, p.578; T.K. Velu Pillai, *Travancore State Manual, IV,* Trivandrum, 1948, p.620

68. Sreedhara Menon, *op.cit.*, pp.298-299

69. Ibrahim Kunju, 'Umayamma Rani', *Journal of Kerala Studies,* II, March 1975, p.23

70. A. Galetti, *op.cit.,* p.53

71. Nagam Aiya, *op.cit.,* I, p.306

72. Canter Visscher Jacob, *Letters from Malabar,* Madras, 1862, p.58

73. T.K. Velu Pillai, *The Travancore State Manual, I,* Travancore, 1940, p.299

Chapter 2

Power Struggle and Fortification in Attingal

K.N.Chaudhuri had rightly pointed out that force was an implicit part of the European trade with Asia, the reason being that profits from armed trading were higher than in the case of peaceful commerce.[1] In fact, west Europeans never came to India as peaceful traders. They had to contend and compete with various conflicting trade and other interests not only in their homelands, but also in India to such an extent that aggressivity became a part of their commercial activities. Thus they felt the need for fortifying their settlements in India, unlike the foreign traders like the Arabs, Persians and the Chinese who had preceded them.

In many parts of the Indian continent including the Mughal empire, the rulers gave permission to the English as well as other west European powers due mainly to the economic advantages that they could derive from their presence in their territories.[2] The Queen of Attingal was no exception to this rule. She, no doubt, allowed the English to fortify at Anjengo with an eye on economic benefits. But she, like many other rulers of India, including the mighty Mughal emperors, never really gave thought to the possibility that a fortified settlement, even though located in a remote and isolated corner, could possess a certain dynamism and had the potential to create an alternative source of authority within her territorial limits in course of time. As a matter of fact, the prospect of short-term economic advantages was so overwhelming in the eyes of the Queen that she preferred to overlook the long-term security threat to her country or was momentarily unaware of the existence of such a threat. This was in spite of the fact that the *Pillas* were always hesitant, suspicious and wary about allowing the English to fortify at Anjengo.

Trade and Fortification

As soon as the historical grant was received, steps were taken to commence the work of fortification at Anjengo. Brabourne always seems to have thought that fortification was necessary in order to trade profitably in Attingal. Already by the month of November 1694, a temporary fortification with pallisades and earth was constructed.[3] The total cost of the fortification was estimated at 7000 pounds.[4] As per the plans of Brabourne, the fort was intended to cover a space of ninety yards square on which 60 to 70 guns were to be mounted.[5] But as the garrison consisting of 34 soldiers and 75 topasses were found to be insufficient to assure the defence of the place, Fort St.George was asked to send more soldiers.[6]

In Attingal as all over Malabar all persons except members of the royal family were prohibited from building with stone or brick. Consequently, the Company found it difficult to obtain artifices.[7] This is in spite of the fact that the Queen had granted the English the right to use stones for fortification. By December 1695, the English managed to procure 70000 stones, though *chunam* was still scarce. Stone cutters, bricklayers, carpenters and smiths were sent overland from Madras. Coolies, labourers, topasses, soldiers and slaves, along with *chunam*, etc. came from Bombay.[8]

Though workmen were sent from Madras and Bombay, Brabourne tried his best to procure as many coolies as possible from Attingal itself. But the attempt was not very successful as the Malabaris did not approve of being trained in skilled workmanship by the masons and stonecutters from Madras. In fact the English found them untractable, obstinate and lazy, for they thought that it was below their status to be taught by Madrasmen. Besides, they would not turn up to the work before

10 or 11 a.m and if reprimanded they immediately left the job and returned to their houses.[9] This only demonstrated the independence of mind of the Malabaris of Attingal. But this was not conducive to the construction work. As a result the work of the fort progressed slowly and continued by fits and starts for five years, though the foundation stone of the fort was laid in the month of October 1696 itself.[10]

Even before the construction of the fortifications had begun, the Court of Directors in London sent instructions to Brabourne asking him to buy as much quantity of pepper as possible since there was a heavy demand for the commodity in Europe and its price had shot up.[11] But Brabourne embroiled with the problems of fortification and related financial burden, was not in a position to meet the demands of the Court of Directors.

In January 1696, he even represented to the Company his inability to buy all the pepper and fulfil the contract with the Queen of Attingal on account of the absence of a strong fort. It was difficult to buy and store large quantities of pepper in the warehouse. There was also the risk of pepper being robbed from the insecure warehouse thatched with palm leaves. This being the situation, the contract with the Queen was not honoured.[12]

On her part, the Queen needing money and probably not wanting to let her pepper rot, sold it off to the Danes.[13] Brabourne was convinced that if the English had a strong fort in Attingal, the Queen would not have dared to sell the pepper to the Danes or any other power in violation of her original contract to sell pepper to the English alone. Construction of fortifications at Anjengo thus became imperative.

Bombay Castle and Fort St.George often obliged Brabourne with money,workers and soldiers. But the Court of Directors in London were more interested in procuring pepper than to tackle the problems faced by Brabourne in completing the fortification or in procuring pepper.[14] They even accused Brabourne of lavishing away precious money in stone walls and fortifications without any benefit.[15]

Thus even after the Queen had given Brabourne the permission to construct the fort, he had no immediate means to complete the fortifications. He was constantly dependent upon his higher authorities in Bombay and Madras for financial aid and the procurement of skilled workers and coolies which naturally delayed the construction work. The cost of the construction had shot up to 10000 pounds.[16]

As noted earlier, the *Pillas* were never reconciled with the idea of fortification by the English in their territories. They had given their consent only grudgingly and after much hesitation. But as the construction work progressed slowly, the *Pillas* were becoming increasingly restive, in spite of the fact that it was through them that the English procured the stones necessary for construction of the fort.[17] They constantly visited the fort sites and ship and tried to obstruct the work. Brabourne was obliged to spend more money on them to keep them at bay and in good humour.[18] He was actually buying peace with the *Pillas* through financial inducements, with the objective of completing the fortifications.

To make matters worse, misunderstandings on money matters had developed between the Company and its broker, Verdamon Beca. It was the habit of the Company to pay custom duties etc., to the Queen through Verdamon though such an indirect payment was not stipulated in the grant.

According to the Company's version Verdamon used to borrow money from the Company which he never returned. Verdamon was accused of swindling the Company's money and not making the payments due to the Queen, though he had received money for it from the Company. Finally it seems that the Company decided to stop giving money to Verdamon, which infuriated the latter greatly and compelled him to adopt a hostile posture against the English. As a result, according to the Company's version, Verdamon seems to have complained to the Queen, in his attempt to set her against the Company, that he had spent much of his own money on the Company, but the Company refused to acknowledge the same, which had prevented him from paying what was due to the Queen.[19]

It seems that Verdamon did not stop with this. He accused the English of having even plundered the Portuguese and Chinese ships. Brabourne himself was portrayed by Verdamon as a pirate, whom he blamed for having instigated the burning and plundering of his ship in the Red sea. This was the reason that he gave for his inability to repay the Queen's debt, convincing her at the same time that he had given huge amounts as presents to the English.[20]

In the present state of our knowledge, we are not in a position to ascertain the veracity of Verdamon's contentions and accusations. But his accusation that during this period many Englishmen were indulging in piracy is a historical fact. Not only the English, but also the other west European powers like the Danes and the French were indulging in piracy in the Indian Ocean and the Arabian sea, especially during the second half of the seventeenth century.[21] In 1686, the English East India company, with the permission of the King of England, James I, had waged a war against the Mughal empire in the Arabian sea and the Bay of Bengal. During this period and until the end of the war in 1689 many Mughal and other Indian-owned ships were raided and plundered by English pirates, especially in the Arabian sea. Piratical activities had continued even after the war.[22]

Verdamon, being the accredited broker of the Company in Malabar was certainly in a better position to be aware of these happenings, for he had lost one of his own ships due to piracy. Piracy was also hampering trade. Naturally he had apprised the

Queen of Attingal of the dangers of piracy which could affect Malabar merchants like himself. The Queen seems also to have been aware of the notorious piratical activities of Captain Kidd, who was actually familiar with Attingal and its Queen.[23] As a result, the Queen and the Malabaris viewed the English activities in Attingal with a certain distaste. They suspected more and more the real character of the entire English population at Anjengo.[24]

Moreover, the Queen began to fear that once the fort was completed, the Company might take measures to recover the money they had given to the *Pillas* and also refrain from paying customs to her.[25] She realised that she would then not be in a position to procure money from the English. She also realised though belatedly the threat to her authority in Attingal posed by the English fortification. Verdamon served only to fuel the Queen's suspicions which hastened her actions against the English.

The Queen wanting to clarify and settle the matters regarding the customs due to her, invited Brabourne to meet her at Retorah. But Brabourne avoided meeting her on grounds of ill-health.[26] The Queen pressed for the payment of customs on pepper. She refused to heed to the Company's version that they had already advanced the money through Verdamon. The Queen further retorted that she expected her money directly from Brabourne and if there was any account or understanding between the Company and Verdamon, it did not concern her.[27]

The Queen once again expressed her desire to meet Brabourne personally to express her affection and to tell him that she did not give any credence to the stories of them being pirates. She also wanted to obtain an explanation from him regarding the complaints of Verdamon who, she believed, was unjustly used by the Company and was unable to pay his debt to her. But Brabourne politely refused again to meet the Queen. He suspected that the Queen had resolved to use her force and destroy the half-finished fort.[28] This prompted Brabourne to hasten the fortification. Officers and soldiers were asked to work on the fort. Guns were mounted on the newly built walls of the unfinished fort to scare away the Malabaris.[29]

It is strange to note that Brabourne who was after the Queen ceaselessly before the accord of the grant in 1694, was now avoiding to meet the Queen in her own territory, in spite of the latter's overtures. The tables were turned somewhat. The Queen naturally could not bear the challenge to her authority in her own territory, even before the fort was completely built. Whatever might be the truth of the Queen's intentions regarding the fort, Brabourne could have clarified to the Queen regarding the payment of customs and Verdamon's complaints. But by avoiding to see her or even give an explanation, the veracity of the accusations of Verdamon seems to have been clear.

The Queen realising at last that Brabourne was simply evading her by false excuses called on the *Pillas* and the heads of the Nairs, the local militia and declared intentions to them to drive the English out of Anjengo and Attingal.[30] But by then the English had mounted guns on the fort. The *Pillas* who had always been against the construction of the fort and the Queen realising the impossibility of undoing the English due to the guns, decided to starve out the English off the fort.[31] Accordingly orders were issued that no goods or provision of any sort should be sold to the English, that whoever was known to have any communication with them should be slain and whoever killed any of the English people or set fire to their houses would be rewarded by the Queen.[32] Moreover, the Queen sent a personal warning to the English to leave the fort for she wanted no thieves to dwell in her country.[33]

As a result some Company servants who went out of the fort to fetch provisions were beaten up by the Malabaris and nobody ever dared to bring provision to the fort. The Malabaris were also encouraged to raid all English factories under the order of the Queen. The Queen and the *Pillas* seem to have been almost certain that the English would not be able to survive for long without provision. In fact, during that time of the year, it was also not possible for any vessel to approach the coast with relief.[34]

Power Struggle in Attingal and its Consequences

Just when the Queen was determined more than ever to oust the English from her dominions, her headmen were poised to embark upon a power struggle. This was due to the old age of the Queen and the fact that she had no legitimate heiress to succeed her in the throne of Attingal. The 'great' *Pilla* Vanjamutta and Cuddamon Pilla were the main competitors for power in the Attingal country. Cuddamon Pilla, who, the English considered as weaker than Vanjamutta, sided with the Queen in their common struggle against the English, perhaps with the ulterior intention of getting the upper hand in the Attingal kingdom in the event of the Queen's demise.[35] On the contrary, Vanjamutta sought the help of the *madambees* of Travancore with the objective of foiling Cuddamon's design, though we do not know for sure if he sought the help of the Rajah of Travancore too. It is interesting to note, on the basis of English records, that Travancore had thrown off their allegiance to the Queen of Attingal during this period.[36] This seems to be the reason why Vanjamutta sought Travancore's help. The rift between the *pillas* came as a blessing in disguise for the English and could only serve their interests in Attingal.

Very soon Vanjamutta sought to befriend the English too in his struggle against Cuddamon. Contrary to the orders of the Queen forbidding all sorts of goods to be brought to the fort, Vanjamutta surreptitiously took two or three boat-loads of provisions to the fort. When the Queen came to know of this, she ordered some of her soldiers to kill the Malabar merchants, who heeding to Vanjmutta and violating her standing orders had delivered provisions to the English. The soldiers looted the merchants houses and abused their women. But Vanjamutta did not remain quiet. He, in his turn, plundered the supporters of the

Queen.[37] This only shows that Vanjamutta had gathered sufficient strength during this period to challenge the authority of the Queen in Attingal. The Queen entered into an alliance with the Queen of Kalliquilone and the Prince of Chenganatta to ward off the threat posed by Vanjamutta and his new allies, the *madambees* of Travancore. She even sought the help of the Dutch.[38]

The English benefitted from the misunderstanding between the Queen and Vanjamutta. That Vanjamutta needed the assistance of the English in his designs against the Queen was proved by his willingness to supply the English with provisions. The English could not have wished for anything better. At this juncture the English needed the support of Vanjamutta more than the latter's need for them. Though it is not clear from the existing records that the English actually exploited the misunderstandings between the Queen and Vanjamutta in their favour, yet they did not let go the opportunity provided by Vanjamutta to defy the Queen's authority. Vanjamutta actually came in handy to the English to fortify Anjengo and prolong their stay in Attingal. It is quite clear that if Vanjamutta too had sided with the Queen, the English would have been put into a very precarious situation.

Realising that an attack on the fort was imminent, the English asked Fort St. George and Bombay Castle to supply them with more soldiers, guns, ammunitions, provisions and stores. Bombay Castle managed to send them topasses and slaves and some ammunitions immediately.[39] The Queen watched their arrival in ships to Anjengo. She was incensed at her own headman for aborting her measures to drive the English out of the country. Her attempts to obtain help from the Dutch proved fruitless. But she was determined to act on her own. Very soon she sent about three or four thousand men to assault the English.[40]

The English had prior intelligence about this intended assault. From the rampart of the fort it was difficult to have a clear view of the countryside as the trees obstructed their vision. They therefore started clearing the ground in front of the fort which was densely wooded. But the Dutch had a cottage about three hundred yards near the fort, with some thirty palmyra trees. The English agreed not to cut these trees, eventhough they blinded the fort.[41]

The men of Attingal of all castes, both Hindu and Muslim, except Vanjamutta and his supporters approached the fort with the intention of storming it. They were led by a Nair captain. They fired at the fort from behind the walls of some houses. They then threatened to seize and burn the Company's warehouse which contained four or five hundred candies of pepper.[42] The English retaliated and killed their Nair captain. The Malabaris retreated to the Muslim quarters of the town, which was set on fire by the English.[43] In the course of the battle, some Malabaris took refuge in the Dutch house. The English threw hand grenades inside the Dutch cottage, which caught fire and was completely gutted to the ground.[44]

This was the first open confrontation between the Malabaris and the English in Attingal. It failed mainly because Vanjamutta did not side with the Queen. The English emerged victorious. They proved the superiority of the English soldiers and guns over the Malabari striking power.

Though the English won, they had unintentionally antagonised the Dutch. The Dutch held the English responsible for their gutted cottage and accused them for having had the time to break open the doors and plunder the goods in the cottage, but were unable to snuff out the fire. They demanded damages. The English apologised.[45]

Thenceforth the English became extremely apprehensive of the Dutch. They realised that they had also wounded the feelings of the Malabaris and the Queen by their actions. It was feared that the Dutch and the Queen would gang up against them. But they nevertheless felt that the Dutch would not dare to break the peace existing between the two nations in Europe.

The failure of the assault convinced the Queen that it was not a joke to defeat the English. She smouldered under the insult. She went away to Quilon proclaiming that she would never return to Anjengo till every stone of the fort was tumbled down. She was furious with her headman Vanjamutta for interfering in her plans of starving the English out of their fort.[46] In fact, Vanjamutta regularly supplied the English with wood and provisions and even promised them that if the Queen did not make peace with them, he would persuade the merchants to sell to the English as much pepper as they wanted.[47]

As the Queen nevertheless persisted in her intention to blockade the fort, Brabourne asked the English to seize all the boats of the Malabar merchants.[48] He thought that under such circumstances, the merchants who were discontented with the Queen's attitude to the Company would pressurise her to make peace with the Company, for the confiscation of the boats with commodities would affect their trade adversely. The Queen would thus be under pressure to listen to them. Brabourne's calculations were right. When the English started confiscating the boats of the merchants, the merchants made a great clamour declaring that by this unprofitable war they were utterly deprived of all their trade.[49] But contrary to their expectations, instead of seeking peace she sought the help of the Dutch. She asked them to issue passes for the ships and boats of her merchants.[50] However, the Dutch help was not forthcoming this time too.

On the other hand, the great *Pilla* Vanjamutta convinced the Queen that in the interests of the merchants it would be better to make peace with the English so that the trade might go on unhampered rather than continuing the unprofitable war. It was even pointed out to her that it was impossible to take the fort or to stop provisions reaching the fort because the sea was open.[51] As

Vanjamutta himself supplied the English with all that they wanted, the English were not in want of anything, except the right to go up and down the country.[52] Meanwhile 30 more English soldiers with arms had arrived at Anjengo. This alarmed the inhabitants greatly for they thought many more were coming.[53]

The Queen taking stock of the situation, finally decided to make peace with the English on condition that she was paid amply. She was naturally under intense financial pressure due to the war, which would have compelled her to claim more money from the English in return for peace. The Company, in their turn, offered 500 dollars on condition that a durable peace might be concluded with aspects of the original grant of 1694 amended in their favour.[54]

The English wanted the original grant to be amended as follows :

1. All the strands between the sea and the river extending southward as far as river mouth to northward as far as farthest end of the Moor (Muslim) town which is about a mile and ¼ should be totally under our obedience.
2. The pepper and other goods taken out of Ruttera house should be restored
3. That the Company on those conditions should, upon the arrival of the first Company's ship, pay the custom of pepper shipped on board the East India merchant the annual present due for 2 years and 5000 *fanams* over all which would amount to about 15000 *fanams*.[55]

However, before a settlement could be arrived at, Umayamma Rani passed away at Retorah of a distemper in the month of July 1698. The Queen as noted earlier did not leave a legitimate heiress to succeed her. Naturally there was confusion and chaos in the country.[56]

The demise of Umayamma Rani removed from the Malabar political scene a formidable opponent to the designs of the English.

A new Queen had to be installed. However, the dowager Queen was soon followed to the grave by the elder of the adopted princesses. After the death of the elder of the adopted princesses, the Junior princess became the only surviving female of the royal family of Attingal. But she was only a adopted princess, not belonging to Attingal. She became anyhow Attingal Mutha-thamburan.[57]

It was widely expected that the adopted princess when she became officially Queen would not command much respect among the people as she was actually a foreigner to Attingal with few dependents.[58] On account of this, it was also expected that she would excessively depend on the *pillas* for the administration of the country. In other words, it became clear that the real power would rest with the *pillas*, especially Vanjamutta and Cuddamon. The English became very cautious henceforth in their dealings with the *pillas*, whose power loomed larger than ever, after the death of the old Queen.

It is interesting to note that the *pillas* of Attingal had conferred with the *madambees* of Travancore, before announcing their decision to install the new Queen in the month of November.[59] This in itself showed the power of the *pillas*. Naturally, the new Queen would be permanently indebted to the *pillas* for their decision. But she was also indebted to the *madembees* of Travancore. Thus her actual power stood largely diminished. The very fact that the *madambees* were involved in her installation as Queen proves a certain ascendancy of Travancore in the affairs of Attingal. In fact, as noted earlier, Travancore was no more obedient to the Queen of Attingal from 1698 itself when Vanjamutta made overtures to them and when the old Queen was expected to pass away at any time.

Brabourne, realising the new power equations in Attingal, sent word to the *pillas* that the Company desired to have a good understading with the Attingal government. The *pillas* sent

Verdamon and a Rajadurai to negotiate with the Company a treaty of peace. The English took hold of the opportunity to attempt and modify certain points in the original grant and to obtain the maximum benefit.[60]

The English wanted to scrap especially the clause about sharing the spoils in case of shipwreck, to which Brabourne had agreed to earlier out of sheer desperation and without much forethought.[61] They only later realised that they had been outwitted by the Queen on this account for when the fort was completed, there would be flurry of activities on the sea and the shore, and there was the likelihood of ships getting wrecked on the coast especially owing to the dangerous surf on the sea. If the original contract was adhered to, then in case of shipwreck the spoils would be divided between the Queen and the Company. This would result in heavy losses to the Company. In view of the fact that there were also some ships which came loaded with gold and silver to be distributed to all the subordinate factories for their monthly expenses, and if such ships got wrecked and if the Queen demanded half the spoils, the Company was sure to incur heavy loss. The incoming ships laden with treasure and the outgoing ships laden with pepper and cloth were both valuable to the Company. Bombay Castle therefore wanted this clause to be scrapped somehow. They also wanted some amendments to the original grant favourable to them.[62]

After some delay, the new Queen was installed by the *pillas*. By January 1700, Verdamon informed the Company that the new Queen and the *pillas* were inclined towards peace.[63] But as they seemed not interested in finalising a treaty, the English could not seek modifications in the original grant at least for time being.

Instead, the English turned their intention towards completing the construction of their fort, in spite of financial constraints. The fort was completed by the beginning of 1699,at an expense of Rs.56,425. It was a regular square with four bastions.

Each bastion had eight guns mounted and each courtin had six or seven guns. Besides there was a line of 20 guns pointing towards the sea. On the whole there were 56 to 60 guns.[64]

From the strategic point of view, the fort was highly secure. On the west, it was bounded by the sea and on the east it was protected by the Vamanapura river which originated from the main range of the Western Ghats and passed through the factory garden before it emptied into the sea. Along this river only country boats could ply, not big ships. The avenues to it from north and south were very narrow. There was no highland near it. It was difficult for ships to ply in the backwateers. The fort was thus naturally defended by the sea and backwater. Attack on the fort could only come from the land which was amply protected by about 60 guns on the fort. An attack from the sea, especially by Malabaris was out of question.[65] The garrison of the fort consisted of about 400 Europeans and 70 to 80 topasses.[66]

The date of the completion of the fort has been a matter of controversy among the scholars. William Logan has not given any specific year. According to him in the year 1684, the English obtained a sandy spit of land at Anjengo and the place was fortified some years later.[67] Alexander Hamilton wrote that the fort was built in 1695.[68] Padmanabha Menon seems to have concurred with him. According to the Glossary of the Madras Presidency it was in 1695 that a factory with fortification was erected.[69] In view of suffcient documentary evidence cited above, it is almost certain that Anjengo fort was finished only in 1699, the foundation of the fort being laid only in 1696.[70] With the completion of the fort, the English were naturally in a much stronger position in Attingal than before, as feared by the old Queen and the *pillas* earlier. But now the new Queen and the *Pillas* had a *fait accompli* to deal with.

The English had not succeeded still in modifying the clauses especially concerning ship wrecks in the original grant. Before that, as feared by the English there was a shipwreck near the coast of Anjengo, in the year 1704. A ship named *Neptune* commanded by Captain Leslie, bound for Madras, fully laden with treasure capsized during the monsoon, on 21 June 1704 at Mannacurra, not far from Cape Comorin. All the crew escaped except one. The ship had carried 30 chests of silver and one chest of gold in addition to a large amount of treasure and some very important boxes of letters containing instructions to all the forts and factories of the English.[71]

As the ship had sunk near the coast there were chances of retrieving all the goods by the month of September or October after the monsoon was over and when the sea would have receded considerably. Simon Cowse second-in-command at Anjengo fort was sent to the vicinity of the wreck to explore the chances of retrieval and also try and recover whatever came ashore.[72]

But the English were bound by the grant of 1694 to divide the spoils of the sunken ship equally between the Queen and the Company. Actually the ship had wrecked in the province of the Rajah of Travancore and not in the dominion of the Queen. But the reigning rajah of Travancore, Ravi Varma, was not a strong ruler to impose his will. The English feared that the treasure might fall into the hands of the *pillas*. They did not also want the confidential letters to fall into the hands of the Dutch or the French.[73]

The *pillas* contended that earlier when the Portuguese and the Dutch vessels had sunk in these parts, the Queen of Attingal had the benefit of the entire wreck. They do not seem to have wanted to change the customary practice which had existed at least from the times of Chau Ju Kua. Ibn Batuta and Abd-er-Razzak had mentioned about it, as noted in the introductory chapter.[74] This only confirms that the Queen of Attingal's writ ran still in Travancore territory in 1704. When Simon Cowse arrived at the spot, he realised that the local people had carried away already all the goods that had come on the shore. The *pillas* who were masters of these regions had even placed guards about two miles on each side of the place of the shipwreck. They managed to take away some money which had loosened from the ship, and also two guns and two anchors. Cowse who wanted to somehow retrieve the box of secret letters, could only lay his hands upon a few pieces of torn letters and other papers.[75]

Brabourne threatened military action and asked the *pillas* to respect the clause in the original grant.[76] This was of no avail because the *pillas* seems to have insisted that the wreck was not in Attingal territory and therefore the grant of 1694 did not apply. Brabourne clamoured for help from the higher Company authorities to retrieve the treasure.[77] Meanwhile Cowse returned to Anjengo with the news that the Malabaris had fortified themselves with 7 guns and that they refused to part with any goods.[78]

As feared by Fort St. George, all English efforts ended in failure since even by December they could not retrieve the treasure and all hopes of retrieving it were lost.[79] All the chested gold and silver was deeply buried in the sea irrecoverably lost to the English. Perhaps even today the treasure may be lying intact at the bottom of the sea off Mannacurra near Cape Comorin. Brabourne, the father of the Anjengo settlement, did not live long. He drowned along with the ship *Chambers Frigate*, one of the strongest vessels used in chasing pirates, on his way to Fort St. David on May 1707, two years after he handed over the chiefship at Anjengo to Simon Cowse in 1705.[80] He was no doubt the man who contributed most to the assertion of English power in south Malabar.

The foregoing reveals many things in various ways. First of all, the Malabaris had proved all throughout the negotiations that led to the grant of 1694 that they were not to be underestimated. They had thought over the implications of the various clauses of the grant. Only when they were convinced that their trade and financial interests were fully protected that they allowed the English to construct the fort. The Queen was the decisive factor in the decision of giving permission to construct the fort, though her headmen felt that there was no need of a fort for trade purposes.

Later the Queen realised her mistake and tried to prevent the English from completing the construction of the fort with the help of the *pillas*. But her old age and the fact that there was no legitimate heiress to the throne contributed to a power struggle among the *pillas*. The English exploited the differences between the *pillas,* which enabled them to survive in the hostile atmosphere and even to deal a swift blow to the Malabaris who did not have much idea of what an awesome task it would be for them to storm the fort mounted with formidable guns.

The Malabaris who had been earlier treated as cowards by the English proved by their daring attacks on the fort that they could be dangerous. Though Queen Aswati Umayamma Rani (Ashure) failed in her attempt to expel the English from Attingal, due mainly to the support extended by her chief headman Vanjamutta to the English, she proved that she was a force to be reckoned with in the region. Her authority was undermined somewhat in her last days in 1698, due to the actions of Vanjamutta, who allied himself with the *madambees* of Travancore, who had thrown off their obedience to the Queen. Later after the death of the old Queen, the *pillas* of Attingal had come to an agreement once again with the *madambees* of Travancore to install a new Queen on the throne of Attingal. Thus Travancore seems to have acquired a say in the affairs of Attingal, though we do not know the exact role of the Rajah of Travancore in its affairs. But the latter was known to be a weak ruler, who, as we know, could not prevent the *pillas*' attempts to retrieve all the treasure of an English shipwreck in Travancore territory in 1704, for the sole benefit of the new Queen of Attingal. This again shows that the Queen was still held in high regard in Travancore and her authority was respected.

Notes and References

1. K.N. Chaudhuri, *The Trading World of Asia and the English East India Company, 1660-1760,* Cambridge, 1978, pp.113-114
2. J.B.P. More, 'Some Maritime Aspects of the Indian Ocean Region, 1660-1760', K.S.Mathew(ed.), *Indian Ocean and Cultural Interaction, A.D.1400-1800,* Pondicherry, 1996, pp.134-135
3. Bombay Letters Received, 1694, John Brabourne, Anjengo to John Gayer, 24 Novemebr 1694, p.82
4. Bombay Letters Received, 1695, John Brabourne, Anjengo to John Gayer, Bombay Castle, 20 March 1695, p.26
5. Bombay Letters Received, 1695, John Brabourne, Anjengo to John Gayer, Bombay Castle, 19 June 1695, p.59; see also John Bruce, *Annals of the Honourable East India Company, III,* London, 1810, p.195
6. Bombay Letters Received, 1694, John Brabourne, Anjengo to John Gayer, Bombay, 29 July 1694, p.11; Fort St. George Records, 1696, Fort St.George to John Brabourne, Anjengo, 13 August 1696, p.113
7. Bombay Letters Received, 1694, John Brabourne, Anjengo to John Gayer, Bombay, 29 July 1694, p.11
8. *Ibid;* Bombay Letters Received, 1695, John Brabourne, Anjengo to John Gayer, Bombay Castle, 14 December 1695, pp.13-14; Bombay Letters Received, 1696, John Brabourne, Anjengo to John Gayer, Bombay Castle, 11 March 1696, p.85; Fort St. George Records, 1697, Fort St. George to John Brabourne, Anjengo, 21 May 1696, p.102
9. Bombay Letters Received, 1696, John Brabourne, Anjengo to John Gayer, Bombay Castle, 27 August 1696, p.166
10. Anjengo Factory Records, 1704-1749, John Brabourne, Anjengo to Court of Directors, June 1704, p.8
11. Fort St. George Records, 1696, Fort St. George to John Brabourne, anjengo, 26 December 1696, p.147
12. Fort St. George Records, 1696, Nathaniel Higgins, Fort St. George, to John Brabourne, Anjengo, 17 October 1696, p.136; Public Despatches to England, 1696, Fort St.George to England, 31 January 1696, p.48
13. Public Despatches to England, 1696, Fort St.George to England, 31 January 1696, p.48

14. Despatches from England, 1696, Court of Directors to President and Council, Fort St. George, 16 January 1696, p.38; Bombay Letters Received, 1697, John Brabourne, Anjengo to John Gayer, Bombay, 4 February 1697, p.37; Fort St. George Records, 1697, John Brabourne, Anjengo to Fort St. George, 13 April 1697, p.54

15. Despatches from England, 1697, court of Directors, London to President and Council, Fort St. George, 26 January 1697, p.36

16. Bombay Letters Received, 1697, John Brabourne, Anjengo to John Gayer, Bombay, 21 August 1697, p.37

17. *Ibid.*

18. Bombay Letters Received, 1697, John Brabourne, anjengo to John Gayer, Bombay, 4 February 1697, p.38

19. Bombay Letters Received, 1697, John Brabourne, anjengo to John Gayer, Bombay, 21 August, p.39; Bombay Letters Received, 1697, John Brabourne, Anjengo to John Gayer, Bombay, 21 August 1697, p.41

20. Fort St. George Records, 1697, John Brabourne, Anjengo to fort St. George, 4 June 1697, p.57; Bombay Letters Received, 1697, John Brabourne, Anjengo to John Gayer, Bombay, 21 August 1697, p.41

21. J.B.P. More, *op.cit.*; See also J.B.P. More, 'West European and Mughal Interaction during the reign of Aurangzeb', Malekandethil Pius & Jamal Mohammed,T.(eds.), *The Portuguese, Indian Ocean and European Bridgeheads*, Tellicherry, 2001, pp.558-586

22. Ibid.

23. John Biddulph, *The Pirates of Malabar and an English woman in India two Hundred Years Ago*, London, 1907, p.48 ; Bombay Letter Received, 1698, John Brabourne, anjengo to John Gayer, Bombay, 14 November 1698, pp.181-82 ; Letter from Fort St. George Records, 1698, Fort St. George to John Brabourne, Anjengo, 5 april 1698, p.37 ; For more details refer to letters from Fort St. George, 1697-1698

24. John Biddulph, *op.cit.*, p.48

25. Bombay Letters Received, 1697, John Brabourne, Anjengo to John Gayer, Bombay, 21 August 1697, p.41

26. *Ibid.*, p.42

27. *Ibid.*

28. *Ibid*; Fort St. George Records, 1697, John Brabourne, Anjengo to Fort St. George, 24 September 1697, p.171; Bombay Letters Received 1697, John Brabourne, Anjengo to John Gayer, Bombay, 21 August 1697, p.43

29. Anjengo Factory Records, 1704-1749, John Brabourne, Anjengo to Court of Directors, June 1704, p.8
30. Bombay Letters Received 1697, John Brabourne, Anjengo to John Gayer, Bombay, 21 August 1697, p.44
31. Anjengo Factory Records, 1704-1749, John Brabourne, Anjengo to Court of Directors, June 1704, p.8
32. Bombay Letters Received 1697, John Brabourne, Anjengo to John Gayer, Bombay, 21 August 1697, p.44; Bombay Letters Received, 1697, John Brabourne, Anjengo to John Gayer, Bombay, 27 August 1697, p.8
33. Fort St. George Records, 1697, John Brabourne, Anjengo to Fort St. George, 24 September 1697, p.171; Bombay Letters Received 1697, John Brabourne, Anjengo to John Gayer, Bombay, 21 August 1697, p.44
34. Fort St. George Records, 1697, John Brabourne, Anjengo to Fort St. George, 24 September 1697, p.172; Bombay Letters Received 1697, John Brabourne, Anjengo to John Gayer, Bombay, 21 August 1697, p.44
35. Bombay Letters Received, 1697, John Brabourne, Anjengo to John Gayer, Bombay, 27 August 1697, p.8
36. *Ibid.*, pp.8-9
37. Fort St. George Records, 1697, John Brabourne, Anjengo to Fort St. George, 24 September 1697, p.172
38. Bombay Letters Received, 1697, John Brabourne, Anjengo to John Gayer, Bombay, 27 August 1697, p.9
39. Letters from Fort St.George, 1697, Fort St. George to John Brabourne, Anjengo,15 November 1697, p.21
40. Fort St. George Records, 1697, John Brabourne, Anjengo to Fort St. George, 24 September 1697, p.172; Anjengo Factory Records, 1704-1749, John Brabourne, Anjengo to Court of Directors, June 1704, p.8
41. Anjengo Factory Records, 1704-1749, John Brabourne, Anjengo to Commodore Neatherland East India Company, Quilon, 22 October 1697, p.17. The Dutch referred to this cottage as their factory
42. Bombay Letters Received, 1697, John Brabourne, Anjengo to John Gayer, Bombay, 27 December 1697, p.67; Fort St. George Records, 1697, John Brabourne, Anjengo to Nathaniel Higgins, Fort St. George, 14 November 1697, p.173
43. Bombay Letters Received, 1697, John Brabourne, Anjengo to John Gayer, Bombay, 27 December 1697, p.67-68

44. Fort St. George Records, 1697, John Brabourne, Anjengo to Nathaniel Higgins, Fort St. George, 14 November 1697, p.173; Anjengo Factory Records, 1704-1749, John Brabourne, Anjengo to Commodore, Neatherland East India Company, 1 December 1697, p.21, 22 December 1697, p.12; Records of Fort St.George, Diary and Consultation Book, 1697, 14 November 1697, p.134

45. Anjengo Factory Records, 1704-1749, John Brabourne, Anjengo to Commodore, Neatherland East India Company, 1 December 1697, p.20; Anjengo Factory Records, 1704-1749, John Brabourne, Anjengo to Commodore, Neatherland East India Company, Cochin, 22 October 1697, p.17; Anjengo Factory Records, 1704-1749, Hendrick Decroom, Commander Neatherland East India Company to John Brabourne, Anjengo, 2 December 1697, p.19

46. Fort St.George Records, 1697, John Brabourne, Anjengo to Nathaniel Higgins, Fort St.George, 27 December 1697, p.173

47. *Ibid.*

48. *Ibid.*

49. Bombay Letters Received, 1697, John Brabourne, Anjengo to John Gayer, Bombay, 27 December 1697, p.68

50. Secretariat Outward Letter Book, 1697-1699, Bombay Castle to John Brabourne, Anjengo, June 1698, p.92

51. Bombay Letters Received, 1697, John Brabourne, Anjengo to John Gayer, Bombay, 27 December 1697, p.69

52. Bombay Letters eceived, 1698, John Brabourne, Anjengo to John Gayer, Bombay, 28 January 1698, p.42

53. Bombay Letters Received, 1697, John Brabourne, Anjengo to John Gayer, Bombay, 27 December 1697, p.69

54. Bombay Letters Received, 1698, John Brabourne, Anjengo to John Gayer, Bombay, 29 February 1698, p.53

55. Bombay Letters Received, 1698, John Brabourne, Anjengo to John Gayer, Bombay, 31 August 1698, p.139

56. *Ibid.*, p.140; Secretariat Outward Letter Book, 1697-1699, Bombay Castle to John Brabourne, Anjengo, July 1698, p.94

57. Shungoony Menon, *A History of Travancore, I,* Delhi, 1878, 1984, p.106 . Adoption to the throne of Attingal had already taken place in the year 1688. K.V. Krishna Ayyar, *A History of Kerala,* Coimbatore, 1965, p.286. The eldest Queen was called Attingal Moothathampuran, the next as Attingal Elaya Thampuran, and the next as Attingal Moonammura

58. Bombay Letters Received, 1698, John Brabourne, Anjengo to John Gayer, Bombay, 31 August 1698, p.140

59. Bombay Letters Received, 1698, John Brabourne, Anjengo to John Gayer, Bombay, 3 November 1698, p.177

60. Bombay Letter Received, 1698, John Brabourne, Anjengo to John Gayer, Bombay, 3 November 1698, p.177

61. Bombay Letter received, 1698, John Brabourne, Anjengo to John Gayer, Bombay, 3 November 1698, p.178; Secretariat Outward Letter Book, 1698, Bombay Castle to John Brabourne, Anjengo, 4 November 1698, p.184, 14 November 1698, p.207

62. Bombay Letter Received, 1698, John Brabourne, Anjengo to John Gayer, Bombay, 14 November 1698, pp.178, 181-182

63. Bombay Letter Received, 1699, John Gayer, Bombay castle to John Brabourne, Anjengo, 16 September 1699, p.30 ; Bombay Letter received, 1700, Bombay Castle to John Brabourne, Anjengo, 21 January 1700, p.44

64. Anjengo Factory Records, 1704-1749, John Brabourne, Anjengo to Court of Managers for the United Trade of the Company, London, 9 September 1704, p.1; Political Consultation, 1812, Resident, Anjengo to chief Secretary, Fort St. George, 29 December 1812, pp.4026-4027; Bombay Letter Received, 1698, John Brabourne, Anjengo to John Gayer, Bombay, 17 Sept.1698, pp.168, 205

65. T.K. Velu Pillai, *The Travancore State Manual*, Trivandrum, 1940, p.62; Edward Ives, *A Voyage from England to India*, London, 1773, p.192; Anjengo Factory General, 1804, Anjengo to Jonathan Duncan, Governor, Bombay, 9 March 1804, p.135

66. Anjengo Factory Records, 1704-1749, John Brabourne, Anjengo to Court of Directors, June 1704, p.8

67. William Logan, *Malabar, I,* Trivandrum, 1887, 1981, p.389

68. Alexander Hamilton, *A New Account of the East Indies*, London, 1728, 1930, p.18

69. K.P. Padmanabha Menon, *History of Kerala, I,* Ernakulam, 1924, p.336; C.D. Maclean, (ed.), *Glossary of the Madras Presidency*, Delhi, 1893, 1982, pp.33-34

70. Secretariat Outward Letter Book, 1699-1702, John Brabourne, Anjengo to Bombay Castle, 6 December 1699, p.11

71. Letter to Fort St. George, 1704, John Brabourne, Anjengo to Thomas Pitt, governor, Fort St. George, 1 July 1704, p.113; Records of Fort St. George, Diary and Consultation Book, 1704, 20 July 1704, p.63

72. Records of Fort St. George, Diary and Consultation Book,1704, 20 July 1704, p.63

73. Shungoony Menon, *op.cit.*, p.106 ; Letters to Fort St. George, 1704, John Brabourne, Anjengo to Thomas Pitt, governor, Fort St. George, 1 July 1704, pp.114-115

74. Letters to Fort St. George, 1704, Simon Cowse, Cotata to John Brabourne, Anjengo, 2 August 1704, p.135

75. Fort St. George Records, 1704, Simon Cowse, Cariapatam to John Brabourne, Anjengo, 28 July 1704, p.229; Letters to Fort St. George, 1704, Simon Cowse, Cariapatam to John Brabourne, Anjengo, 28 July 1704, p.117; Letters to Fort St. George, 1704, John Brabourne, Anjengo to Thomas Pitt, Fort St. George, 17 July 1704, p.132

76. Letters to Fort St. George, 1704, John Brabourne, Anjengo to Simon Cowse, Cariapatam, 31 July 1704, p.238

77. Letters to Fort St.George, 1704, John Brabourne, Anjengo to Thomas Pitt, fort St.George, 17 July 1704, p.131-132, 9 September 1704, p.192; Public Department, Fort St.George, 1704, Fort St.George to John Brabourne, Anjengo, 30 November 1704, p.164

78. Fort St.George Records, 1704, John Brabourne, anjengo to Thomas Pitt, Fort St.George, 15 August 1704, p.236

79. Letter to Fort St.George, 1704, fort St.George to John Brabourne, Anjengo, 16 December 1704, p.164

80. Despatches to England, 1706, John Brabourne, anjengo to Court of Directors, London, 6 October 1706, p.63; Despatches to England, 1708, Fort St.George to England, 1 October 1708, p.95. Fort St.David was in Cuddalore on the Coromandel coast.

Chapter 3

The Attingal Revolt

Immediate Economic Grievances :

As long as the old Queen of Attingal lived, the English had a person with considerable authority with whom they could negotiate the conditions to carry on with their trade. But her sudden death took the English unawares. They were not able to negotiate the peace treaty or modify certain clauses in the original grant. This left them in a state of uncertainty about their future.

Besides the departure of Brabourne from Anjengo in 1707 deprived the English of a person who had guided English fortunes in Attingal almost single-handedly for more than a decade, in spite of opposition from various quarters. Brabourne was succeeded by Simon Cowse who was until then second-in-command. The latter was esteemed to excel even Brabourne in the knowledge of the different interests of the country. He even had perfect knowledge of the Malayalam language.[1]

It seems generally that until the end of the seventeenth century the object of the English in Malabar was straight forward trade, more specifically the purchase, the transport to Europe and the sale of goods there.[2] It was not different in Attingal. But it appears that by the beginning of the eighteenth century, the English Company's presence in Malabar underwent a qualitative change. Instead of working to promote the Company's trade, the English servants of the Company indulged more and more in private trade. In fact, the English East India Company directors in London themselves decided to allow private trade so that the Englishmen under their service could make some extra money for themselves.

This was thought to encourage them at the same time to work for the promotion of the trade interests of the Company.[3] But this decision had far-reaching consequences in the Malabar, for thenceforth the English could indulge directly in the country trade which was until then dominated by the merchants of Malabar, especially the Mappilas. In fact, they were competing with the Malabar merchants for a share in the local trade.

It appears that in Attingal, the English factors were paid a higher salary than in the rest of India.[4] But this never deterred them from trading locally on their own account. They behaved more like middlemen rather than agents. Very soon their private trade began to encroach on Company trade to such an extent that Bombay Castle had to send an order to the English factors in Attingal to refrain from all private trade in pepper.[5] This order had no effect at all. But the decision to allow officially the company servants to indulge in private trade boomeranged on the Company as most of the Company servants amassed huge wealth and became more or less independent. No regulations emanating from London could prevent English private trade in Malabar.[6] Misappropriation of Company's money through private pepper trade became the trend during John Kyffin's period who succeeded Simon Cowse as chief of Anjengo in 1712. Kyffin was even accused of having underhand trade dealings with the Company's rivals, the Ostenders.[7] As a result he was dismissed and was replaced by William Gyfford in 1719, who had already made a name for himself as a successful private trader. He accompanied by his young and attractive bride duly took up residence at Anjengo.[8]

Moreover, Kyffin, unlike his predecessors was less tactful in his dealings with the *Pillas*. He was ignorant of the enmity that existed between the great *Pilla*, Vanjamutta and Cuddamon *Pilla*. So without proper knowledge of the Attingal affairs, he chose to gratify the great Pilla Vanjamutta alone, which naturally displeased the other *pillas*.[9] Taking advantage of Kyffin's ignorance of local affairs, Vanjamutta even extracted money out of Kyffin on the imagined pretext that Cuddamon Pilla had been angered by his permitting pepper to come to the fort and promising to quieten things down.[10]

But William Gyfford was no better than Kyffin. He even excelled Kyffin in dishonesty as far as his trade dealings were concerned and in imprudence in his overall dealings with the Malabaris.[11] He systematically double-crossed the Company as well as the Malabar pepper merchants. The merchants were given money in advance by the Company to bring in large quantities of pepper. The usual practice was that the merchants did not bring the entire quantity in one bulk as they had to collect them from various sources. They accepted receipt only for the first consignment they brought to the fort. They never demanded receipts for the successive consignments.[12]

Gyfford began to exploit the confidence that the Malabar merchants had placed on the English. He demanded pepper delivery from those merchants who had already completed the delivery. In the absence of proper receipt, they could not argue their case legally. This amount was entered as debt in the name of the respective merchant.[13] As the English East India Company had the monopoly of the pepper trade in the region, the Malabar merchants were obliged to sell the pepper that they had collected from various sources to the English alone. Otherwise they had no option but to allow the pepper to rot.[14] Thus the English in Attingal under Gyfford embezzled the merchants unscrupulously.

At the same time Gyfford cheated the Company also by making false entries in the factory books, especially with regard to the pepper bought by the Company.[15] On one occasion one Chetty Conacopilla pawned two chests of copper with Gyfford for Rs.3535 at 12 per cent interest. He empowered Gyfford to sell the same if the money with its interest was not repaid by 30 March

1719. Gyfford sold the entire copper and spent the money for his personal use.[16]

Besides making wrong entries in the factory books, Gyfford even resorted to using false weights and thereby weighed more pepper into the warehouse than the original contract.[17] All the pepper thus procured was sent to the neutral market in a ship called, *Thomas* which belonged to Thomas Cooke, brother of Mrs.Gyfford.[18] Gyfford thus double-crossed both the Company and the Malabar merchants who incurred heavy loss. The merchants could have obtained a higher price by selling the pepper to the Dutch. But owing to the monopoly enjoyed by the English they did not dare to sell it openly to others eventhough smuggling of pepper to other parts of the country and selling them to the Dutch were not uncommon.[19]

Naturally the merchants of Malabar, who consisted of both Hindus and Muslims, were not at all happy with this state of affairs, where their interests were undermined by the English private traders who were also Company officials. They were not in a position to obtain redressal of their grievances either from the English who were out to exploit them to the hilt, nor from the Attingal Queen and her chiefs, who were generally gratified by the English, as noted earlier.

Religious Grievances

It appears that from the time when Gyfford became the chief at Anjengo, the behaviour of Englishmen with the inhabitants of Attingal, both Hindus and Muslims took a turn for the worse. In 1720, the official interpreter or linguist of the Company, Ignatio Malheiros, a Roman Catholic of Portuguese descent, who probably had a grouse to settle with Muslims, instigated some English lads to pelt with eggs and filth at some Muslims who passed by.[20] When the matter was reported to Gyfford, he instead of punishing the interpreter, apprehended the Muslims and imprisoned them. This unjust and intolerant action, which smacked of racial and religious arrogance appears to have wounded deeply the feelings of the Muslim community of Attingal. But they chose not to react immediately to this grave provocation. It is worth noting that Ignatio Malheiros was an important official employed by the factory. He not only functioned as a translator, but on several occasions he mediated between the Company and the Malabar powers, especially the Queen of Attingal and the Rajah of Travancore. This resulted in the linguist becoming very friendly with the latter. [21] That a person of this status behaved in such an irresponsible and disdainful manner would have certainly infuriated the Muslims much more.

During this period, the English provoked the Hindus too unnecessarily. Usually the English had some slaves in the fort, probably hailing from the lower Hindu castes or outcastes. Once the English without any obvious reason, compelled a Nambudiri Brahmin to shave off the beards of their slaves, an act which the Brahmins could not perform in those days without losing caste.[22] This affair affecting a member of the highest caste in the then social set-up of Malabar caused great consternation and alarmed the Hindu community, especially its higher castes.

The Hindus were offended further when the Portuguese interpreter, Ignatio Malheiros, obtained possession of some Hindu temple lands, known as Cottadally, in a money-lending transaction from persons who had no power to dispose of it. He purchased it for 90000 fanams. It was a very large tract of farm land, the circumference of which was about three miles and was very fruitful and rich in coconuts and toddy, arrack and betel trees.[23] The possession of the temple lands by a Portuguese Christian, at the service of the English infuriated the Hindus greatly. Cuddamon Pilla took up the cause of the Hindus. He along with many others 'burnt the gamel demanding likewise that the linguist (interpreter) should be delivered to their mercy for his daring to purchase Cottadally'.[24]

The preceding incident shows that the Hindus of Attingal were not passive spectators of English high-handedness. They were quite capable of reacting firmly. But this appears not to have halted English interference in the affairs of the Malabaris, for in 1721, English company records maintain that both Gyfford and Ignatio Malheiros were believed to have whipped up some Nairs, belonging to the martial class of Malabar, for some unknown reason.[25]

Matters reached a critical stage at the annual Easter dinner given by Ignatio Malheiros at his own house. Men of different communities attended the dinner. It so happened that Muslim traders came to the fort to transact business with Simon Cowse, the former chief, who was still a Company servant at Anjengo. As he was not available, the traders went to the interpreter's house to sit and wait. It appears that while they were waiting there, the interpreter's servants threw 'colour powder' upon the Muslim merchants in a very nasty way.[26] To add insult upon injury, the intepreter's mistress threw coloured water on the merchants' face and body, which was uncovered to the waist according to the manners of the country. Stung by the insult, one of the merchants drew his sword and wounded the woman. He would have killed her, but he was overpowered, probably by the interpeter's men or servants and carried away forcibly to the fort. It seems that the Muslims of Malabar like their Hindu counter-parts had many strange customs and beliefs. For them, the contact of coloured water or powder with their bodies was a symbol of pollution. As a result they had to pay money in order to be accepted into their caste again.[27] There might be some truth in this belief for otherwise there was no reason for the Muslim to have reacted so violently.

However, when the above incident was reported to Gyfford, he instead of punishing the interpreter's servants and mistress, ordered the Muslims who had come to the fort probably to retrieve their companion and seek justice, to be turned out of the fort, after their swords were insultingly broken over their heads.[28] This incident seems to have mobilised the inhabitants of Attingal, both Hindu and Muslim, against the English. They took up arms with the intention of attacking the Englishmen in the fort of Anjengo in order to avenge the insult heaped on the Muslim merchants. Alarmed by the aggressive designs of the Malabaris, the English asked and received reinforcements from Madras and Bombay.[29]

Meanwhile there was confusion prevailing in the palace of the Queen of Attingal. The principal *pillas* prevented the rightful heiress of the deceased old queen from ascending the throne. Instead, they installed illegally someone of their own making. This was naturally against the wishes of the common people.[30] The *Pillas* expected the English to pay to the unlawful Queen the annual presents promised in the original grant. The Company officials including Gyfford insisted on paying the dues to the legitimate Queen, for they feared that if they make presents to the pretender there was chance that they would be obliged to pay once again when the legitimate Queen was re-installed. As the *Pillas* persisted in their demands, the company finally decided to forward the presents to the illegitimate Queen. But as the company did not have immediate stock of *chequeens*, which was the money usually paid for presents, they offered to pay the equivalent in fanams or dollars. But the *pillas* refused to accept it and began harassing the Englishmen.[31] Gyfford was convinced that the natives were bent upon attacking them. He decided to send away the pepper stocked at Betture factory, which was established prior to that of Anjengo. But before that, the infuriated Malabaris had set fire to it. It was never rebuilt.[32]

Skirmishes between the Malabaris and the English settlers continued for some months in which, according to Fort St.George records, several Malabaris lost their lives.[33] The Queen of Attingal Amutamburan attributed the reason for the skirmishes to the Company, who had given shelter to a certain Comadevarmur who had become an outcaste. This according to her had angered the Malabaris more than anything else.[34] Giving shelter to an outcaste was considered to be a grave offence in those days in south Malabar.

In January 1721, reinforcement from Cochin arrived at Anjengo in Attingal consisting of four ships of soldiers. Besides, Walter Brown was despatched from Bombay to restore peace, with 300 men. They were sent to Cherringa where the inhabitants were particularly hostile towards the English. All these preparations seem to have had their effect on the Malabaris who abandoned any attack on the Englishmen or the fort for the time being.[35]

On her part, the Queen probably realising the grave situation, chose to restore normalcy in her country. She sent her chief headman, Vanjamutta Pilla to patch up the differences between the English and the Malabaris. Vanjamutta met the Company officials, Walter Brown, Gyfford, Captian Macrae, Cocksedge and 12 other soldiers and promised them to settle the differences amicably and also provide them with pepper. The officials presented Vanjamutta and his *Kariakars* (managers) with 140 chequeens.[36]

This time the Company officials conscious of the blunder committed earlier by John Kyffin who by befriending Vanjamutta alone, antagonised the other *pillas*, decided to confer also with Cuddamon Pilla, the second most influential among the *pillas* of Attingal.[37] But this happened only after the meeting with Vanjamutta. Consequently, everything appeared to have returned to normal. At this juncture, it is worth asking if the Muslim merchants and the Hindus, especially the Nairs, forgave really the insults heaped upon them by the English and if the former really forgave Gyfford and his colleagues for swindling them so blatantly.

The Revolt

The practice of carrying presents to the Queen of Attingal had been abandoned for the previous seven years. The Company officials decided to revive this custom and settle all the differences with the inhabitants.[38] When the *Pillas* came to know of this, they immediately approached the English and demanded the presents on behalf of the Queen. They assured Gyfford that they were demanding the presents by the Queen's order and even offered receipt in her name.[39] But Gyfford refused to entrust the presents to the *Pillas*. He flushed with the hope of having peace and pepper at the same time and wanting to ingratiate himself more with the country government, announced that he would personally carry the total presents for seven years to the Queen Amutamburan. The annual presents for seven years at the rate of 75 venetians per annum besides presents to the Pillas amounted to Rs.17000.[40]

Accordingly on 14 April 1721, accompanied by all the English merchants and factors and taking all his best men about 150 in number, along with a number of coolies and topasses, Gyfford set out to the palace of the Queen, which was about four miles up the river. He left back only a few invalids to guard the fort.[41] The party advanced with much pomp and splendour with sounds of trumpets and drums. They reached the palace of the Queen, where they were received by an enormous crowd of people who gave them a friendly reception. Gyfford never suspected any sort of treason, but thought that the crowd had assembled as spectators to watch the ceremony.[42]

Simon Cowse who had come along with Gyfford consulted the Queen's headmen regarding the delivery of presents, to whom they should be delivered and what amount to each person of distinction. Cowse's suspicion was aroused when he who knew Malayalam perfectly, heard whispers and delays on the part of the Malabaris.[43] His fears seem to have been confirmed when he was told that the chief headman Vanjamutta was drunk and they must have to wait till he was fit to receive them. Cowse suspecting foul play appears to have wanted the English to return to the fort at once. But Gyfford was not ready to believe Cowse. Instead he beat him and confined him as prisoner in the Queen's palace itself.[44]

The ceremony of handing over the presents was done with much pomp under the supervision of Cuddamon Pilla in the absence of Vanjamutta.[45] The Dutch records maintain that after the ceremony, the Queen pressed the party to spend the night at her court. Pretending that she was unable to accomodate the whole party in one place, the Queen assigned different lodgings to them so that they were scattered and rendered unable to assist each other in case of need.[46] However, the English records maintained that the Queen intervened to pacify Gyfford and Cowse and advised them all to return to their fort, fearing that their quarrelling might lead to some misfortune.[47]

Gyfford to show his goodwill ordered his soldiers to fire a salvo. But to his utter dismay he found that the ammunitions carried by the soldiers were tampered with and as a result they were utterly defenceless.[48] Gyfford, realising the dangerous and helpless situation they were in, seems to have managed to entrust a letter to a friendly Malabari addressed to the store-keeper of the fort, Captain Sewell, apprising him of the situation.[49]

That night the Malabaris assembled there rose in open revolt and surged upon the Englishmen, who were drawn up in an enclosure.[50] Not a single European lived to see the next day. The principal English officers of the party, Gyfford, Burton Fleming and the interpreter, Ignatio Malheiros were reserved for cruel death. Gyfford's tongue was torn out and nailed to a log of wood and sent floating down the river.[51] Ignatio Malheiros' body was gradually dismembered so that he died a slow and terrible death. Simon Cowse however, managed to disguise himself in a country dress and tried to escape, but he was confronted by a Muslim merchant who owed him money.Cowse offered to acquit him of his debt, but to no purpose. He was done to death and thus the debt was settled.[52]

Of the entire party 17 topasses (probably including some coolies) managed to escape the massacre, but they too were severely wounded, some of them having received eleven or thirteen wounds each but none without any.[53] Pandemonium had broken out already among the English ranks in the fort when they received Gyfford's note, sent through a Malabari. They were literally terror-struck when the wounded men confirmed the revolt and the massacre. It is worthwhile to note at this juncture that Gyfford in his enthusiasm to please the Queen had taken all the able-bodied men with him leaving in the fort only boys and pensioners less than forty in number.[54]

As a result the defence of the fort was considerably weakened. Anyhow preparations were afoot to defend the fort, fearing an imminent attack by the Malabaris. English officers in the fort were Robert Sewell, who was a Storekeeper cum Adjutant cum Captain, Lieutenant Peter Lapthorne, ensign Thomas Davis and the gunner, Samuel Ince. The first three seem to have been of not much use. It was Samuel Ince who seems to have taken the initiative to ship off the three English women whose husbands were slain, along with their children to Quilon and Madras.[55] This included Mrs.Gyfford.

By then, they had received a reinforcement of seven men and a consignment of provision in two small ships from Cochin.[56] With the arrival of these seven men, there were 47 soldiers in all to defend the fort. Precautions were taken to protect the houses in the fort from the fire-arrows of the Malabaris by dismantling the roof. This left them open to bear the excessive heat of the day and the rain and cold of the night.[57] Further they shifted seven hundred bags of rice with salt fish from the ware-house to the fort, along with the Company's treasure which was in a large iron bound chest. These provisions could last for a month. Besides, urgent appeals were sent to the English at Calicut and Tellicherry for reinforcement.[58] Following the appeals, on 1 May an ensign and fifty-one men collected by Adams from Calicut and Tellicherry joined the Englishmen at Anjengo.[59] This bolstered the defence against an eventual Malabari attack.

It is surprising to note that the Malabaris did not chose to attack the fort immediately after the revolt and the massacre. This seems to have given some time to the English to organise their defence more effectively. By the time the Malabaris gathered outside the fort, with the apparent intention of evicting the English once for all from Attingal country, the English seemed to have been better prepared to repulse any attack. The Malabaris began by firing fire-arrows with the intention of setting fire to the dismantled palm-leaf roofs. All non-Malabari houses in Anjengo were set on fire and plundered according to the English records, except the Company's warehouse which still contained goods worth one hundred and fifty thousand fanams.[60]

On 24 June, the Malabaris launched a planned attack on the fort from three sides.[61] We do not know how many Malabaris were involved in this vigorous attack. They had actually entrenched themselves on one side close to the fort. Sensing the danger to the fort, the English tried to dislodge the Malabaris, but failed in the attempt, though they claimed to have killed and wounded many of them.[62] But later unable to face the mortar shot at them from the flag staff and the bastions, they decided to retreat. They came back after some time and attacked the fort with guns and rantackers from the river side. The English used grenades to repulse the Malabaris from their positions. Three or four were killed and several of the attackers were wounded, while some leapt into the river and were drowned. According to the English records, many English soldiers were wounded, but none were killed in the attacks launched by the Malabaris against them. Though the Malabaris continued to impose a land blockade of the fort, they refrained from their attempts to dislodge the English from the fort.[63] By this time, a second reinforcement of 80 Englishmen along with provisions and ammunitions was sent down by Adams from Calicut.[64]

Aftermath of the Revolt

The revolt and the massacre that ensued appear to have been carefully planned by the Malabaris of Attingal. Realising fully well, that it was impossible to attack and dislodge the English as long as they were within the fort, the Queen's subjects chose to fall upon them, when almost the entire English garrison was outside the fort in the Queen's palace. The Queen pleaded ignorance of the entire affair. She wrote to the governor of Fort St.George in June 1721 the following :

'On the 14 April the governor (Gyfford) with several other gentlemen came with 150 soldiers to see me, when they arrived at my house, the above named Codervompilla with some inhabitants combined together and fell upon them and cut them off which was unknown to me or any of my attendants.'[65]

The Queen actually blamed Codervompilla who was none other than Cuddamon pilla for the massacre and the revolt. She however attributed the actions of Cuddamon Pilla to the incident which took place months back, when the English incurred the wrath of the *Pillas* by giving shelter to an outcaste by the name of Comadervomur. The Queen profusely apologised on behalf of her subjects. She actually wrote to Madras the following :

'...as soon as I heard what a treacherous thing the inhabitants had been guilty of to the English especially at such time, I with my family and Chief man Vanjamuttapilla fled into another's (king of Quilon) dominion.'[66]

The Queen even gave her word of honour to the English that she would not return to her kingdom unless the English came back and lived in Attingal as before. She also promised to extend all her help to punish the rebels. She along with Vanjamutta Pilla even promised to furnish the Company with all the necessary provisions to compensate for the actions precipitated by the Nairs and the Muslims.[67] Under these circumstances, a peace deal was clinched between the English and the Nairs and Muslims, which permitted many old Englishmen and the widows of the slain soldiers to return to Attingal. Nevertheless, it is surprising that the English did not take the law into their own hands to personally apprehend and punish the rebels. English records maintain that this was because they realised that the massacre was partly the outcome of the nasty behaviour of their own Company servants towards the Malabaris.[68]

There are many contradictory opinions among the historians regarding the number of Englishmen who went to the Queen's palace to give the presents. Alexander Hamilton held that Gyfford took with him two of his council and some others of the factory. Jacob Canter Visscher's statement regarding the number of persons is ambiguous. John Biddulph wrote that on 11 April, accompanied by all the merchants and factors and taking all his best men, about one hundred and twenty in number and the same number of coolies, Gyfford proceeded to the palace of the Queen. William Logan on his part stated that on 15 April, Gyfford and ten other persons went to make the presents to the Queen.[69]

Velu Pillai, the historian of Travancore, reiterates the statement made by Alexander Hamilton. According to him Gyfford was accompanied by two members of his council and a major portion of the garrison. Nagam Aiya also concurs with Hamilton's statement. Henry Davison Love does not give any specific number, although he held that the greatest part of the garrison went to Attingal. A recent work mentions that the party was attacked and Gyfford and ten of his companions were murdered. Padmanabha Menon corroborates Biddulph's version. According to Sreedhara Menon the number was 140.[70] However, in the light of sufficient documentary evidence in the form of East India Company factory records and the actual letter written by the Queen of Attingal to the Company officials after the massacre, it becomes quite clear and certain that the actual number of Englishmen who proceeded to the Queen's palace was more than one hundred and fifty, which included 150 soldiers.[71] All of these soldiers were massacred in the combined revolt of the Hindu Nairs and the Muslims.

Another controversy among the historians was regarding the venue of the massacre. Most of them are of opinion that the massacre took place when the party was en route to the palace of the Queen. Alexander Hamilton did not give any direct reference to the venue. Biddulph indirectly hinted that the massacre took place while the party was on their way to the Queen's palace. Henry Davison Love held that the party was attacked by the Malabaris on the way. Velu Pillai stated that they were brutally murdered in the course of their journey. Nagam Aiya reiterates Hamilton's version. Sreedhara Menon and Ibrahim Kunju concur with Velu Pillai's statement[72] These views stand disproved, as there are sufficient documentary proofs in the form of Fort St.George records, the letter written by the Queen, John Wallis' treatise and the Dutch records which prove beyond doubt that the massacre took place at the Queen's palace and that too, after the customary presents were handed over to the Queen ceremoniously.[73]

Historians have also differed in their analysis of the cause of this revolt against the English, which was no doubt one of the earliest of its kind in the Indian subcontinent. The main point of debate has been whether this uprising was triggred off by religious grievances or personal vendetta or the connivance of the Queen of Attingal. There is however no unanimity of opinion among the historians as to the real cause of the revolt. Biddulph puts the blame on the Muslim merchant who had an old score to settle with William Gyfford. In Jacob Canter Visscher's opinion the revolt was the outcome of the insult heaped on the Hindu community. He also upheld the role played by the Queen. He referred to her as 'the artful princess'. Alexander Hamilton claimed that the *Pillas* were the brain behind the massacre.[74]

However the analysis of the happenings that led to the revolt in the foregoing pages brings out clearly that the immediate cause of the revolt was the mismanagement and ill conduct of William Gyfford. The intervention of Gyfford in the internal affairs of the Malabaris was a radical departure from the traditions of non-intervention of John Brabourne. A state of excited feelings and bitter antagonism caused by Gyfford prevailed among the Malabaris.

Gyfford's insulting dealings especially, with the Muslims who were the principal merchants of the region, provided the latter with enough reasons to see the departure of the English, who were actually competing with and obstructing their trade, as noted earlier. This stands confirmed even by the English Factory records.[75] Besides Gyfford's dealings with the Hindu sections of the population were not any better as we have seen. They along with the Muslims were nursing their grievances waiting for the right opportunity to wreak their vengeance over the English.

As pointed out earlier, the chief headman Vanjamutta had befriended the English against Cuddamon Pilla in the competition for power when the old Queen Ashure was nearing her death. Naturally Cuddamon was never very happy with this situation where the English were allying with Vanjamutta. When John Kyffin became the chief of Anjengo in 1707, he chose to gratify only Vanjamutta with presents and ignored Cuddamon Pilla.[76]

After the death of the old Queen, the new Queen had been installed on the throne of Attingal by the *Pillas*. When Gyfford succeeded Kyffin, things have not changed much. The new Queen actually sent Vanjamutta to conclude peace with Gyfford, Walter Brown and others.[77] This time too Cuddamon was sidelined.

Though the English later decided to meet Cuddamon too, with the object of coming to a good understanding, nothing concrete had seemed to have taken place. All these events had the potential to increase the hostility of Cuddamon against the English.

On the other hand, Vanjamutta had been quite friendly with the English, not only before the death of the old Queen, but also after her death. In 1698 he had actually sided with the English even against the wishes of the Queen who along with Cuddamon *Pilla* wanted to evict the English from Attingal. Besides, if Vanjamutta had been the brain behind the revolt in the Attingal palace, then there is no reason for him to have got drunk during such an important event as the revolt, when the rebels would have expected his orders and participation. But Vanjamutta simply faded away from the revolt into his drunken state. Later he even fled with the Queen to the neighbouring dominion, from where he promised along with the Queen, to help the English with provisions.

However, the Queen's involvement in the revolt is not very clear. Though the Dutch records maintain that the Queen of Attingal was the brain behind the revolt, there are no conclusive proofs in the English records, of her being even one of the instigators of the revolt. Instead, her sympathetic attitude towards the English after the massacre proves to some extent her non-involvement in the revolt, though she might have had an inkling of it when she advised Gyfford to leave the palace immediately after the ceremony. Anyhow the English themselves never believed that the Queen had a hand in the revolt.[78] She had fled with Vanjamutta to the neighbouring territory of the King of Chenganatta or Quilon, who had always been very friendly and helpful to the English. It is noteworthy that it was her brother, the King of Quilon who was the first to send condolences to the English at Anjengo for the massacre.[79]

Both the Queen and the English accused Cuddamon Pilla for having masterminded the revolt. In a letter the Court of directors of the Company in England, the massacre was attributed to 'the treachery of our blackfriend Cuddamon Pilla'.[80] In this he was no doubt assisted by the Muslims. As pointed out earlier, Cuddamon Pilla had always a sense of personal hostility against the English. Previously in 1698 he sided with the old Queen Ashure in taking up arms against the English. Presently, the dissatisfaction of the Muslims and the Nairs with the arrogant behaviour of the English and Gyfford and their treacherous methods of dealing with the Malabar merchants in particular provided the necessary ingredients which Cuddamon Pilla put to good use to organise the revolt.

Considering the number of Englishmen killed in the revolt, it is quite probable that the rebels were significantly numerous. Taking note of the fact that William Gyfford and Ignatio Malheiros were subjected to the crudest barabarities, there is no doubt that the rebellion was also in a way the outcome of the brashness of these two and the haphazard way in which they behaved with the Malabaris. When their arrogance became unbearable, the Nairs and the Muslims, under the leadership of Cuddamon Pilla joined together to strike the blow. As a matter of fact, the revolt itself was the result of the combination of several grievances and factors on the economic, political, social and religious planes.

The *Pillas* were never reconciled with the idea of allowing the English to construct a fort in Attingal. In the course of time, the company officials exploited and ill-treated the Muslim merchants in particular. Besides the English ridiculed local sentiments on the religious and social planes, which served as immediate causes for the revolt.

It cannot possibly be supposed that such a skilfully devised plan was worked out momentarily by the aggrieved Malabaris. It was evolved in anticipation of the pending annual present. However, the revolt, though it taught the English a bitter lesson, ended in a failure, in so far as its immediate aim was concerned. According to the Company records the aim was to force the English to withdraw from Anjengo and Attingal.[81] It failed because the revolt did not enjoy the support of all the chief *Pillas* and the Queen. Cuddamon Pilla, though powerful and influential, seems to have been alone in spear-heading the revolt. His isolation and the eventual lack of support from the other *Pillas* was more than sufficient for the revolt to peter out subsequently.

Probably, the Malabaris under the direction of Cuddamon never had the intention of driving the English away from Attingal once for all, but only they wanted to avenge the insults heaped upon them, as noted earlier. This seems to stand confirmed by their decision to attack and harass the Englishmen in the fort, several days after the revolt and massacre. If their intention had been to drive the English away from Attingal, they would have launched an attack on the fort immediately after the revolt, when they were in a stronger position while the English were completely decimated and weakened.

However, the revolt brought to the fore the fact that the Queen was no more in total control of the affairs of her country. It undermined irreversibly her strength. One of the two main *Pillas,* Cuddamon pilla, did not heed to her directives. He was acting according to his own sweet will without the traditional consent or concurrence of the Queen, as during the time when the grant was given to the English in1694. The Queen relied heavily on Vanjamutta, who, as we know, had established a working relationship with the *madambees* of Travancore earlier. This was not a good sign for the future independent status of the Queen as sovereign of Attingal.

The much publicised Black Hole tragedy of Calcutta, where 146 English men, women and children were ushered into a small room, out of whom 123 died of suffocation, fades into insignificane when compared to the Attingal revolt and massacre, which occurred about two and a half decades earlier.[82] Recent researches have established that the Black Hole tragedy was blown out of proportion and largely imaginary.[83] On the other hand the Attingal massacre and revolt possess authentic proofs in the English factory records and the Queen's letter. However, this is one of the earliest recorded instances in the entire history of the English in India, of hundred and fifty Englishmen being brutally massacred as part of a more elaborate revolt, in which Hindus and Muslims of Attingal in south Malabar, combined to punish and evict the English.

Notes and References

1. John Wallis, 'A Short treatise by way of essay of Attinga, 1727', 7 September 1727, p.21.
2. J.H.Parry, *Trade and Dominion – The European Overseas Empires in the Eighteenth Century,* London, 1971, p.65.
3. Despatches from England- 1705, England to Fort St. George, 12 January 1705, p.67
4. Secretariat Outward, 1698, Bombay Castle, to John Brabourne, Anjengo, 27 June 1698, p.96.
5. *Ibid.*
6. Despatches from England-1705, Fort St. George to John Brabourne, Anjengo, 12 January 1705, p.67.
7. John Biddulph, *The Pirates of Malabar and an English Woman in India two thousand years ago,* London, 1907, p. 274 ; John Wallis, *op.cit.,* p.23; Factory Records, Miscellaneous- 1718-1719, William Kyffin, Anjengo to President and Council of Bombay, 11 January 1718, p.12.
8. John Biddulph, *op.cit.,* pp.267 – 268; Talboys, J. Wheeler, *A History of the English Settlements in India,* Calcutta, 1878, p.79; John Keay, *The Honourable Company. A History of the English East India Company,* New York, 1991, p.253
9. John Wallis, *op.cit.,* p.21.
10. *Ibid*, p.22
11. Biddulph, *op.cit.*, pp.267-268
12. Anjengo Factory Records- 1704 – 1748, John Wallis, Chief Anjengo to Bombay Castle, 13 December 1723, p.33.
13. *Ibid.*
14. Manohar Malgonkar, *Kanhoji Angrey,* Bombay, 1959, p.151.

15. Anjengo Factory Records- 1704 – 1749, James Salisbury, Factor, Anjengo to William Phipps, Bombay, 28 December 1728, pp.88-89.

16. *Ibid.*, p.89

17. Manohar Malgonkar, *op.cit.*, p.156.

18. *Ibid.*

19. Anjengo Factory Records- 1704 – 1749, Nathaniel Whitewell, Secretary, Anjengo to President and Council of Bombay, 22 February, 1726, p.41 ; A. Galletti, *Dutch in Malabar*, Madras, 1911, pp.71– 72.

20. Jacob, Canter Visscher, *Letters from Malabar*, Madras, 1862, p.31.

21. *Ibid;* Political Consultations, 1809; Sebastien Diaz Fernandez, Linguist, Anjengo to Committee at Fort St.George, 31 October 1809, p.2457; Anjengo Diary, 1755, George Scott, Chief, Anjengo to Fort St.George, November, 1755, p.29

22. Jacob Canter Visscher, *Letters from Malabar*, Madras, 1862, p.45.

23. John Wallis, op.cit, p.26. The farm purchased by Ignatio was called Cottadilly. He purchased it for 90000 fanams. It was 'a very large tract of land, the circumference of it about three miles, and its extent from North to South about one..... this spot of ground was very fruitful in coconuts and toddy, arrack and betel trees', pp. 64 – 65.

24. *Ibid.*

25. Foreign Records Miscellaneous- 1721, Midford and Salisbury, Anjengo to President and Council of Bombay, 6 February1721, p. 69. The record which comprises of letters of William Gyfford to various Company officials is not available in India. The present author found it in India Office Library Records, London.

26. John Wallis op.cit p. 24, « the natives sat on the porch of the interpreter's house and ate a betle as it was customary for all strangers to eat a betle »; Biddulph, John, *op.cit*, p.275; Wallis,John, *op.cit,* p.24.

27. Wallis, John, *op.cit.*, p.24.

28. *Ibid,* p.23.

29. Records of Fort St.George, Diary and Consultation Book- 1720, Chief, Anjengo to Fort St. George, 31 August 1720, p. 159; Factory Records Miscellaneous- 1720, Bombay Castle to William Gyfford, Chief, Anjengo, 15 April 1720, p. 129.

30. Factory Records Miscellaneous - 1720, William Gyfford, Anjengo to Bombay Castle, 17 February 1720, p.25.

31. *Ibid.*, p.26.; The Company decided to get the chequeens from Calicut to pay the presents to the Queen.

32. *Ibid.*, p.27; Factory Records Miscellaneous, 1720, William Gyfford, Anjengo to Bombay Castle, 17 February 1720, p.27
33. Records of Fort St. George, Diary and Consultation Book-1720, Chief, Anjengo to Fort St. George, 31 August 1720, p. 159
34. Records of Fort St.George, consultation Book, 1721, 18 November 1721, p.92
35. Public Consultation, 1721, Fort St. George, to Anjengo, June 1721, p.154
36. *Ibid;* Factory Records Miscellaneous, 1721, William Gyfford, Anjengo to Bombay Castle, 25 January 1721, pp.35,38
37. Factory Records Miscellaneous, 1721, William Gyfford, Anjengo to Bombay Castle, 25 January 1721, p.38
38. John Wallis, *op.cit.*, p.27; Records of fort St.George, Diary and Consultation Book, 1721, Anjengo to Fort St. George, 11 May 1721, p.71
39. Alexander Hamilton, *A New Account of the East Indies,* Edinburg, 1728, pp.332-333
40. John Wallis, *op.cit.*, p.27; Anjengo Factory Records, 1704-1749, Alexander Orme, Anjengo to Bombay Castle, 13 December 1723, p.30
41. *Ibid;* John Biddulph, *op.cit.*, p.277
42. Jacob Canter Visscher, *op.cit.*, p.28; Wallis, John, *op.cit.*, p.28
43. John Wallis, *op.cit.*, p.28
44. John Biddulph, *op.cit.*, p.277; Factory Records Miscellaneous, 1721-22, Midford, Anjengo to Bombay Castle, 6 February 1722, p.69
45. John Wallis, *op.cit.*, p.28
46. Jacob Canter Visscher, *op.cit.*, p.46
47. Factory Records Miscellaneous, 1722, Midford and Salisbury, Anjengo to Bombay Castle, 6 February 1722, p.70
48. John Wallis, *op.cit.*, p.28
49. John Biddulph, *op.cit.*, p.278
50. John Wallis, *op.cit.*, p.29
51. John Biddulph, *op.cit.*, p.279
52. John Wallis, *op.cit.*, p.29
53. Despatches to England, 1719-1729, fort St. George to England, 3 February, 1722. p.68
54. John Biddulph, *op.cit.*, p.280

55. Records of fort St. George, diary and consultation Book, 1721, Anjengo to Fort St. George, 17 May 1721, p.76; Factory Records Miscellaneous, 1721, Robert Sewell, anjengo to Bombay Castle, 26 April 1721, p.51; Public consultation, 1721, Fort St. George to Anjengo, May 1721, p.132. Even in this grief stricken state of mind, Mrs. Gyfford carried off the factory records, official papers and whatever money she could lay her hand on. She even tried to entice Peter Lapthorne but Sewell prevented her – Anjengo Factory Records, 1704-1749, Alexander Orme, Anjengo to fort St. George, 13 December 1723, p.32

56. Factory Records Miscellaneous, 1721, Military Officers, Anjengo to President and Council, Bombay, 26 April 1721, p.49

57. *Ibid.*,

58. *Ibid.*, pp.49-50; John Biddulph, *op.cit.*, p.282

59. John Wallis, *op.cit.*, p.31

60. Factory Records Miscellaneous, 1721, Military Officers, Anjengo to President and Council, Bombay, 26 April 1721, p.50

61. Factory Records Miscellaneous, 1721, Peter Lapthorne, Anjengo to Mrs. Gyfford, Bombay, 3 August 1721, p.54

62. *Ibid.*

63. *Ibid.*, p.55; John Biddulph, *op.cit.*, p.285; John Wallis, *op.cit.*, p.30

64. Factory Records Miscellaneous, 1721, Blackett Midford, Anjengo to President and council, Bombay, 14 November 1721, p.57

65. Fort St. George Records, 1721. A translate of a Malabar letter from the Queen of Attingal to the governor of Fort St. George, June 1721, p.92. See Appendix. This letter is not referred to in any book by historians. The present author found it in Fort St. George Records, Tamilnadu Archives

66. *Ibid.*

67. *Ibid*; Factory Records Miscellaneous, 1721, Blackett Midford, Anjengo to President and council, Bombay, 14 November 1721, p.60

68. Factory Records Miscellaneous, 1721, Blackett Midford, Anjengo to President and council, Bombay, 14 November 1721, p.61; Factory Records Miscellaneous, 1721, Bombay Castle to the Court of Directors, London, 28 December 1721, p.145

69. Alexander Hamilton, *op.cit.*, p.333; Canter Jacob, Visscher, *op.cit.*, p.46; John Biddulph, *op.cit.*, p.277; William Logan, *Treaties, engagements and other papers of importance relating to British Affairs in Malabar*, Madras, 1879, 1891, (111), p.19

70. Velu Pillai, *A History of Travancore,* Trivandrum, 1935, p.10; Nagam Aiya, *The Travancore State Manual, I,* Trivandrum, 1906, p.325; Henry Davison Love, *Indian Record Series – Vestiges of Old Madras,* II, London, 1913, p.214; Ibrahim Kunju *Medieval Kerala History,* Trivandrum, 1975, pp.123-124; K.P. Padmanabha Menon, *History of Kerala, I,* Ernakulam, 1924, p.337; Sreedhara Menon. *A survey of Kerala History,* Trivandrum, 1984, p.207

71. Fort St. George Records, 1721, p.92; Public Despatches to England, 1722, Fort St. George to the Court of Directors, London, 3 February 1722, p.68. See Appendix

72. Alexander Hamilton, *op.cit.,* p.333; Pillai, Velu, *op.cit.,* p.10; Nagam Aiya, *op.cit.,* p.325; Sreedhara Menon, *op.cit.,* p.207; Love, Henry Davison, *op.cit.,* p.214; Ibrahim Kunju, *Rise of Travancore,* Trivandrum, 1976, p.87; John Biddulph, *op.cit.,* p.277

73. Fort St. George Records, 1721, Anjengo to Fort St. George, May 1721, p.71; See Appendix; John Wallis, *op.cit.,* p.28

74. John Biddulph, *op.cit.,* p.287; Visscher, Jacob Canter, *op.cit.,* p.31; Alexander Hamilton, *op.cit.,* pp.332-333

75. Factory Records Miscellaneous, 1721, Bombay Castle to Court of directors, 28 December 1721, p.145

76. Bombay Letters Received, 1697, John Brabourne, anjengo to John Gayer, Bombay, 27 august 1697, p.8; John Wallis, *op.cit.,* p.21

77. Facory Records Miscellaneous, 1721, William Gyfford, Anjengo to Bombay Castle, 25 January 1721, p.35

78. Factory Records Miscellaneous, 1721, Salisbury, anjengo to the Resident and council, Bombay, 6 February 1722, p.70

79. Factory Records Miscellaneous, 1721, Bombay Castle to the court of Directors, 28 December 1721, p.145; See also Appendix; Leena P.K., 'The History of the English East India Company's Settlement at Anjengo', Phd.dissertaion, Calicut University, august 1989, p.146

80. Factory Records Miscellaneous, 1721, Bombay Castle to Court of Directors, 28 December 1721, p.145

81. *Ibid.*

82. Ishwari Prasad, *India in the Eighteenth Century,* Allahabad, 1973, p.90

83. Ramakrishna Mukherjee, *The Rise and Fall of the East India Company, Bombay,* 1955,1973, p.261. The truth of the story has been doubted on many grounds.

Chapter 4

Attingal Declines and Travancore Rises

The years that followed the revolt were a period of instability and uncertainty. The Attingal massacre and the rude shock it gave the Company continued to haunt the English. The affairs of the Company were in a state of confusion. The undercurrent of rivalry between the *Pillas* and the helplessness of the Queen adversely affected the interests of the Company. The *Pillas* had to be reckoned as a power in the region and the Queen was lacking in influence in dealing with them effectively. In consequence the country was plunged into a series of internal feuds.[1]

Midford succeeded Gyfford as chief of Anjengo with directives to re-settle the Company of Anjengo after the calamity that had befallen them and obtain satisfaction from the Attingal Queen and government for the loss incurred in human lives and trade.[2] The Malabaris expected the forces of Midford to wreak vengeance on those who were responsible for the revolt by launching an attack.[3] But contrary to all expectations, Midford's reaction to the Attingal revolt in which 150 Englishmen were killed, was mild and muted. Moreover during this critical period, the the Company's forces, instead of confronting the Malabaris who had revolted against them, were diverted against the Angrias (pirates from the northern Maratha country). This naturally diminished considerably their prestige and rendered them contemptible in the eyes of the Malabaris.[4]

At this juncture the atmosphere in the country was not at all conducive for favourable trade. The Queen of Attingal Amutumbaran's reduced power in the changed circumstances and the volatile nature of the *Pillas* had a destablising effect on the whole country. However the Company under Midford, instead of waiting or even working first for the return of a certain stability in the region, was simply bent upon making immediate money on pepper by contracting with Vanjamutta pilla for 1000 *candies* of pepper. This only resulted in the enhancement of the price of pepper.[5]

Very soon Alexander Orme succeeded Midford. So the responsibility of restoring amicable relations with the Queen of Attingal fell on his shoulders. In September 1722, he entered into a treaty with the Queen. The main provisions of the treaty were :

1. The ring leaders in the attack on Gyfford were to be punished and their estates to be confiscated
2. The Queen was to reimburse the Company for all the losses caused by the attack on Anjengo
3. The Company was to have exclusive right to the pepper trade and be empowered to build factories in the Queen's dominions whenever they pleased
4. The Queen was to return all arms taken in the outbreak and furnish timber to rebuild the church that had been burnt
5. The Company was expected to supply soldiers to the Queen to carry on war against her enemies.

It is interesting to note that this treaty was guaranteed by the Queen's brother, the King of Quilon.[6] Though this once again proves that the Queen's power had eroded to some extent, it is nevertheless surprising that she did not call upon the Rajah of Travancore, who was traditionally obedient to the Queen to guarantee the treaty. This might be because of the fact that though historically Attingal was the maternal house of the Rajah of Travancore, yet the Queen was not directly related to the Rajah. Besides, she was regarded as a foreigner to the royal family of Attingal by the inhabitants. She actually owed her appointment as

Queen to the *Pillas*. All these factors seemed to have diminished considerably her prestige not only in Attingal but also in the whole region.

The English too were conscious of the fading power of the Queen. They were particularly worried about their trade interests. Though the Company had already entered into a treaty with the Queen of Attingal by which she was promised with military aid to suppress her enemies, yet the Court of Directors' disapproval on lavishing money on unprofitable military ventures put the Company servants in Attingal on guard.[7] Besides, the Queen of Attingal had never been able to prosecute those who participated in the Attingal revolt due mainly to the opposition of the *Pillas*. Surprisingly, Vanjamutta himself who had always sided with the English, even during the revolt, prevented the Queen from punishing one Cockoor, a Muslim inhabitant of Permadura, who participated in the Attingal revolt, though later he blamed the Carriacar for that.[8]

In the face of the fading power of the Queen who was literally controlled by the *Pillas*, the English sought for other alternatives to protect their trade and other interests. This seems to have brought them into contact with the Rajah of Travancore more than anything else. It is highly doubtful if the English would have dared to open direct contacts with the Rajah, if the present Queen was as strong as the old Queen, having a direct line of relationship with the Rajah.

At this time, the reigning Rajah of Travancore was Unni Kerala Varma (1718-1724). He was known to be a weak ruler.[9] His nephew was Martanda Varma, whose counsels prevailed in the court of Travancore. Martanda Varma was not favourably disposed towards the *Pillas*. He and the Travancore royal house and court were conscious of the fact that the Queen of Attingal's power had eroded to such an extent that she could do nothing to ensure peace in the region, in spite of the treaty that she had entered with the English. Probably they feared also the growing influence of the Pillas in Travancore itself, given that it was with the concurrence of the *madambees* of Travancore that the *Pillas* had installed the present Queen on the throne of Attingal.

So the Rajah probably on the advice of Martanda Varma chose to check the activities of the *Pillas*.[10] But taming the *Pillas'* power in the region single-handedly was no joke. As a result they decided to seek the help of the English, who in their turn turned towards Travancore with the hope of protecting their interests. T.K.Velu Pillai asserts that it was Martanda Varma who was the man behind the King's decision to befriend the English East India Company.[11] Thus considerations of mutual interests and benefits resulted in the negotiations of a treaty between Martanda Varma as the Prince of Neyattingara, the acknowledged representative of the Rajah of Travancore, and Alexander Orme on 25 April 1723. Its provisons were :

1. The Company was allowed to erect a fort at Colachel under the orders of the king of Travancore who should bear the cost of construction of the fort and also pay for the people placed in it.
2. The Company was obliged to supply the artillery and ammunitions of war for the fort.
3. The Company was permitted to build a mint for coining of *fanams*

In addition, the government of Travancore agreed to remain 'in league and united in good friendship with the Honourable Company'.[12] Three months later another agreement was entered into, this time by the King of Travancore himself and Alexander Orme by which the King agreed to punish those who were involved in the Attingal revolt and massacre.[13]

The treaty of April 1723 was a water-shed in the history of south Malabar, though the contention of K.M.Pannikar cannot be conceded that it was the first ever treaty negotiated by the English East India Company with an Indian State, in the light of what we have seen above.[14] What the English could never obtain from the Queens of Attingal, for the past more than three decades, ie., the privilege of coining *fanams,* they obtained from the Rajah of Travancore within a very short period. In return, the Company agreed to supply artillery and ammunition in exchange for pepper and other spices.[15] It has to be noted at this juncture that just about six months back the Company had entered into a treaty with the Queen of Attingal to supply her with soldiers to put down the rebels and enemies. But the Company chose not to honour this treaty, mainly under pressure from the Court of Directors. Instead, the Company was determined to honour their commitment to the Rajah of Travancore that they would supply him with arms and ammunitions and also men.

Later, on 30 July 1724, the Rajah of Travancore seems to have given even a grant to the English, assuring them that none other than the English will be permitted to establish settlements in his territory.[16] The King of Travancore thus sought to consolidate his relationship with the English.

That Martanda Varma was fascinated by the superior western military discipline and artillery is another matter.[17] But the historical fact was that the English had made a deliberate choice to strengthen the hands of the Rajah of Travancore, at the expense of Attingal, because he corresponded more to the promotion of their needs and interests than the Queen of Attingal in the changed atmosphere. The Company seems to have realised that only if the king of Travancore had full power in his hand, they could enjoy a free and full trade in future. It was because of this factor that the Company resolved to put down the enemies of the King, in spite of the expenses involved.[18] They seem to have favoured the rise of a 'despotic monarch who would assign to them monopolies of the produce they came seeking and could enforce the same with a strong arm'.[19] These factors more than anything else, not even the ambition or intelligence of Martanda Varma, seems to have laid the foundation for the rise of Travancore in Malabar.

The King of Travancore on his part swung into action to please the English. He pledged himself to compel Cuddamon to tender in writing public pardon for the fault he was guilty of against the Company. He pledged also to establish a godown at Kulaccal and not to supply any other European nation any goods which were necessary for the English. He further agreed to order for the supply of 1000000 piece goods every year in various kinds and to permit the Company to collect the customs on all imports and exports. In the customs account, the Company was to pay the King 6000 *fanams* annually in gold or other articles on account.[20]

The Queen of Attingal realising that the Rajah of Travancore had asserted himself independently by concluding a treaty with the English decided to befriend the English in her turn in a more pronounced manner. This realisation though belated could be taken as an attempt by the Queen to stem her diminishing fortunes in the region.

Accordingly on 18 March 1726, the Queen of Attingal with the consent and concurrence of Vanjamutta and Cuddamon, the two main headmen, granted the English permission to set up a factory at Eddawa.[21] This was done with an eye on augmenting further the customs duties of the government and cement the relationship with the Company, who had begun to flirt with the Rajah of Travancore.[22] In return for the factory at Eddawa, the Company had to pay the Queen 5000 *fanams*, the Princess (her daughter) 2000 *fanams*, Vanjamutta 1000 *fanams*, Cuddamon 1000 *fanams*, the Queen's Rajadurai and Annavy 1000 fanams and Adichen Concoply (the accountant probably) 200 *fanams*. In the instrument of ratification, the Queen clearly stated that this grant had been made for obtaining the favour and help of the Company.[23]

In spite of this grant, the English were not in a position or did not want to strengthen their contacts with the Queen mainly because of the frictions created by the *Pillas* in the region and the establishment of friendly relationship with the Rajah of Travancore. Not only did the *Pillas* fight between themselves but also sometimes turned against the Queen and the English. The great *Pilla* Vanjamutta who had been continuously an ally of the Queen since quite some time gradually turned against her and also the English. He even began harassing the English, whom he had always helped since the time of the old Queen, when pepper was required by the latter.The Queen also was not happy with Vanjamutta for his opposition to stone-cutting at Nadogundy for the Company's building. She conferred with Cunjee Ally, the sister of Cuddamon about Vanjamutta's opposition to stone-cutting. She even went to the extent of sending one Cunjan of Calliel Vidill to assist stone-cutting. She also assured protection to the Tiyya workmen who were involved in the cutting and transport of stones by sending some Nairs.[24]

Further, probably in order to assert her authority she demanded the customs that was due to her according to previous agreements. The Company promised to pay provided she sent them a receipt for it signed by both Vanjamutta and Cuddamon, not only because they were customarily involved in all public affairs, but also because they had a share in the customs.[25] Thus the English without helping her militarily to put down all her enemies according to the treaty of September 1722, chose to play up the differences between them and delay the payment. The Queen did not like the English implicating the *Pillas* in affairs which she considered her own.

In fact the Queen asserted that the *Pillas* were entitled only to a gratuity when she received her annual presents and not to any part of her customs.[26] She was perfectly right in this assertion for nowhere do we have a written evidence either in the grants or in the treaty that the *Pillas* had a share in the customs. As a matter of fact the Company had decided to lower her prestige and power in Attingal and in the region, by insinuating that she was not in a position to protect them and assert her own right as the sovereign without the concurrence of Vanjamutta and Cuddamon, who were actually vying with one another for more power. It should not also be forgotten at this juncture that Vanjamutta had always been helpful to the English especially in times of great peril as in 1697 and also in 1721. So it was quite natural that the English had some sympathy for him and did not want to let down their old friend altogether.Thus the English seem to have set the Queen more unintentionally than wantingly, against her own headmen, the *Pillas*.[27]

The neighbouring powers of Attingal, the Kings of Chenganatta and Peritally watched the power struggle in Attingal, sometimes taking the side of the Queen, sometimes that of the the *Pillas* according to what was most advantageous to them.[28] Meanwhile the *Pillas* ie., the *madambees* of Travancore followed the example of those in Attingal and began to throw off their allegiance to the King of Travancore. According to the English records, Vanjamutta was the brain behind the *madambees,* defiant attitude. The *madambees* in their turn helped the *Pillas* of Attingal when occasions arose.[29]

It appears that the *Pillas* of Attingal and Travancore began manœuvres for the destruction of the young prince, Martanda Varma, who had earlier obtained the support of the English through the treaty of April 1723. Vanjamutta was especially bent upon eliminating the young prince. Martanda Varma had to remain in disguise and proceed from place to place to escape from the clutches of the *Pillas.* He finally sought refuge at Attingal with the Queen.[30] The English seem to have played a role in bringing the King of Travancore to Attingal. According to their records, it was Alexander Orme who was instrumental in bringing Martanda

Varma into Attingal to fight the *Pillas*, by lending large sums of money to the King of Travancore without the consent of his superiors.[31] Neither the *Pillas* nor the Queen of Attingal knew about it. In the process Orme seems to have succeeded in setting not only the Queen of Attingal as noted earlier, but also the King of Travancore against the *Pillas*. This he seems to have done because he was conscious of the fact that the English did not have sufficient forces to wage any war in Attingal.[32] Besides, he seems to have also been instrumental in bringing the influential prince of Travancore, Martanda Varma, who was not directly related to the Queen of Attingal, closer to the latter, probably in his efforts to eliminate the *Pillas*.

It appears that the *Pillas* angered by the Queen's attitude in drawing closer to the King of Travancore decided to kill the Queen and her little son, Rama Varma, who was a heir to the Travancore throne. As a result, it is held that an attempt was made in 1728 on the lives of the Queen and her little son when they were travelling from Attingal to Trivandrum. But owing to the intervention of the Queen's consort Koil Thampuran, she and her son escaped. But Thampuran was killed in his bid to save the royal family.[33]

The above incident provoked the Queen of Attingal and the King of Travancore to declare a war against the *Pillas* of both Attingal and Travancore. Thus the royal families of Attingal and Travancore came together after several decades in a common bid to suppress the *Pillas* under Vanjamutta who threatened their power. Cuddamonpilla who had always vied for power with Vanjamutta chose to join the Queen of Attingal and the King of Travancore to crush Vanjamutta. The Queen had a personal grudge against Vanjamutta who, she thought, was the brain behind the revolt of the *Pillas* of Travancore against Martanda Varma and under whose probable instigation she and her son were targeted for assassination.[34] Vanjamutta becoming an inveterate enemy of the Rajah of Travancore and the Queen of Attingal, the Queen had no other option but to go against Vanjamutta with the combined forces of Travancore and Attingal. She even demanded the help of the English in this combined operation.[35] But this alliance with Travancore was bound to have its repercussions in the short as well as long run.

Many open encounters and skirmishes took place between the two without any decisive result. Martanda Varma burnt Vanjamutta's palace and razed his fort of Pallichal.[36] Vanjamutta complained that Martanda Varma had burnt his palace and fort of Pallichal together with about 500 houses that were within the fort, when none of his family were there to defend it. The Queen later claimed responsibility for the destruction of the fort of Pallichal. Vanjamutta vowed to avenge himself for this act. He was anxious to know whether the English were for him or against him. He insisted that the English should not take sides with the Queen. He informed them that he was not instrumental in the obstruction of stone-cutting for the building in the fort as accused previously by the Queen.[37] But the English who had entered earlier into a treaty with the King of Travancore, who in his turn had sought refuge in Attingal fleeing the *Pillas,* would not commit themselves openly.

Later Vanjamutta in consultation with the King of Peritally, and his *Pillas* decided to burn the Queen's palace at Capi in retaliation for Prince Martanda Varma's action against Pallichal.[38] Consequently the Queen sought assistance from the English, according to the understanding with them in September 1722. But the English seem to have been still not sure as to who will get the upper hand in the tussle for power between the *Pillas* and the Queen. So they did not want to throw in their lot fully with any Malabari power openly, which could only be detrimental to their own interests. So in the midst of these conflicts, keeping in mind the dangers to pepper trade that would arise if Vanjamutta was antagonised and also fearing another major attack on the fort, the English decided to observe strict neutrality.[39] Therefore, they informed the Queen that in case they sided with her, the *Pillas* would definitely burn and destroy the English factory at Eddawa. They also informed her that as they were in no way concerned with the quarrel, they did not want to interfere and undermine peace.[40] It was a way of telling her that she had to manage by herself her conflict with the *Pillas* without the open help of the English. Thus the English kept the *Pillas* too guessing about their attitude in the ongoing conflict.

However, the Queen in her turn informed the English that the *Pillas* had already destroyed her palace at Capi and that she was expecting them to invade Attingal. She therefore requested them to deliver her arms.[41] She also wanted 2000 *fanams* to pay her soldiers, for she was also under financial pressure. She assured that she would remove all the obstacles to pepper trade and ensure free flow of pepper and promised to clear all pending accounts.[42]

Meanwhile Vanjamutta had defeated Martanda Varma and obliged him to retreat to the frontiers of Travancore. He thus established himself as the foremost power in Attingal at the expense of the Queen of Attingal.[43] Growing impatient with the unfavourable attitude of the English towards him, Vanjamutta threatened to destroy Eddawa factory and demanded 10000 *fanams* as annual presents from the English as he considered himself as the new King of Attingal. According to English records, Vanjamutta seems to have had an inkling during this time about the role of Alexander Orme in bringing Martanda Varma to Attingal to fight him.[44] But the Queen put her foot down and dissuaded the English from fulfilling the wishes of Vanjamutta by pointing out that Cuddamonpilla following the example of Vanjamutta would demand similar presents which was not at all legitimate, for it was the custom to give annual presents to the Queen and not to anybody else.[45]

However, as the Queen was no more able to give any assurance to the English regarding their factory at Edawa and as the latter were determined to preserve it, it was decided to befriend Vanjamutta.[46] On the other hand, Cuddamonpilla who had always vied for power against Vanjamutta and who had always been against the English and was considered the brain behind the Attingal revolt decided to patch up his differences with Vanjamutta. He did not want any more to cater to the Queen's interests which had become linked with Travancore.[47]

But in the meantime, Martanda Varma who had fled back to Travancore under pressure from Vanjamutta, was making preparations to undo the *Pillas,* who constituted a threat to even the authority of the King of Travancore, given Vanjamutta's alliance with the *madambees* of Travancore. Besides Travancore was also as usual under pressure due to incursions into its territory from the east. In order to counter these threats and incursions, the Rajah of Travancore decided to seek help from the Nayak of Madura. Further the King of Travancore, influenced probably by Martanda Varma, the Prince of Neyattingara, had chosen to enter into agreements with the English in 1723 itself. When things were thus, Unni Kerala Varma, the King of Travancore died in 1724. He was succeeded by his younger brother Rama Varma who was a junior uncle to Martanda Varma.[48] The King of Travancore and Martanda Varma, who, as we know, were embroiled in troubles with the *Pillas* were looking for avenues to quell the *Pillas*. They therefore decided to befriend the powers in the east in their efforts to counter the *Pillas*.

In 1726, Rama Varma on the advice of Maratanda Varma took a very momentous decision in the history of Travancore, by offering his allegiance like his predecessors to the Nayak of Madura and solicited his help in exterminating the *Pillas*.[49] The King himself left for Trichinopoly in the Tamil country accompanied by Martanda Varma and other officers and paid homage to the Nayak.[50] He agreed to pay a sum of Rs.3000 annually as tribute to the Nayak for supplying a suitable force to punish the rebels.[51]

After some discussion and enquiries, Rama Varma was successful in obtaining a force consisting of one thousand cavalry, under the command of Venkatapathy Naiken, and two thousand Carnatic sepoys, headed by Thripathy Naiken and others. With help from Madura and having earlier procured some arms and ammunitions from the English, Martanda Varma intimated the English at Anjengo on 10th November 1728, his intention of setting out to Trivandrum at the head of a great force to confront the *Pillas* and *madambees*. On 11th November he attacked the *Pillas* with 3000 men. Unable to bear the onslaught, the *pillas* fled.[52]

On 18 November Martanda Varma himself informed the English in Attingal that the *Pillas* had been defeated and they had fled. He asserted that he himself had killed fifteen of the *Pillas,* at the cost of only one of his men. But Vanjamutta was not among those killed. He also reported that a number of *madambees* had sued for peace and they had promised to pay him 6000 *fanams* and repair the Capi palace with stone walls and to restore all the guns that they had taken out of that fort.[53] Immediately after crushing the *Pillas*, Martanda Varma visited the English at the Anjengo fort, probably in order to prove to them that he was the real authority in the region. The English reciprocated by saluting him with seven guns and sent him a present of five venetians.[54] Martanda Varma's power was definitely on the rise after his victory over the *Pillas*.

Sensing this new development, the French who were settled in Mahe in north Malabar from 1721 visited the King of Travancore, Rama Varma with presents of 15 yards of scarlet clothes, three fire-locks and 25 *pagodas*. They sought permission to settle at Eddawa and Colachel. The King replied that Eddawa was already given to the English and as for Colachel he would consider it later.[55] Even the Dutch Commodore at Cochin offered to build a fort in Travancore to protect the King against what he termed his enemy, the English.[56] The King of Travancore, most certainly under the advice of Maratanda Varma refused all these overtures of the Dutch and the French, preferring to maintain his good relationship with the English.

Martanda Varma's victory over the *Pillas* allowed the King of Travancore and the Queen of Attingal to assert their authority jointly in the region in a more forceful manner. As a result, they sent their representatives, the Dalawa and Crisna Annavy to the English at Anjengo to discuss and settle customs dues from the Company, which they had refused to pay earlier to the Queen on the pretext that she should have the signatures of Vanjamutta and Cuddamon. This time the English had other excuses. The English chief, Alexander Orme told that he had augmented the number of forces and swelled the charges of the garrison on account of the troubles between the Queen and the *Pillas*. As a result he had incured heavy expenditure and loss, not only for the maintenance of a special force for the security of Attingal, but also because their trade had suffered due to the inability of the King of Travancore or the Queen of Attingal to protect it.[57]

He also reminded the Dalawa that no reparation had been made as yet for the massacre of Englishmen at Attingal in 1721 and notwithstanding so many treaties and agreements with both the Queen of Attingal and the King of Travancore the perpetrators of the massacre were still at liberty and therefore it was not reasonable to make any payments to the Queen. But the Dalawa retorted by asserting that the war waged by the King of Travancore against the *Pillas* was itself extremely costly and was done only to chastise the perpetrators of the Attingal massacre.[58]

Even at this juncture when the power of Travancore was ascending, the Queen of Attingal continued to enjoy a certain independence. In fact, John Wallis who became the new chief of Anjengo fort, still had direct dealings with the Queen. In order to win her over to his side, he decided to revive the custom of carrying presents to the Queen, which was actually abandoned after the

Attingal revolt.[59] The ties between the Queen and the English continued even later. On 5 April 1729, the Queen entered into another agreement with the English, by which the latter agreed to present 75 venetians to the Queen annually in return for all the pepper in the country. Besides, they were to pay a custom duty of 5 *rajees* (50 *chakrams*) for every *candy* of pepper, from which she allowed 20 per cent to the Company. The Queen further agreed to assure the transportation of the pepper to the fort free of all embarassment in the region. The English in their turn agreed to pay the customs on pepper only to the Queen and not to anyone else in the country, given that the power of the *Pillas* had been suppressed to a great extent by Martanda Varma.[60]

Thus a relative peace conducive to the development of trade was re-established in Attingal. The earlier fear of the English of the Queen losing her power because of the *Pillas* was found to be baseless. So they pursued with further negotiations with the Queen. She even agreed to pay damages to the English for the loss they suffered during the Attingal revolt of 1721 ten years ago. As a result the Queen of Attingal and the King of Travancore jointly decided to cede the revenue-yielding gardens of Cottadali and Palatady to the English.[61] This joint cession to the English however proves the increasing cooperation between Attingal and Travancore in the management of the affairs of Attingal. It attests to some extent the diminishing influence of the Queen, though her sovereignty was still recognised by the English, in spite of the gradual ascendancy of the King of Travancore.

Expansion of Travancore

At the death of Rama Varma in 1729, prince Martanda Varma ascended the throne of Travancore.[62] Though only 23 years old, he was well-versed in the art of warfare and statecraft, as we have seen. His contacts with the Nayak of Madura, probably influenced Martanda Varma to become more ambitious in his internal as well as external dealings. He re-organised the state administration and finances on a firmer footing. As king he was the head of State. He had a prime minister (*Valia Sarvadhikariakar* or *Diwan*) directly answerable to him. There was a chief secretariat with a Secretary (*Neetezhuthu Pillay)* and an under-secretary*(Rayasom Pillay*), assisted by several *rayasoms* or clerks and *Kanakku Pillamars* or Accountants. Officers known as *Sarvadhikariakars* (district collectors) had jurisdiction over districts. Political correspondence with foreign powers was carried out by the prime minister. There were various government departments headed by *Rayasoms.*[63]

In this administrative set up the King's power was almost absolute, for no important matter was to be decided or executed without the consent and final approval of the King.[64] This was a drastic departure from previous methods of administration and political control, were the King's power was extremely curtailed.[65]

Having thus consolidated to a great extent his internal power, Martanda Varma turned once again his attention towards the remaining *Pillas*, who still adopted a hostile posture to his government. Actually the *Pillas* brought into their fold the late King Rama Varma's sons known as Kunju Thambies alias Papu Thamby and Raman Thamby, who had held high position during the life time of their father, but who were now reduced to the level of ordinary nobles by Martanda Varma. Probably wanting to retrieve their former position, they decided to ally with the rebelling *Pillas* to overthrow Martanda Varma and recapture power.[66] Taking the cue from Martanda Varma himself, who had earlier contacted the Nayak to assert his authority, the *Thambies* approached the Pandyan kingdom of Trichinopoly for assistance. Alagappa Mudaliar promised help and he actually came with a force and encamped at Pullikurichi. But Martanda Varma sent his deputies Ramayyan and Narayanayyan who seemed to have tactfully convinced Alagappa that the claims of the Thambies were unfounded and false. Sreedhara Menon holds that Alagappa was bribed by Martanda Varma to return home. Alagappa seems to have reprimanded the Thambies and returned with his force to Trichinopoly, loaded with presents from Martanda Varma.[67]

Having thus warded off a Tamil intervention in the affairs of south Malabar, Martanda Varma realised that he had to act quickly, to counter the Thambies and the *Pillas*. He re-organised his army which consisted of the Maravars (a Tamil caste known for its warlike nature) and the Nairs, the traditional militia of Malabar. Regiments of infantry with fire-arms were formed and maintained. Fortifications were built at vantage places, garrisoned by detachments. Spies were appointed throughout the country and from them Martanda Varma received intelligence about each and every movement of the *Pillas*.[68]

As a result, 42 *Pillas*, *madambees* and chiefs were caught, tried, and sentenced to death. They were all hanged at a place known by the name *Mukhamandapam*, a few miles north-west of Kalkulam. Even Papu Thamby and Raman Thamby were executed on his orders. He also ensured the elimination of the entire kith and kin of those who were opposed to him. He even gave orders to seize the women and children and hand them over to the fishermen, thus making them outcastes, according to the then prevailing customs.[69]

Thus by the year 1734-35, Martanda Varma wiped out the *Pillas* who defied his authority. Golleness, the Dutch commander recorded in his memoir that it was with the help of the English that Martanda Varma was able to suppress the rebellion of the *Pillas*.[70] Though English soldiers did not directly participate in the operations against the *Pillas,* yet it is certain that they provided arms and ammunitions to Martanda Varma.

Flushing with victory over the *Pillas* and probably thinking that some of the surviving *Pillas* like Vanjamutta might have found refuge in the neighbouring kingdoms, from where they could regroup and attack Travancore once again, Martanda Varma seems to have been left with no other alternative but to subjugate the neighbouring kingdoms. In consequence in 1734, he attacked Elayadathu Swarupum in which Peritally kingdom was absorbed. The conquest of Peritally and Elayadathu Swarupam literally doubled the dominions of Travancore. In the same year, Martanda Varma attacked the King of Kayamkulam who fell in the battle on 10 June 1734. The King of Kayamkulam being the uncle of the King of Chenganatta or Quilon, the latter waged war against Travancore to avenge the death of his uncle.[71]

The Dutch East India Company that had factories both at Kayamkulam and Quilon realised the danger to their settlements if Martanda Varma grew very powerful. Till then they had observed a neutral policy in the quarrels between Travancore and Kayamkulam. But in the face of a rising menace which could compromise their trade interests, they finally decided to ally with the kings of Quilon, Cochin and Porcad with the intention of cutting to size the growing power of Travancore.[72]

The Dutch sent a messenger to Martanda Varma insinuating that all his annexations were unjust. But the King, who was in good terms with the English, retorted with a stern warning that they need not meddle in affairs which did not concern them. The Dutch did not retaliate immediately for they knew that the King might seek the help of the English. Instead, they wrote a threatening letter to the English at Anjengo asking them to remain neutral in the war that they had already declared against the King of Travancore. In fact, about the same time they had begun their attack on Quilon with their ships. In the war that followed, Martanda Varma was forced to retreat. The Dutch then went on to destroy and burn Attingal, whose Queen had become an ally of the King of Travancore.[73]

Vanjamuttapilla who had earlier escaped the general massacre of the *Pillas* by Martanda Varma chose the moment to settle his old score against the King of Travancore by allying with the King of Quilon. The King of Travancore obtained arms from the English at Anjengo, in spite of the fact that the new chief of Anjengo, Charles Whitehill wanted to adopt a neutral attitude in the disputes between the King of Travancore and the King of Quilon. But Dutch plans to take possession of some land near the English factory of Eddawa, where much of the pepper was stored at that time, obliged Charles Whitehill to send 50 Englishmen there as a precaution. The Dutch were also informed that the coast of Eddawa down to Brinjohn belonged to the English.[74]

But the Dutch seemed to have obtained reinforcement from Ceylon. They landed at Colachel, and from there they commenced an attack. They also attacked Attingal, with the help of the King of Chenganatta and probably also Vanjamutta. But it was a disaster and they lost a good number of men. As a result, neither the Dutch nor the King of Quilon did attempt any further attacks on Attingal.[75] The Dutch were extremely unhappy with the English for their violation of neutrality and alliance with the King of Travancore. But the English maintained that they did not break neutrality and that they could claim an ancient and just title to the seashore from Eddawa to Brinjohn, where they possessed indisputable authority to hoist their flags.[76] The Dutchman, Gollenesse retorted from Quilon insultingly in the following terms :

'we know that in Eddawa and Brinjohn...you have little houses or huts which you call factories...we have enquired of knowing persons in this matter the same and they clarify us that your jurisdiction extends about three steps round your factory.'[77]

During this period, besides the Dutch, even the Nayaks of Madura to the east of Malabar, turned against the English, and began to ply in ships and sloops threatening the people along the sea-coast. The English again decided to provide arms and ammunitions to the King of Travancore against any attack from the Nayaks of Madura. At the same time, the English had to contend against the Dutch fleet which began to forbid all vessels from calling at Anjengo and even arrested some Malabar pepper merchants, who were sent off to Batavia, the Dutch headquarters in the east, as slaves.[78]

After lying low for sometime, the Dutch with fresh re-inforcements invaded Travancore from the south, when the King was on his northern expedition. They landed at Tengapatam, Cadiapatam and other places in south Travancore and began harassing the inhabitants.[79] As a major part of the Travancore forces was deployed in the north, the entire country between Colachel and Kottar surrendered to the Dutch who, seeing no opposition, made preparations to advance further north in Travancore.[80] Consequently, the King of Travancore abandoned his northern expedition and rushed back.

As the English help was not forthcoming sufficiently, the King of Travancore sought the help of the French, who as noted earlier, had already made overtures to the King. He concluded a treaty with the French by which the latter bound themselves to assist the Rajah against his enemies. He agreed to grant them Colachel, that they had demanded earlier and also some lands in other parts of the coast for building fortifications and factories and allowed them to trade with Travancore. The French promptly arrived with two ships and two brigantines and landed with about one hundred men on 12 March 1740. But the French authorities in Mahe did not want to run the risk of waging war against the Dutch, who claimed to hold a commercial monopoly at Colachel. Besides the French at Mahe were at war with the neighbouring prince of Badagara. So they asked the French ships to reach Mahe to fight the Prince of Badagara to the great displeasure of the king of Travancore, who sent three letters and an ambassador to Mahe to convince the French to change their decision.It appears also that in March 1741, Martanda Varma sent his deputy Narayanayyan to Pondicherry with the intention of getting French help against his enemies in Malabar. However, the English alarmed by this new development where they ran the risk of losing the confidence of the Rajah of Travancore if they did not assist him adequately, sought help from the English fort at Tellicherry, who sent them an officer, with a gunner and forty men with ammunitions.[81] This thwarted the attempts of the King of Travancore in allowing the French to make further inroads into Travancore at the expense of the English.

With English help forthcoming, the Rajah of Travancore constructed several batteries within forty yards of the Dutch forts.[82] In August 1741, the small Dutch garrison at Colachel was attacked by the Rajah's troops and the provisions including rice were destroyed. Owing to lack of provisions, the Dutch garrison surrendered on 7 August 1741.[83]

This victory did not bring much accolades to the Rajah of Travancore as it was known to everyone that it was lack of provision which compelled the Dutch to give up Colachel. Anyhow the battle of Colachel had shattered Dutch hopes of conquering Travancore. In fact many prisoners numbering about 350, which included Dutch as well as Malays, entered the service of the Rajah of Travancore. The most distinguised among the Dutch prisoners were Duyvenschot and Eustache Benedict de Lannoye. The former was appointed to command the Rajah's forces and the latter, who was in fact a Frenchman was appointed Commander-in-chief of the Rajah's forces which is said to have comprised of 50000 men. Thus the Rajah, who was endowed with a great sense of foresight and clairvoyance, not only utilised the arms and ammunitions of European origin to further his interests, but also made use of the expertise of the Europeans in strengthening his military might and in disciplining his troops.He even consulted de Lannoye in all his military adventures and endowed him with great wealth and property. It seems that it was because of de Lannoye's influence with the Rajah that the French obtained the permission to settle at Colachel, an important cloth manufacturing centre, situated near Anjengo. [84]

While the Dutch were awaiting to get new forces from far away Batavia, the Rajah besides obtaining arms and ammuntions from the English, was also expecting some assistance from the French.[85] Formal peace between the Dutch and the Rajah of Travancore was concluded only in the year 1743. The peace treaty containing 27 clauses was signed at Mavellikara on 22 May 1743, between Maratanda Varma and Commander Reinicus Siersma on behalf of the Dutch. The Dutch were compelled to recognise all the claims of the Rajah of Travancore. This naturally entailed the dropping of all their schemes for large territorial acquisition on the west coast of India for the moment.[86]

After his victory over the Dutch, the Rajah of Travancore annexed Kayamkulam to his kingdom. The fort and palace of the King of Kayamkulam were seized. He also turned his attention to those northern states like Ambalapuzha, Cochin, Purakkad and Vadakkumkur.[87] Moreover, Martanda Varma, following his policy of expansionism resolved to take direct control over the kingdom of Attingal too, which had been an independent entity since a long time, as we have seen. However, even in 1743, the English at Anjengo decided to pay the customary annual presents due to the Queen for four years from 1740 to 1743 amounting to 15450 gallion *fanams*. But it was during 1743, that the power of the Queen was totally wiped out. She was even arrested and imprisoned.[88]

Her authority and her administrators were replaced by that of the Rajah of Travancore and his own administrators. In fact, the English records even assert that the Rajah of Travancore had taken control of even the revenue of Attingal into his own possession and placed a young prince on the throne of Attingal to govern it, while the Queen was stripped of all power, with only the right to an annual maintenance and the annual presents. The English maintained a non-interfering stand when Martanda Varma usurped Attingal kingdom.[89] Contrary to the unfounded claims of Sreedhara Menon, as noted earlier, there is no record to prove that the Queen of Attingal was subservient to the Rajah of Travancore, till its forcible annexation by Martanda Varma. Sreedhara Menon perceives in the absorption of Attingal, not the annexation of an independent state, but only an administrative action pursued by Martanda Varma in exercise of a legitimate power vested in him as the sovereign of the kingdom and the head of the royal house of Venad. But we have shown on the basis of sufficient documentary evidence that Attingal Queendom was independent at least from the time of the arrival of the Portuguese on the Malabar coast, if not earlier, and its Queen had even joined forces with the Queen of Quilon in 1519 to expel the Portuguese, at a time when the Rajah of Travancore was only a small king.

In 1748, the Rajah's officers demanded the annual presents of the Queen of Attingal to be brought to the Rajah of Travancore.[90] This gave a rude jolt to the Company officials. Earlier even though the Rajah absorbed the Attingal kingdom, the presents were always made to the Queen of Attingal. The Rajah now chose to totally abolish the traditional privileges of the Queen. He not only 'usurped the Queendom', but had overrun all the neighbouring Princes to the very border of the Cochin country.[91]

Soon the Rajah himself informed the English that thereafter all the presents which were to be given to the Queen of Attingal should be given to him. However, the English were reluctant to carry the presents to the Rajah because they thought that he had become very insolent and predatory in his demand. They argued that since the presents of the Queen were founded on ancient privileges, which were abolished by the Rajah, he had no right to demand such presents.[92]

When arguments were going on in full swing, the Queen of Attingal herself, probably under pressure or a change of mind, intervened on behalf of the Rajah. She informed the English that she was contented that the King of Travancore should receive the annual presents due to her.[93] Thus the English had no option but to make the presents to the Rajah. They, however, decided to make them on fresh demand.[94] Thus it seems that the subjugation of Attingal to the Travancore kingdom was brought about through the relationship that developed between the Queen of Attingal and the King of Travancore, from the time the latter sought refuge in Attingal and both of them decided to turn against the *pillas* who challenged and threatened their authority. The Queen Amuthamburan seems to have realised that she was no more in a position like her pedecessor to contain the *pillas*. She also became conscious of the rising power of the King of Travancore who too had problems with the *pillas* and *madambees*. Naturally considerations of mutual interest led to mutual cooperation and understanding. But the decision of the Rajah of Travancore to annex Attingal was certainly not to the liking of the Queen of Attingal. She opposed it. As a result she was imprisoned. But later she seems to have toed the line of the Rajah to the detriment of her own Queendom. Thus the only independent kingdom, where only females had the right to rule, came to an end.

In 1750, the marriage ceremony of the second heir of Travancore with the Princess of Attingal was celebrated. As usual presents were demanded from the Company on this occasion.[95] The new chief at Anjengo, Thomas Byfeld had an audience with the Rajah of Travancore lasting for four hours, during which time he put forth a number of grievances. The main point raised by him was the loss suffered by the English in being debarred from the liberty of trade for the previous two years. He brought to the notice of the Rajah the clandestine purchase of pepper by the Dutch in his territory, who were his enemies. He even mentioned the frequent visits of the French to his court for forming a settlement in Colachel. This, he emphatically pointed out, was in violation of the grant of 30 July 1724. In fact it appears from Ananda Ranga Pillai's diary that the Raja of Travancore had promised help to the French against the English in 1748. Later in October 1750,

Martanda Varma had despatched two emissaries by the name of Sora Marakkayar and Malu Pillai, to Dupleix, the French governor of Pondicherry. Again in 1751, he sought French help to put down his enemies.[96]

Another point raised by Byfeld during the conference, was the violation of ancient sea rules by the Muslim boat-owners and merchants, the Marakkars and the *pillas*. According to the ancient rules, no vessel belonging to the subject of Attingal should navigate without passing the Anjengo fort to give their identity and their destination. But this was not being observed. The Rajah agreed to look into all these allegations and thus the conference broke up. This was the first instance when the Chief of Anjengo had a prolonged conference with the Rajah.[97]

In the same year, the Queen of Attingal Amuthamburan died at the age of 79. The English at Attingal fired twenty half minute guns from the ramparts of the Anjengo fort, with flags at half mast and an order was issued by beat of drums forbidding fishing or keeping open shops within the space of five days which was customary on such occasion.[98]

The unification of south Malabar by Martanda Varma, at the expense of various rulers and chieftains of south Malabar as well as the Dutch was largely a military achievement. It entailed a lot of violence, killings and bloodshed, probably unparalleled in the whole history of south Malabar until then. The French traveller, Anquetil Duperron who had been in Travancore during Martanda Varma's reign tells us that the Rajah was sometimes cruel. Conscious of this historical fact, Martanda Varma seems to have sought ways to attenuate its effect on his own conscience and on his newly unified and expanded kingdom. It is here that the Brahmin priests came to his help. Under their advice, he initiated certain measures in accordance with the prescription of the Vedas to expiate his crimes and also for the general prosperity of his kingdom. He celebrated the *Murajapom* ceremony. After celebrating it, he dedicated his kingdom to Lord Sri Padmanabha, the royal deity of Travancore, and declared that from that day onwards he was the vassal of Sri Padmanabha Swamy.[99]

After the death of the old Queen of Attingal, Martanda Varma celebrated, again on the advice of his Brahmin priests for his own renativity, another costly ceremony called *Hiranyagarbhadhanam*, in 1752. This was a unique ceremony in the sense that a golden cow wieghing 267 pounds of pure gold was made and after many rituals the Rajah would enter it through the nose and remain for three days inside the cow and on the fourth day he would emerge out of it from under the tail.[100] After this, the golden cow was cut into pieces and distributed among the Brahmins who conducted the ceremony. On this occasion, congratulatory presents were sent to him by the Dutch at Cochin and the English at Attingal.[101]

The significance of the ceremony was always a point of debate among scholars. Nagam Aiya, Shungoony Menon and Velu Pillai are unanimous in their opinion that this was a coronation ceremony. Though D.D. Kosambi had asserted that several south Indian kings of tribal origin performed this ceremony, yet it is certain that the later Rajahs' of Travancore did not perform identical ceremony for their enthronement.[102]

The second version was that it was an ennobling ceremony, the object of which was to raise the Rajah of Travancore from the inferior *Shudra* to the superior *Kshatriya* caste. Tradition ascribes that the Rajah of Travancore was not a *Kshatriya*. Only the Rajah of Cochin was a *Surya Kula Kshatriya,* while the Kolattiri and Zamorin of northern Malabar and the Travancore Rajahs were not pure *kshatriyas*. After the performing of this ceremony the Rajah is said to attain the status of *Kshatriya*. A third version is that of Anquetil Duperron who asserts that the Rajah performed this ceremony in order to elevate himself from the status of Nair to that of the Brahmin, for he badly wanted to dine with the Brahmins. From the time he performed this ceremony, Duperron asserts that the Rajah started dating his letters from the day of his rebirth and dined with Brahmins of his country, but not with the other Brahmins who considered the act of the Travancore brahmins as cowardly.

From Manucci's accounts we come to know that such a ceremony or similar ceremony was performed even earlier during the second half of the seventeenth century. The intention of the Rajah was to enjoy the privileges of a Brahmin. The Brahmins seem to have opposed this move, in spite of the large sums of money that he promised them. Coming to know from the Brahmins that he could attain Brahminhood if he was born anew in the stomach of a cow, the prince caused a golden cow to be made secretely, placed himself in the belly of the cow in a large hall in the presence of the Brahmins. He then issued from the cow and bellowed like a new-born calf. Finally the Brahmins gave in and the prince is believed to have at last obtained what he desired, and enjoyed the privileges of Brahminhood, and after him his posterity likewise. But as we know that the posterity were not Brahmins and that Martanda Varma performed a similar ceremony in 1752, this version does not stand the test of enquiry.

A final version was that by E.H.Nolan, who stated that the ceremony was performed merely as an expiation for the sins committed by Martanda Varma earlier. Fra Paolina San Bartolomeao who was in Travancore during the last quarter of the eighteenth century, had made a thorough enquiry into the reasons that motivated Martanda Varma to celebrate the *Hiranyagarbhadhanam.* He rejects the theory advanced by Anquetil du Perron and his likes, as a small fable that had been borrowed by him thoughtlessly from the subjugated people who were then enemies of the Rajah of Travancore. Instead, he asserts on the basis of convincing evidence, that Martanda Varma in the course of his conquests of the neighbouring territories had destroyed many a temple and idol. This great sin could be erased only by performing a unique ceremony, which consisted in constructing a gold cow and pass through it to become pure. Martanda Varma did exactly that and the gold cow existed still in 1787 in the king's treasury. Donandi, the captain of the king affirmed having shown it to Fra Paolina. All these have also been attested by other witnesses including Fra Paolina himself and Father Cruz Fernandez, a Malabar priest, who had left precious memoirs on the wars of Vira Martanda Pala (Martanda Varma), which Fra Paolina made use of to come to his conclusions. He had also made use of many other letters and memoirs in the archives of the Verapoly mission regarding Martanda Varma's wars.[103] Thus it becomes quite clear that the version of E.H.Nolan and Fra Paolina San Bartolomeo is the correct version, exposing the reasons for the celebration of the *Hiranyagarbhadhanam* ceremony.

The holding of such costly ceremonies for one reason or the other, did not however prevent Martanda Varma from annexing or conquering more terrtories. The Dutch realising the futility of waging war with the Rajah of Travancore on account of the heavy expenses involved and because it was detrimental to their trade interests, preferred to strike a deal with the Rajah, according to which they would provide ammunitions to the Rajah to continue with his scheme of expansion, if they obtained a certain quantity of pepper below market price.[104] As a result they concluded another treaty on 15 August 1753. According to the terms of the treaty, the Dutch promised not to stand in the way of the expansion of Travancore and were to supply arms and ammunitions worth 12000 rupees every year. In return, Maratanda Varma agreed to supply 3000 *candies* of pepper at the rate of 65 rupees per *candy* from Travancore and Attingal, and another 2000 *candies* at 55 rupees from the principalities he had conquered.[105] In fact, the treaty of 1753, helped him to conquer Tekkumkur, an independent kingdom,

Vadakkumkur, Purakad (Porcad) and portions of Cochin kingdom between Purakad and Arukurry. It is significant to note that after concluding the treaty with the Dutch and consolidating his power in south Malabar, Martanda Varma began to disregard de Lannoye, who until then played a key role in his military designs. Anquetil Duperron who had partly attributed the victories of Martanda Varma to de Lannoye, had taken note of this factor. He writes that Martanda Varma did not consult de Lannoye anymore from 1757.[106]

Subsequently the Travancore forces were able to defeat the forces of the Rajah of Cochin, who had taken up the cause of the exiled *rajahs* of Tekkumkur, Vadakkumkur and Ambalapuzha. In the meantime the Zamorin of Calicut had entered Cochin territory in the north. This literally pushed Cochin into the hands of the Rajah of Travancore. As a result in 1757 (as in 1753), a treaty of alliance was concluded between Travancore and Cochin. Travancore promised help to Cochin in its wars against the Zamorin on condition that if Travancore were to capture any territory, other than those which originally belonged to the Rajah of Cochin, they should go to Travancore. In return the Cochin *rajah* undertook not to render any help to the dispossessed princes or to enter into any kind of relationship with them. This treaty, however, demonstrates the expansionist aims of Martanda Varma, even beyond the Cochin frontiers, so that it would not be an exaggeration to conclude that Martanda Varma's ultimate aim was to unify the entire region of Kerala or Malabar. Mohibbul Hasan, has on the basis of Dutch records, asserted that the Rajah of Cochin had become a mere puppet in the hands of Martanda Varma through this treaty.[107]

Some Observations :

The death of the old Queen Aswati Umayyama in 1698 without any legitimate heiress led to the enthronement of the adopted princess as the new Queen of Attingal. This new Queen known as Amuthamburan did not have any direct line of relationship with the king of Travancore. Nevertheless she remained a sovereign in her own right and was never answerable to the King of Travancore. She also had direct dealings with the English like the former Queen. But she owed her installation as Queen to the *pillas*. As a result their power in the country had increased and she was increasingly unable to rein them in.

The Attingal revolt in which the *pillas* and her men played a prominent role eroded her authority as the Queen to a great extent. In September 1722 she entered into a new treaty with the English. But the English, conscious of the waning power of the Queen due to the defiance of the *pillas* and worried about their trade interests, turned towards the Rajah of Travancore to stabilise the situation in the region. In April 1723, they entered into a treaty with the Rajah mainly to procure pepper in exchange for arms and ammunitions. Later they strengthened their relationship with Travancore by obtaining a grant from the Rajah in July 1724. In the meantime, the *pillas* of Attingal, along with the *madambees* of Travancore were challenging the established authority both in Attingal and Travancore. This brought the King of Travancore, especially his influential nephew, Martanda Varma and the Queen of Attingal closer. They joined hands to put down the *pillas* and *madambees*.

In 1728, Martanda Varma marched against the *pillas* and routed them. But the Queen of Attingal still retained her independence and sovereignty. This is attested by the fact, that she entered once again into a treaty with the English on 5 April 1729, without any reference to or approval of the Rajah of Travancore and the English agreed to pay her annual presents as before. In the light of what we have seen above, there is no cogent reason to believe Velu Pillai, when he makes a biased assertion that the Rajah of Travancore had every right to seize power because the Queen of Attingal had no political authority, and such power that she exercised was nothing more than what was delegated by the lawful Rajah of Travancore.[108] The actual historical facts go against his unfounded contentions.

But the whole scenario changed when Martanda Varma ascended the throne of Travancore in 1728. Within a few years of his accession to the throne, Travancore which was only a small principality until then, rose to become the most powerful kingdom in Malabar, with a centralised authority in the name of the King and a powerful army, with modern arms and ammunitions and even commanded by European officers. The King realising that there was no political domination without economic domination, took over the entire pepper trade in his hands. In order to impose his political and economic domination, he wiped out the remaining *pillas*, defeated the Dutch and conquered all the territories rich in pepper. In the process, he amalgamated the Attingal Queendom with the Travancore kingdom as late as 1743 and abolished the privileges of the ageing Queen.

Notes and References

1. Factory Records Miscellaneous, 1722, Bombay Castle to the Court of Directors, 11 May 1722, p.159
2. John Wallis, 'A Short Treatise by way of Essay of Attinga on the Malabar Coast,1727', 7 September 1727, p.35
3. *Ibid.*, p.34
4. *Ibid.*
5. *Ibid.*, pp.34-35
6. John Biddulph, *The Pirates of Malabar and an English Woman in India Two Hundred Years Ago*, London, 1907, p.288
7. *Ibid.*, pp.289-290
8. John Wallis, *op.cit.*, pp.40-41
9. Vaikathu Pachu Moothathu, *Thiruvithamkur Charitram*, Cochin, 1867,1986, p.33
10. Shungoony Menon, *A History of Travancore,I*, Delhi, 1878, p.108

11. T.K. Velu Pillai, *The Travancore State Manual, II,* Trivandrum, 1940, pp.251-252
12. William Logan, *A Collection of Treaties, Engagements and other papers of importance relating to British Affairs in Malabar, III,* Madras, 1879, 1889, p.9
13. *Ibid.,* p.11
14. K.M. Pannikar, *A History of Kerala,* Annamalai, 1960, p.229
15. *Ibid.*
16. Anjengo Factory Records, 1750, 9 May 1750, p.182
17. Shungoony Menon, *op.cit.*
18. William Logan, *op.cit.*
19. William Logan, *Malabar, I,* Madras, 1887, 1951, p.350
20. William Logan, *A Collection of Treaties, Engagements and other papers of importance relating to British Affairs in Malabar, III,* Madras, 1879, pp.11-12
21. Anjengo Factory Records, 1750, Diaries and Consultation, 1750, 4 February 1750, p.68
22. Nagam Aiya, *The Travancore State Manual, I,* Trivandrum, 1906, p.328
23. John Wallis, *op.cit.,* p.41
24. *Ibid.,* pp.12-13,46
25. *Ibid.,* pp.43-44
26. *Ibid.,* p.44
27. *Ibid.,* pp.36-37,44-45
28. *Ibid.,* p.15
29. *Ibid.*
30. *Ibid.,* p.16 ; Nagam Aiya, *op.cit.,* p.328
31. John Wallis, *op.cit.,* pp.36-37
32. *Ibid.,* pp.36, 38
33. Vaikathu Pachu Muthathu, *op.cit.,* p.37 ; T.K. Velu Pillai, *A History of Travancore,* Trivandrum, 1935, p.11. It seems that in recognition of the faithful conduct of the Koil Thampuran, grants of land embracing the whole village called Killimanoor was given to his family.
34. John Wallis, *op.cit.,* p.15
35. *Ibid.,* pp.15, 47-48

36. Anjengo Factory Records, 1704-1749, Alexander Orme, Anjengo to Bombay Castle, 20 April 1728, p.54
37. John Wallis, *op.cit.*, pp.46, 47, 48, 50
38. *Ibid.*, p.50
39. *Ibid.*, p.17 ; Anjengo Factory Records, 1704-1749, Alexander Orme, Anjengo to Court of directors, 20 April 1728, p.54
40. Anjengo Factory Records, 1704-1749, Alexander Orme, Anjengo to Court of directors, 20 April 1728, p.54
41. Anjengo Factory Records, 1704-1749, Queen of Attingal to Alexander Orme, Anjengo, 8 November 1728, p.68
42. *Ibid.*, 7 November 1728, p.84; Anjengo Factory Records, 1704-1749, Queen of Attingal to Hezekiah King, Anjengo, 8 November 1728, p.68
43. John Wallis, *op.cit.*, p.53
44. *Ibid.*, pp.36, 53
45. *Ibid.*, p.54
46. *Ibid.*, pp.54-55
47. *Ibid.*, pp.58-59
48. Shungoony Menon, *op.cit.*, p.108; A.P. Ibrahim Kunju, *Rise of Travancore : A Study of the Life and Times of Martanda Varma,* Trivandrum, 1976, pp.13, 87-88
49. Shungoony Menon, *Ibid.*, p. 109; Robert Sewell, (ed.), *A Sketch of the Dynasties of Southern India,* Madras, 1883, p.98; R. Bishop Caldwell, *A History of Tinnevely,* New Delhi, 1982(reprint), p.253
50. *Ibid.*
51. *Ibid;* Nagam Aiya, *The Travancore State Manual,I,* Trivandrum, 1906, p.327
52. Anjengo Factory Records, 1704-1749, Martanda Varma to Hezekiah King, Anjengo, 10 November 1728, p.68 ; P.K. Leena, 'The History of the English East India Company's Settlement at Anjengo', Phd.dissertation, Calicut University, 1989, p.191; Shungoony Menon, *op.cit.*, p.109; Caldwell, *op.cit.*, p.253; Robert Sewell, *op.cit.*, p.98
53. Anjengo Factory Records, 1704-1749, Martanda Varma to Hezekiah King, Anjengo, 10 November 1728, p.68
54. *Ibid.*, pp.68-69
55. Anjengo Factory Records, 1704-1749, Rajah of Travancore to Chief, Anjengo, 21 November 1728, p.69

56. Anjengo Factory Records, 1704-1749, Queen of Attingal to Chief, Anjengo, 10 December 1728, p.78
57. Anjengo Factory Records, 1704-1749, Martanda Varma to Hezekiah King, Anjengo, 10 November 1728, p.69; John Wallis, *op.cit.*, pp.36-37; Anjengo Factory Records, 1704-1749, Queen of Attingal to Chief, Anjengo, 10 December 1728, p.77
58. *Ibid.*
59. Letters to Fort St.George, 1729, John Wallis, Anjengo to Fort St.George, 18 July 1729, p.90
60. Anjengo Diary, 1803, Traslate of an agreement written in silver Ola by Princess of Attingal and Hezekiah King, Anjengo, 5 April 1729, pp.15-16, see Appendix
61. William Logan *op.cit.*, p.19
62. Vaikathu Pachu Muthathu, *op.cit.*, p.37
63. Nagam Aiya, *op.cit.*, pp.329-330, 334
64. *Ibid.*, p.330
65. Selections from the Records of the Madras Government, Dutch Record No.14, 'Memoir Written in the year 1677 A.D. by Hendrick Adriaan Van Rheede, Madras, 1911, p.32
66. Shungoony Menon, *op.cit.*, p.116
67. Vaikathu Pachu, Muthathu, *op.cit.*, pp.39-40; Caldwell, *op.cit.*, p.254; Shungoony, Menon, *op.cit.*, pp.115-118; A. Sreedhara Menon, *A Survey of Kerala History*, Kottayam, 1967, p.274.
68. T.K. Velu Pillai, *op.cit.*, p.17; Caldwell, *op.cit.*, pp.253, 255; Menon, Shungoony, *op.cit.*, pp.115-118
69. Vaikathu, Pachu, Muthathu, *op.cit.*, p.43
70. *Ibid.*
71. A. Galetti, (tr.&ed.), *The Dutch in Malabar*, Madras, 1911, p.55; T.I. Poonen, *Dutch Hegemony in Malabar and its Collapse(A.D.1663-1795)*, Trivandrum, 1978, p.94; Caldwell, *op.cit.*, p.255
72. A. Galetti, *op.cit.*, p.23; Anjengo Factory Records, 1704-1749, Charles Whitehill, Anjengo to Court of Directors, 18 February 1739, p.145; T.I. Poonen, *op.cit.*, p.96; see also, Ibrahim Kunju, *op.cit.*, p.35
73. A. Galetti, *op.cit.*, p.83; Anjengo Factory Records, 1704-1749, Charles Whitehill, Anjengo to Court of Directors, 18 February 1739, p.145; for details of war see also T.I. Poonen, *op.cit.*, pp.96-97

74. Anjengo Factory Records, 1704-1749, Charles Whitehill, Anjengo to Court of Directors, 15 October 1739, pp.147,159; Public Department, 1739, Fort St.George to Charles Whitehill, Anjengo, 9 August 1739, p.75

75. Anjengo Factory Records, 1704-1749, Commodore, Cochin to Charles Whitehill, Anjengo, 9 December 1739, p.161

76. *Ibid;* Anjengo Factory Records, 1704-1749, Charles Whitehill to Commodore, Cochin, 12 December 1739, p.161

77. Anjengo Factory Records, 1704-1749, Gollenesse, Quilon to Stephen Law, Governor, Bombay, 12 March 1740, p.180

78. Anjengo Factory Records, 1704-1749, Charles Whitehill, Anjengo to Court of Directors, England, 18 February 1739, p.137

79. Nagam Aiya, *op.cit.,* p.342

80. A. Galetti, *op.cit.,* p.83

81. Anjengo Factory Records, 1704-1749, Anjengo to the Court of Directors, 18 February 1740, pp.151,153; A. Martineau, *Les Origines de Mahé,* Paris, 1917, p.x; Kunju, Ibrahim, *op.cit.,* pp.89-92; A. Martineau, *Dupleix et L'inde Française,* vol.II, Paris, 1923, pp.10-14; Dodwell & J.F.Price(eds), *The Private Diary of Ananda Ranga Pillai, 1736-1761,* vol.I, p.155; A.P. Ibrahim Kunju, *Rise of Travancore: A Study of the Life and Times of Martanda Varma,* Trivandrum, 1976, pp.89-92

82. Letter to fort St.George, 1741, Anjengo to Fort St.George, 11 July 1741, p.142

83. T.I. Poonen, *op.cit.,* p.98; Galetti, A., *op.cit.,* p.83

84. A. Galetti, *op.cit.,* p.25; Nagam Aiya, *op.cit.,* p.358; Shungoony Menon, *op.cit.,* p.165. De Lannoye was called *Valiya Kappithan*, the great Captain of the Travancore force; Anjengo Factory Records, 1704-1749, anjengo to court of directors, 8 December 1741, p.200; Anquetil Duperron, *Voyage en Inde 1754-1762,* Paris, 1997, p.199; J.Placid Podipara, (tr), *The Varthamanapusthakam,* Roma, 1571, p.15

85. Letter to Fort St.George, 1742, anjengo to Fort St.George, 2 September 1742, p.134

86. A. Galetti, *op.cit.,* p.24

87. K.M. Pannikar, *op.cit.,* p.245; Sreedhara Menon, *op.cit.,* pp.275, 278-79

88. Secretariat Inwards (Letter Book), 1743, Charles Whitehill, Anjengo to Bombay Castle, 23 May 1743, p.165

89. *Ibid.*, 22 October 1743, p.245; Secretariat Inward Letter Book, 1743, Anjengo to Bombay Castle, 23 May 1743, pp.166, 168

90. Secretariat Inward Letter Book, 1748, Bouchier, Anjengo to Bombay Castle, 25 February 1748, p.53

91. Secretariat Inward Letter Book, 1749, Bouchier, Anjengo to Bombay Castle, 23 May 1749, p.213

92. *Ibid;* Secretariat Inward Letter Book, 1749, Bouchier, Anjengo to Bombay Castle, 14 September 1749, p.261

93. Foreign Powers Extract Selections, 1796. A list of olas delivered by R.Bouchier on his resigning the Chiefship to.Thomas Byfeld, Anjengo, 4 February 1750, pp.128-129

94. Anjengo Factory Records, 1749, Rajah of Travancore to Bouchier, Anjengo, 16 November 1749, p.28

95. Anjengo Factory Records, 1750, 9 May 1750, p.177; 21 April 1750, p.131

96. *Ibid.*, 9 May 1750, pp.179, 182; Dodwell & Price(trs.), *op.cit.*, VI, pp.23-24; VII, p.410; VIII, p.44

97. *Ibid.*, p.181; Anjengo Consultations, 1751, Rajah of Travancore to Byfeld, Anjengo, 7 February 1751, p.191

98. Anjengo Factory Records and diaries, 1750, At a consultation, 18 March 1750, p.219

99. Shungoony Menon, *op.cit.*, pp.169,171; this ceremony consists in the lighting of the sacred lamp.One hundred thousand lamps were lighted to the chanting of prayers by the Brahmins. Martanda Varma celebrated it in a grand style at an outlau of two lakhs of rupees. See also, Duperron, Anquetil, *op.cit.*

100. Anjengo Factory Records and Diaries, 1751, At a consultation, 16 June 1751, p.265; Anquetil Duperron, *op.cit.*

101. *Ibid.*

102. Nagam Aiya, *op.cit.*, p.361; Shungoony Menon, *op.cit.*, p.57; T.K. Velu Pillai, *op.cit.*, p.25; D.D. Kosambi, *The Culture and Civilisation of Ancient India in Historical Outline,* London, 1965, p.171

103. E.H. Nolan, *The Illustrated History of the British Empire in India and the East from the Earliest Times to the Suppression of the Sepoy Mutiny in 1859,II,* London, n.d., p.160; K.P. Padmanabha Menon, *History of Kerala, I,* Delhi, 1924, 1982, p.536 ; D.D. Kosambi, *op.cit.*; Anquetil Duperron, *op.cit.*, pp.194,199-200; William Irvine, (tr.), *Storia Do Mogor or Mogul India, 1653-1708,* by Niccolao Manucci, vol.III, London, 1907,

pp.274-75; Paulin de Saint Barthélémy, *Voyages aux Indes Orientales,* vol.I, Paris, 1808, p.320

104. T.I. Poonen, *op.cit.,* p.117

105. Ashin Das Gupta, *Malabar in Asian Trade, 1740-1800,* Cambridge, 1967, p.34; A. Galletti, *op.cit.,* p.24

106. T.I. Poonen, *op.cit.,* p.11; Anquetil Duperron, *op.cit.*

107. Sreedhara Menon, *op.cit.,* pp.279-280; Ibrahim Kunju, *op.cit.,* pp.160-161; Hasan Mohibbul, *History of Tipu Sultan,* Calcutta, 1951

108. T.K. Velu Pillai, *op.cit.,* p.299

Chapter 5

Trade in Attingal and Travancore

At this juncture, it would not be out of place to digress into the realm of trade in the Queendom of Attingal and the Kingdom of Travancore, with special reference to the English. This would bring to light not only the various aspects involved in the trade of the region and its ups and downs, but also the connection between trade and politics, especially with regard to the Kingdom of Travancore.

The foundation of European trade with Malabar was the direct result of the growing commercial and economic necessities in Europe. At the end of the fifteenth century, Malabar had evolved a system in which trade flourished and different communties lived without friction.[1] With the arrival of Vasco da Gama at Calicut in north Malabar, the state of affairs in Malabar was in for a change. By the beginning of the sixteenth century, the Portuguese had established themselves as a trading body in Malabar largely at the expense of Muslim traders, with the aim of seizing absolute control over Malabar's trade in pepper.[2] Their relations with Malabar lasted for over a period of 150 years.

Soon the commercial supremacy of the Portuguese yielded to the Dutch.[3] It was the spice trade of Malabar which had first led the Portuguese and then the Dutch to enforce a commercial monopoly,[4] in a region where free trade was the norm since ages. The English did not lag far behind. Since the penetration of the Portuguese, they had devised ways and means to trade with Malabar. Though they were late comers, they were able to etch their name more effectively in the commercial map of Malabar for many years to come.

Pepper was the mainstay of early European trade with Malabar. Trade in cotton, coir, tobacco and timber also assumed some importance later. Lead and cowries were other articles of trade. However, pepper was the most important commodity as it was used in Europe by all who could afford the luxury of a seasoning.[5] Besides it could be retailed in very small quantities which meant that it was within the reach of the common people. Thus partly through the ease with which it could be purchased and sold and partly due to its widespread consumption in Europe, pepper remained the staple commodity of the English in their trade with Malabar, which began during the second half of the seventeenth century.[6]

The trade of the English in the territory of the Queen of Attingal and the adjoining regions can be divided broadly into two phases. The first phase began in the year 1694, when the Queen granted the English the entire pepper produce of the country, which coincided with the establishment of an English factory at Anjengo. This continued till the year 1743 when the Rajah of Travancore annexed the Attingal Queendom. The second phase started with the acquisition of the exclusive rights of trade in pepper and other commodities by the Rajah of Travancore, until the Anjengo factory itself was abolished and the Travancore kingdom itself was subordinated to English rule in India.

The First Phase

Pepper was grown in so much abundance in Attingal, that the Queen was called the 'pepper Queen' and the country was known as the 'mother of pepper'. Pepper grows well in the low lands but far more abundantly in the elevated tracts and along the hills and mountains. Pepper is not planted in open areas but in close neighbourhood of trees. Pepper plucked from the trees was laid out in the sun to dry. After a few days this pepper becomes black. This dry and black pepper was what was wanted in Europe and was considered fit for export. A healthy vine would live for about 25 years and would yield the best pepper for six or seven years.[7]

The pepper ready for export was put in mat bags each containing from 65 to 128 pounds.[8] There were different varieties and different ages of pepper. To gauge the age of pepper when it was brought by the merchants for sale proved to be very difficult, as very often it was not the planters who brought it up but the merchants. However, the English were not bothered about the age of pepper. Their concern was only to obtain maximum pepper from Malabar to take it over to Europe.[9]

Prior to the establishment of a factory at Anjengo in Attingal, the Court of Directors of the English East India Company in London, had asked their Company servants to augment the pepper trade on the Malabar and use all means for the conservation of pepper.[10] As early as 1687, Thomas Mitchell, who later became the chief of the English factory at Tellicherry in north Malabar, had come to Attingal, the dominion of the Queen, and purchased more than 1200 *candies* of pepper. For purchasing this much pepper, he had to bribe the Queen by carrying presents worth 3000 dollars.[11]

According to the Queen of Attingal's grant of 1694, the English could purchase all the pepper her country produced. The Company officials however had no direct dealings with the Queen. They contracted with the country merchants advancing money to them. These merchants brought pepper in boats to the Company's warehouse in Anjengo For every *candy* that the Company procured from the merchants the Queen was paid a custom of 5 *rajas*, as stipulated in the grant.[12] By this method, the Company could procure only the quantity contracted for, nothing more nothing less.

However, a second type of pepper procurement existed through private collections. A large quantity could be procured by making on-the-spot payment without any deduction.[13] This type of pepper purchase though lucrative was very often detrimental to the former method of contracting pepper. Any one could buy it from the merchants. Very often more money was paid for it, and thereby merchants were lured by the Company officials to sell pepper this way. The drawback was that the excess pepper thus purchased went into the personal trade of the Company officials.[14]

Private Malabar merchants also found it easier to make quick money through selling off their pepper privately to the Company officials at a higher price rather than go into the labyrinth of rules and regulations which had to be adhered to if they entered into pepper contracts with the Company officials. As a result there was large scale smuggling in pepper by private merchants. This situation was tolerated by the Court of directors in London, in spite of misuses by the Company servants and the flouting of pepper contracts by Malabar merchants.[15]

In the early period of English trade with the Queen of Attingal, the price of pepper ranged between Rs.65 to Rs.95 per *candy*.[16] Initially there was no fixed yearly supply of pepper to the Company in Attingal. Whatever the Company servants could procure from the Queen was sent to England in ships. It was only later that the Company began to enter into agreements with the Queen for a fixed yearly supply of pepper.

In 1697, trade had come to a standstill due to resistance from the Queen and the Malabaris. In 1700, there was scarcity of pepper owing to leanness of crops as well as smuggling of pepper in large quantities on the backs of oxen to the Tamil country. As a result the cost price of a *candy* shot up to 27 dollars.[17] From 1701 onwards, the trade was never smooth. The *Pillas* of Attingal who had enthroned a new Queen at Attingal obstructed trade in the region in general. Besides European piracy was rampant on the Malabar coast during this period, which had a negative effect on trade. But the Company somehow pulled on. As a result, in 1719, when Travancore was reeling under severe famine conditions the

English at Anjengo were able to ship 200 *candies* 13 *maunds* and 20 pounds of pepper to England.[18]

The Attingal revolt of 1721 completely shattered and dislocated trade in the region for a year or two. The year 1725 saw an abundant crop of pepper. The Anjengo factory was able to procure about 800 *candies* of pepper which were laden on board a ship and the commander was asked to proceed to Cochin to get 200 *candies* more.[19] Whenever there was a deficiency of pepper, the Court of Directors created an uproar. They usually pulled up their factors in the Malabar for the deficiency. The latter blamed the merchants and the merchants blamed the season. But when there was abundant supply of crops, the Court of Directors was highly pleased.

The year 1726 saw pepper trade in Attingal being threatened by the Dutch who had contracted with private merchants for large sums. The Dutch seized the English boats coming in with pepper and vice versa. The English started sending armed cruisers to detect the Dutch ships.[20] Meanwhile the English Company was also threatened by the *pillas* who blocked the pepper from coming to the fort. In 1727, the situation was the same. The year's crop was also bad. Besides, the Dutch continued to intercept the Malabar merchants who carried pepper to the English. On one occasion, a merchant went to Chatanore in Peritally kingdom to purchase pepper. On knowing this, the Dutch sent three soldiers to intercept him dead or alive. But the English nevertheless managed to procure a large quantity of pepper from the local merchants in May 1727.[21]

In 1727, the Queen of Attingal also demanded arms and ammunitions from the English in return for pepper.[22] At the same time she promised to remove all the obstructions in the pepper trade. In 1728, the pepper contracted for was 291 *candies* 9 *maunds* and 26 pounds.[23] The demand for arms and ammunitions in return for pepper became a permanent fixation in all the future agreements in pepper trade from this period onwards.

The years 1728 and 1729 were restless years for trade in Attingal, for the Queen and the *pillas* were engaged in warfare against one another. During the war, the *pillas* cut down and destroyed a great number of pepper vines. Thus there was a stagnation in pepper supply. Only 200 *candies* were purchased by the English in 1729. Between 1730 and 1736 the quantity of pepper purchased by the English was more than doubled from 313 *candies* in 1730 to 761 *candies* in 1736.[24]

Attingal reeled under famine in 1727. So severe was the famine that the Malabaris gathered pepper even before it reached maturity and sold to the Company for money. They did not even garbel the pepper fearing loss of weight.[25]

By 1739, there were fresh disputes between the Dutch and the English which affected pepper trade. The Dutch managed to instill fear in the minds of the pepper merchants if they dared to carry pepper to the English in Attingal. Pepper merchants who lived in Eddawa, informed the Company that the Dutch at Cochin had threatened them with death and slavery if they dared to carry pepper to Anjengo.[26]

In 1729, Martanda Varma had ascended the throne of Attingal. He quelled the *pillas* and annexed various territories to his kingdom. He also confronted the Dutch. On 7 August 1741, Martanda Varma vanquished the Dutch and made further conquests subsequently. He established a new centralised bureaucratic state. To finance this State, he built a commercial department which gradually established a strict monopoly in the trade of pepper.[27]

In the meantime, very heavy smuggling in pepper went on in Attingal. Pepper was being carried away by country people to Surat and Cambay.[28] Some English Company servants like Rickards from Bengal made enormous purchases of pepper illegally.[29] Besides, the French and the Portuguese also indulged in illegal pepper purchases. In spite of all this, the English managed to contract with pepper merchants for 300 *candies* by advancing Rs.3680 to them.[30]

In 1743 Martanda Varma took over the authority and the revenue of Attingal into his own possession. He completely abolished the power of the Queen. She bore only the title and had no power. The entire pepper trade of Attingal passed into the Rajah's hands. The English were told that the Rajah had decided to take upon himself the entire pepper trade in the country.[31] Thus ended the first phase of trade in Attingal, with the Rajah of Travancore taking over Attingal and together with it, its pepper trade.

The Second Phase

The annexation of Attingal and other principalities by the Rajah of Travancore brought about a drastic change in pepper trade in Malabar. The King appointed his own merchants to procure pepper. He refused to allow anyone else to bring pepper to the English other than his own agents.[32] This meant major changes. Henceforth, the King was the sole trader of pepper. He had the right to all the revenues and customs. The merchants appointed by him became very important. The English were told which merchants they must contract with. Besides the merchants were ordered as to whom they should supply.[33]

There was no precedent to such policies. This was a blow to the European traders. The English East India Company considered this development as wholly adverse to their interests. Bombay Castle, however, instructed the Company officials in Attingal to adhere to the old method of contracting for pepper. But the Rajah had other ideas of trade. He made another move with a view to break the treaties entered with the Queen since 1694. He simply gave permission to the French to trade in Retorah. This was in open breach of all privileges granted to the English both by him and his predecessors. However, for some time between

1744 and 1746, certain areas within the kingdom of Travancore were indicated by the Rajah as their limits and in this area the merchants they chose to deal with could buy any amount of pepper.[34]

While the Rajah of Travancore was bent upon establishing his authority over the entire pepper trade, the English in their turn constantly strove to steer clear of his reach. They resorted to other clandestine means of collecting pepper, especially smuggled pepper. For instance there was one Pulapetta, inhabitant of Porcad, who resided near the English factory at Eddawa where a great part of the Company's pepper was collected. Pullapetta used to buy up all the pepper and bring it to Anjengo under the denomination of Dutch pepper and sold it to the English factors there.[35] This was in spite of the fact that the Rajah had imposed severe punishment against the Malabaris who indulged in smuggling. Smugglers of pepper were either killed or lost their nose, ears and eyes. But later on this sentence was commuted to life imprisonment.[36]

In 1746, though there was plentiful crop, side by side heavy smuggling in pepper was going on. The Company informed the King of Travancore that a certain Ramen Annavy had shipped off huge quantities of pepper illegally.[37] But the King seems to have been more interested in procuring arms than punishing the smugglers. He actually retorted phlegmatically that the English were always asking for pepper, but never complied with his request for arms. The English chief at Anjengo claimed that the earlier contract between the Company and Travancore was purely for pepper and that if the Company had supplied then arms to His Majesty, it was purely a friendly gesture. He firmly declared that the Company was no more in a position to supply arms as the English were engaged in war in Europe. He further insinuated that the existing pepper scarcity would not be there if the Rajah gave permission to everybody to bring pepper to them rather than his chosen ones. The Rajah however remained unaffected. He even sarcastically retorted that though in the old contract there was no stipulation made for arms to be supplied to Travancore, there was also no mention of how many *candies* of pepper the English were to have annually.[38]

In 1747, the English Company did not obtain much pepper. The King on the other hand sold large quantities of pepper to the Portuguese. It was believed that 200 bags of pepper were sold to them, each bag containing 150 *candies* of pepper. Such an enormous quantity was sold in violation of all the former treaty obligations.[39]

The English, however, refused to face the fact that freedom of trade had ended in Travancore. They continued to remonstrate the King. In the month of September 1747, the chief of Anjengo alerted the King about the violation of treaties by him. But the King coolly replied that he had the right to sell what was his own.[40]

The realisation by the English that the King was determined to abolish all ancient privileges dawned much later. He even debarred the Company from pepper trade. In a nutshell, the King's resolution was 'no warlike stores no pepper'. The officials of Anjengo informed Bombay Castle that the King was growing more insolent and peremptory in his demands' and had taken over the whole trade of the country. They informed Bombay Castle of the absolute necessity of entering into a new treaty with the King for pepper trade in future.[41]

The Company's procurement of pepper thus remained suspended in the year 1749. Bombay Castle asked Anjengo officials to continue with their remonstrances with the King. But this produced no effect. However, it seems that subsequently in the year 1749, the Rajah entered into an agreement with the English chief at Anjengo for 500 *candies* of pepper at the rate of 75 rupees.[42]

The Company realised that there was no prospect of making another pepper contract with the King except on his own terms.[43]

The merchants suddenly turned out to be of little significance. It was the King who supplied pepper to the English. In 1750, the minister of the King visited Anjengo fort and held talks with the English officials. He confessed to having been the cause of the Company being debarred from pepper trade for the last two years and that he was sent to settle matters. He put forth a few propositions. He demanded the annual present to the Queen of Attingal and insisted on a supply of 400 arms. He further insisted on paying only Rs.75 per *candy*. Besides he agreed to contract for only 500 *candies*. He also demanded advance for pepper supply.[44] The chief of Anjengo did not respond concretely to these propositions. But he declared his inability to supply the King more than 200 arms.[45]

The King was never responsive to the appeals of the English. He said he wanted nothing but warlike stores to defend his country against his enemies, in which case he promised to supply them as much pepper as he could collect in his dominion. The Company tried their best to enhance the pepper supply to 1500 or 200 *candies*. The chief of Anjengo even held a lengthy conference with the King of Travancore during which he represented in the strongest terms the great loss the Company incurred by sending their ships dead freighted home. He even offered to raise the rate of pepper per *candy* to Rs.80. But no argument could prevail to part with pepper even at Rs.80 per *candy*.[46]

The English were aghast at the open flouting of the pepper contract by the King. They reminded him that he had to oblige the Company for their friendly assistance in past times. Suddenly the King agreed to supply 500 *candies* of pepper at the rate of Rs.75 per *candy* on previous terms, and if more was required to complete the tonnage of the expected ship, the same would be delivered. But contrary to all expectations, once again the King refrained from fulfilling his commitment. It was discovered later that the

Dutch were purchasing pepper at an exhorbitant rate. Naturally the King would have preferred to deal with the Dutch and make more profits than to sell the pepper to the English at a lower price.[47]

The year 1752 saw Martanda Varma immersed in war once again with his neighbours. He was in dire need of arms. He agreed to deliver 1500 *candies* of pepper in exchange for 400 fire-arms, flints, old irons and saltpetre.[48] During this period, the daily correspondence revolved around the difficulties of procuring pepper and warlike stores: As the Dutch were promised by the King through the treaty of Mavelikara in 1753, an increasing share in the pepper trade, the English Company decided to enter into a fresh contract with the King for 1600 *candies* of pepper in return for some arms.[49] But the *Dalawa* brought down the quantity to 1000 *candies*. Besides he insisted on the supply of 200 fire-arms for every 500 *candies* of pepper. The English decided to send the linguist to apprise the Rajah that the terms proposed by the *Dalawa* were not acceptable to them and that they were willing to contract for 1500 *candies* of pepper each year.[50] Surprisingly the Rajah agreed to this latter proposal.

However, he started his old game of delaying pepper delivery. He asked the linguist to advance him money for the 1500 *candies* of pepper as he was in dire need of money. He also requested 25 fire arms. The English offered Rs.20000 for pepper, but refused to satisfy his request for arms. The King was very pleased about the money but he sulked for arms. He wrote that the Nairs of his army were without arms.[51]

In 1756, the King persisted in his refusal of pepper. But at the same time he requested for 225 fire arms and 60 *candies* of lead. The English did not comply. The King then tried to cajole unsuccessfully the chief at Anjengo to enter into a perpetual treaty. He declared that he would not deliver a grain more than what was stipulated in the current contract. But the new chief of Anjengo, George Scott refused to be cowed down by the incessant threats of the King and expressed his inability to make fresh contract till the completion of the present one. The King then tried to bait the chief stating that if the Company adhered to his proposal, then he would deliver them 3000 *candies* of pepper. By this time, the English had become fed up with the unkept promises of the King. As they had a long list of unfulfilled pepper contracts, they refused to fall into his trap. As expected the King reverted to his ancient threat that he would not consent to weigh off a grain of pepper more at Anjengo.[52] Bombay Castle observed that in the course of 11 months the Company had received only 270 *candies* 2 *maunds* and 2 pounds which fell very short of the contract.[53]

By the month of December 1756 pepper delivery had come to a virtual halt. The King's *karyakars* (managers) blamed the rains for the delay and promised to deliver pepper as soon as the rains abated. They did deliver, but only eight *candies* at Eddawa warehouse. The English were very much perturbed by the fact that the King of Travancore was the sole merchant in south Malabar, who delivered only such quantities as he pleased without regard to the nature of the contract. Besides, he could stop to honour the pepper contract whenever he pleased. As a result the English were virtually at the mercy of the King in matters of trade.[54]

But towards the end of the year 1757, the King directed nevertheless his *karyakar* to fulfil the current contract. Thus pepper was delivered frequently by the *karyakar* to the English. In November 1757, the chief of Anjengo made known to the King the Company's desire of entering into a new pepper contract. He reminded the King to consider the services rendered by the Company during the wars with Tinnevely and to accede to his proposal.[55] The King finally agreed to enter into a new pepper contract with the Company by profusely apologising for the delay in previous supplies.

On 6 July 1758, the English entered into a contract with the King for 1500 *candies* of pepper at the rate of Rs.82 per *candy* and again another contract was entered into in 1759 for 2000 *candies*.[56] But in 1759 Maratanda Varma passed away to the great relief of the English. He was the architect of monopoly trade in pepper in south Malabar. He perfectly understood the link between pepper trade and his political authority, which pushed him to take over the entire pepper trade of south Malabar. Neither the English nor the Dutch could do anything about it as long as he lived. In fact, they had to submit to the frequent requests for arms in exchange for pepper and also to the other exigencies and unpredictabilities of the King.

Things did not improve very much for the English with the new King Rama Varma, who hailed from the royal family of Kolattiri, ascending the throne of Attingal. But by the end of 1760, the new king too was not able to deliver even one third of the original contract. Moreover he was in dire financial difficulty. In order to obtain a speedy delivery of pepper, the Company advanced him Rs.10000 through a merchant called Medumpilla Meter.[57] But even by 1761, only 799 *candies* of pepper were delivered. As usual, the King was reminded of the past favours bestowed on Travancore by the English. This time a warning was even tendered to the King that if he persisted in his harassment, then the English had no other option but to withdraw from Travancore. Fearing that things might get out of hand, Rama Varma immediately sent Crisna Pilla to meet the English chief at Anjengo. Crisna Pilla gave a detailed account of the pepper produce of Travancore which was around 8000 *candies*, though for the past two years, the yield had decreased to 4000 *candies* for various reasons.[58]

Crisna Pilla's account was, of course, too good to be true, for the Company knew that the country did produce abundant pepper. But it appears that even as late as 1801 the Travancore Rajah made sure that the English Company officials never saw the pepper gardens. In 1764, a new contract was concluded for 2000 *candies* of pepper at the rate of Rs.82 per *candy*. From 1765 to 1770, pepper supply was somewhat balanced viz., 200 *candies* at the rate of Rs.82 per *candy* in return for warlike stores. For every 500 *candies* of pepper the Company was to supply 200 stands of arms.[59] Thus the policy of exchanging pepper for arms was continued by Rama Varma.

From 1771 to 1773, pepper trade was affected due to clandestine sale of pepper to Carnatic and also to the Danes.[60] From 1774 to 1777, pepper trade was further affected as the country was under threat of an invasion by Hyder Ali, the sultan of Mysore. There was a steep decline in pepper supply from 2000 *candies* in 1779 to 1000 *candies* in 1782.[61] From 1784 onwards Travancore was neck deep in war with Tipu Sultan, the son of Hyder Ali, who had ascended the Mysore throne on his father's death. The confrontation with Hyder Ali and Tipu Sultan involved a lot of expenditure for the Rajah. As a result, trade slackened and the pepper contract was not fulfilled. The English were in dire need of pepper as the ships were calling at Anjengo.[62]

During the years 1785 to 1792, trade in Malabar including Travancore was severely dislocated due to the invasion of Tipu Sultan. The calamity lay not so much in the terror he spread but in the deliberate measure he adopted against traditional commerce in Malabar. He destroyed the pepper vines in Travancore. The effect on trade was soon felt. In the turmoil, the Company could obtain only a few *candies* of pepper by fits and starts. In 1788, in spite of the dislocation of trade caused by Tipu Sultan, the Company entered into a new contract with the Rajah of Travancore for the delivery of 1400 *candies* of pepper.[63]

Every effort seems to have been employed to induce the Rajah to enter into a permanent contract for pepper and to take in exchange a considerable quantity of European goods if possible. But even by March 1789 not one grain of pepper was delivered into the Company's warehouse, though the English had information that pepper was collected in Ponderah, in spite of Tipu Sultan's depredations. But the King instead of heeding to the request of the English for the delivery of the pepper from Ponderah seems to have sold large quantities of pepper secretly to Quilon.[64]

In June 1791, the Rajah entered into a new contract for 2000 *candies* of pepper.[65] This contract too remained unfulfilled, partly because the workers who weighed pepper never turned up before eleven or twelve a.m. and as a result they could hardly weigh 15 to 20 *candies* a day. This was brought to the notice of the King pointing out that if the workers came at sunrise they could weigh around one hundred *candies* of pepper per day.[66]

Thus while the English Company officials had perpetual trouble in procuring the requisite pepper, they were also fighting Tipu Sultan, who posed a challenge to the rising English supremacy in south India. In 1792, Tipu was defeated by the English. As a result northern Malabar province came under the control of the English. This annexation changed the power equations in the region and posed a direct threat to the authority of the Travancore Rajah, though the latter was always in friendly terms with the English.

In 1794, Major Dow, supervisor of Malabar province, arrived in Travancore and forced the Rajah to enter into an agreement for 4000 *candies* of pepper.[67] The Rajah was in financial distress during this period, due mainly on account of the expenditure that he would have incurred during the wars. He requested the English for a loan of ten lakhs of rupees at an interest of 6 per cent. But the Chief of Anjengo insisted that in return for the loan, the Rajah must adhere to the previous pepper contracts.[68] It appears that a little later, he requested the English once again to advance him six lakhs of rupees as loan in exchange for the delivery of 1000 *candies* of pepper annually. The amount was to be adjusted in pepper price. The Company refused the loan to the Rajah. When Jonathan Duncan visited the Malabar coast about the same time, he again requested for a loan of two lakhs of rupees. Duncan sympathised with the Rajah and requested the Chief at Anjengo to take two lakhs from the treasury of Anjengo and pay the amount to the Rajah.[69] The chief, however, was unable to raise the amount as the Rajah was already indebted to the Company for Rs.147642.1.12.[70]

The Rajah of Travancore continued to supply large quantities of pepper to non-Malabari foreign merchants and made constant excuses to the Company for failing to provide pepper for which he was bound. A certain Murdock Brown and the Dincur merchants of Mahe were among his most important customers. Brown purchased huge amount of pepper from Travancore. His activities seemed to have been designed invariably to further his private interest. The Company had delivered no authority to him to trade in pepper.[71] Anjengo officials promptly asked the *Dewan* of Travancore to stop supplying pepper to Brown. A protest was also issued to Brown. He owned up his fault and stated that as he saw pepper being taken by the Danes and smuggled to Calicut and Tellicherry, he was under the impression that there was plenty of pepper in the country and thought his purchase would not interfere with the Company interests at Attingal. He apologised profusely for his conduct.[72]

In 1796, Travancore was again under threat of attack by Tipu Sultan. Steps were taken to ensure the Company's pepper trade. Measures were taken to transport pepper to Cochin in fifty boats. Temporary godowns were built at Quilon and Cherringa for all the pepper lying on the beach to be dried and for all the pepper from Anjengo.[73] For a while the pepper trade on the coast was suspended.

But towards the end of 1796, four of the Company's ships had berthed at Anjengo and it was imperative that these ships be filled with pepper. The Rajah in his usual fashion dilly-dallied. By 1797, the court of directors in London had become so concerned at the continued high price of pepper that they ordered the appointment of a special committee to enquire into the reasons.[74]

The Chief at Anjengo decided to revise the rate of pepper by finding out how much pepper the Rajah actually sold to private merchants. After investigating it was found that the price received from private traders ranged from Rs.165 to Rs.175. The English therefore tried to convince the Rajah to contract for Rs.145, reminding him once again of the friendship subsisting between him and the Company. The Company also decided to stipulate that until the full quantity of 3000 *candies* was delivered, the Rajah was not to be entitled to more than Rs.115 per *candy*. The Rajah agreed to enter into a new contract at the market price. He stated that at times when the season failed, he had even purchased pepper at a high price of Rs.200 per *candy* from other regions and delivered to the Company incurring heavy loss. He implored the English at Anjengo to save him from such losses, pointing out that other foreign merchants bought pepper at prices ranging between Rs.165 and Rs.180.[75]

Pepper trade came to a standstill in the year 1798 due to the demise of the Rajah of Travancore. The English approached Dewan Kesava Das for the delivery of pepper. But nothing seems to have come about.[76] But the new King Bala Rama Varma was no better than his predecessors when it came to fulfilling pepper contracts. He gave all possible excuses for untimely delivery.

However, for the first time during this period, Anjengo warehouse was full with unsold pepper. It was decided to shift the same to the warehouse at Quilon in order to receive the current year's pepper at Anjengo. This meant only one thing, that is for the first time the demand for pepper had started dwindling. There was a pepper glut at Anjengo at a time when Dewan Kesava Das passed away.[77] The Rajah seems to have been ignorant of the pepper glut, which had the potential of seriously affecting the economy of his country and also his authority.

Instead, the Rajah in the meantime informed Duncan, the English governor at Bombay that he had weighed 2750 *candies* of black pepper and had deposited it in the warehouse. The balance of 250 *candies* was to be delivered soon. He gave even his fullest assurance of fulfilling every clause in the pepper contract.[78] However, in spite of the assurance, even by May 1800, pepper delivery was not effected. But the Rajah seemed to care nothing for treaty or contract. The Rajah seems to have purposely delayed pepper delivery as the contract rate was Rs.115, whereas he could get Rs.145 from private adventurers. The chief of Anjengo asked the new *Dewan* nevertheless to fulfill the pending pepper delivery. Otherwise he threatened to exact from them a penalty of Rs.57.50 per *candy* for non-compliance.[79] The Rajah blamed the season for not being able to complete the pepper delivery. But the chief would not believe and even threatened to impose penalty for deficit quality of pepper.[80]

The year 1801 saw numerous changes taking place in the court of the Rajah. Velu Thampi had been appointed as the new *Dewan*. The Malabar province was transferred to the Madras government after the defeat and death of Tipu Sultan. The Rajah was in such acute financial difficulty that he was even forced to sell his private jewels to raise money for fulfilling his engagements with the Company. He was so desperate for money that it was known that he forced his subjects to sell him pepper without paying even a single rupee. This affected the pepper trade adversely as the merchants refused to bring pepper for sale to the Rajah.[81] The English realised that this time the Rajah was genuinely in a very tight spot. He had mismanaged the country. As a result the commercial concerns were in doldrums. Old vines were dead and a few pepper vines which were planted to replace the old vines were unfruitful. The English became convinced that thereafter a diminution in pepper delivery must be annually expected.[82]

From 1802 onwards the Company's interest in pepper began to wane. Nevertheless, in 1803, an article of agreement was entered between Macaulay, the new English Political Resident of Travancore and Velu Thampi according to which the Rajah agreed to sell to the Company each year for five successive years 3000 *candies* of pepper.[83]

However, pepper trade was declining rapidly. The Court of Directors in London wrote to the Commercial Department at Anjengo about future pepper purchases. According to them, commercially speaking a contract for a term of years was objectionable for, if the market price was lower than the contract price, then the Company must purchase more pepper from the market. Besides, they had realised that Travancore pepper was inferior to the produce of British Malabar province. But the pound weight of pepper at the Company's sales was however sold for exactly the same sum, whether it was from British Malabar or Anjengo. They further stated that the right of preemption of the surplus pepper of Travancore even at contract price was only an imaginary benefit, not a real advantage. This was so as a *candy* of Travancore pepper at Rs.127 per *candy* would cost on board a ship Rs.139, according to the estimate made by the Accountant General.[84]

At this time, the price of pepper began to fall in England too. It fell to seven pence per pound and appeared to be on the decline. There was also a pepper glut in the market. There was old stock in the East India House at London which was sufficient for more than two years sales for home consumption and exportation on an average of the deliveries of twenty years. Besides there was an equal quantity which remained at their warehouse which was the property of buyers at former sales which was not disposed of. Therefore, in the light of the excess supply of pepper in the absense of any demand, it was decided that no pepper was to be provided by Anjengo during 1807 –1808 except the quantity to be received under the contract with the Rajah of Travancore. As the contract would expire in 1808, the Court of Directors expressed their wish not to renew the same until the terms were submitted to their consideration.[85]

The Rajah had feared that the pepper contract would never be renewed. But the proposition of renewing the contract after the terms were considered gave him a ray of hope. He intimated the chief at Anjengo that if the pepper contract was not renewed, then it would spell his ruin. Besides, he informed him about his financial bankruptcy. He did not have money even to pay the first subsidy of the government.[86]

The chief, however, visited the Rajah to discuss the instructions received from the Court of Directors. Those present at the meeting were the Rajah's own interpreter, Soobayah, and the Company's linguist, S.D.Fernandez and the Diwan Velu Thampi. The Rajah was informed about the Company's intention to debit on the wastage of pepper delivered from 1804 onwards. The Company knew at this juncture that the Rajah would fall in with their wishes, lest the pepper contract was not renewed. As expected the Rajah consented to the above proposal. But he insisted on renewing the pepper contract. The Rajah's proposal was submitted to the Court of Directors through Bombay Castle.[87] However, the Rajah was informed of the improbablility of a new pepper contract as the price of pepper in Europe had reached rock bottom level.

In 1809, Travancore reeled under the uprising of Velu Thampi. Trade came to a standstill. The Rajah owed enormous sums amounting to Rs. 632430 to the Company. He was asked to provide speedy liquidation of the amount. Earlier outstanding amount used to be adjusted in pepper purchases. But the Company no longer required any pepper from Travancore. Thus at Anjengo pepper ceased to be purchased officially by the Company.[88] This was an abrupt fall from the prestigious position the pepper trade had commanded in earlier times in Attingal and Travancore. The Court of Directors intimated Bombay Castle about the futility of procuring pepper from Malabar.[89]

Other articles of trade

Side by side with pepper trade, but less in importance was the trade carried on in Travancore by the English in cotton, coir, timber, lead, cowries, indigo and tobacco. Next to pepper the most important article of trade at Attingal was cotton, while the rest was of very marginal importance.[90] So we will have a look into only the cotton trade in Attingal and Travancore.

Cotton was produced in sizeable quantities in Attingal. From the early days of English settlement in Attingal, musters of country cloth was sent to Bombay to be sent to England. The cloth produced in Attingal was very cheap compared to those produced at Surat or at Madras. Production per annum was around 25000 pieces.[91]

Even though the Europeans, came to south Malabar mainly for pepper, the English realised the profitability of dealing in cloth. They constructed a separate warehouse for cloth, where cloth was received from the Malabar merchants and stocked.[92] Cloth merchants compared to pepper merchants were very poor. They were usually advanced some money before making deliveries.

In 1723, musters of long cloth and *sallampores* were sent to Bombay. Bombay castle was very appreciative about the Travancore clothes, in spite of the fact that production of cloth was stunted by nature, as it rains for five months of the year.[93]

In 1736, Bombay Castle asked the English factors in Attingal to contract for 10000 pieces of cloth. Out of this quantity only 6080 pieces could be delivered on time, the cause of the delay being the vagaries of climate.In 1738, Bombay Castle ordered the chief of Anjengo to contract for another 10000 pieces of cloth. By 1739, they obtained 1150 pieces of cloth in the warehouse.[94] In the same year, Charles Whitehill, the chief at Anjengo contracted with cloth merchants, Nelliampam and Danucem Chittys of Cotata for 10000 pieces of cloth to be delivered within two months to be shipped to England. Again in the year 1740, the Company received 1150 pieces of several assortments of cloth.[95]

But cloth was not a regular item of trade at Attingal. Contract for cloth was entered only when the need arose. Thus it was years later in 1748, ie., after the annexation of Attingal Queendom to Travancore that the English decided to procure large quantities of cloth. But unfortunately the dryness of the season raised the price of cotton and thread so high that the merchants did not manufacture them.[96]

Other nations like the Dutch and the French purchased cloth from Travancore. Since the English did not have a monopoly of this article like pepper and as they were not interested in it, they did not threaten the merchants. During the year 1749, Travancore manufactured only small quantities of cloth.[97] As there was no year to year contract made in cloth trade, there was only occasional mention of this trade in the English Company records.

In 1761, merchants of Cotata entered into an agreement with Thomas Whitehill, chief of Anjengo for 20000 pieces of cloth. After this contract, there was a gradual abandonment of cloth trade at Anjengo. The settlement which received a small annual supply of long cloth and sallampores abruptly discontinued this trade from 1770 onwards.[98]

Cloth trade was again resumed on a firmer footing only in 1795. It was confined not only to long cloth and sallampores but to all varieties that were found suitable to the European markets The Court of directors gave instructions to Bombay Castle to order the chief of Anjengo to procure 15000 pieces of long cloth and 15000 pieces of Sallampores for the ensuing season, and also to collect a complete set of samples of every species of piece goods made there not only for export but for local consumption, together with an account of the prime cost of each sort and the quantities that might be procured.[99]

This time the chief of Anjengo realised the necessity of contracting directly with the Rajah of Travancore rather than with the merchants. Local merchants were very poor and they did not attach much importance to contracts. After advancing huge sums of money to them with a written contract, he knew that the Company will be in a state of predicament owing to the unreliability of the merchants. The Chief also felt that if the Rajah did not participate in this business, he might try to throw obstacles in the way of completing it. Besides, during 1795, he had his doubt of fulfilment of the contract as small-pox was raging on the coast and many weavers had succumbed to the disease. There was thus a shortage of weavers which affected trade.[100] In 1796, the Rajah of Travancore entered into a contract with John Hutchinson, the Resident or chief of Anjengo, for furnishing the Company with 48000 pieces of cloth. In the following year, a fresh contract was entered between the English at Anjengo and the Dewan of Travancore for 50000 pieces of cloth, but by 1798, deliveries were not made. The Rajah, however, asked Dewan Kesava Das to deliver the cloths to the Company without any more delay.[101]

The reason for the delay was ascribed to shortage of weavers. People from other parts of the country came to Travancore to entice the weavers by offering them better salary. Thus many weavers migrated from Travancore to other parts.Weavers were essential for twisting the cloths and as they were taken away, the merchants could not fulfil the contract. The *Dewan* was asked to be vigilant and to issue strict orders against others coming into Travancore to inveigle away the weavers, so that he would not be deprived of the means of fulfilling the cloth contract with the Company.[102]

In September 1799, the English entered into fresh contract with the Rajah for 50000 pieces of cloth, even though 26676 pieces of cloth of previous delivery were still pending with the Rajah. Out of the 50000 pieces of the new contract, the Rajah promised to deliver at least 12000 pieces without delay.[103] The year had nearly come to a close, and out of 12000 pieces only 5761 pieces were delivered and there was a pending quantity of 6033 pieces of cloth. The Rajah put the blame on the weather conditions for the delay in delivery and also on the northern merchants on whom he depended for the delivery of cotton. He also attributed the rapid increase in the price of cotton for the delay. But the English threatened to stop cloth contract with the Rajah forever, if he did not adhere to the tenor of the contract.[104] In spite of the delay in fulfilling the current contract, the *Dewan* wanted the English to enter into a new contract and advance some money too. The English refused to enter into a new contract without fulfilling the old one. They also declined to accept the Rajah's desire to revise the price of the contract.[105]

The Company officials were in a dilemma, as the Rajah neither fulfilled the contract nor allowed them to contract with others. Parry, the Resident at Anjengo, informed Bombay about this "dog in the manger" attitude of the Rajah. He also wrote that other manufacturers of cloth in the country were prepared to sell them to the Company at the same rate as then paid to the Rajah of Travancore.[106]

As the Rajah persistently expressed his desire to enter into a fresh contract, Parry threatened to exact a penalty on former unfulfilled contracts. He firmly stated that unless the outstanding 10866 pieces were received, no new contract would be entered at all. The Company had in their warehouse in 1800, 3419 pieces of cloth.[107] It is rather surprising that in spite of blatantly flouting the contracts and always resorting to excuses for the delay in delivery, the English continued to deal with him.

The Court of directors issued orders to the English at Anjengo to confine henceforth their purchases to only *sallampores*. In 1802, Parry entered into a contract with the Rajah for supplying two sorts of *sallampores* at a lowest rate of Rs.5 per piece. This contract was annulled in 1803. Subsequently the Court of Directors ordered 2000 pieces of *sallampores* to be procured at Rs.6 per piece and accordingly by the year 1804, more than 2000 *sallampores* were purchased.[108] After this year there was no more mention of any cloth contract entered with the Rajah in the English records. Thus the cotton trade of the English with Travancore Rajah came to a standstill very much like that of pepper.

By 1811, the English trading settlement at Anjengo in Attingal had nearly wound up. The Rajahs of Travancore seem to have never foreseen the possibility of a pepper glut in the European market. Neither did they realise that the price could fall so drastically so as to make the whole trade unprofitable for Travancore. Martanda Varma's objective of taking over the pepper trade as a State monopoly in order to assert his political authority was short-lived. His strategy of basing the economy of Travancore on pepper alone was a failure in the long run due mainly to economic vicissitudes in Europe and availability of pepper of better quality in north Malabar, out of his control. When pepper was no more an economic force to be reckoned with in Travancore, it also lost much of its political value. Surprisingly, the economic downslide in Travancore coincided also with a downturn in its political fortunes. Besides the fact that on the one hand the Rajahs of Travancore hardly took into account the fall in the demand and the price of pepper in their political and economic calculations, on the other they had incurred a lot of expenditure mainly due to the wars and also on account of purchases of territories and forts. But the English never really seem to have taken these factors into account when they pressed the Rajah to honour the contracts or for the repayment of the debts. These factors contributed very much to the weakening of the Rajah's hands. We would go into these latter aspects, especially the wars in which the Rajah of Travancore was involved, in a more detailed manner in the next chapter.

Notes and References

1. K.M. Pannikar, *Malabar and the Portuguese,* Bombay, 1929, p.24
2. Jan Kieniewicz, 'The Portuguese Factory and Trade in Pepper in Malabar during the 16th century', *Indian Economic and social History Review,* Vol.VI, No.1, March 1969, p.63; M.J. Rowlandson, *Tuhfat ul Mujahidin,* London, 1833
3. Edward Thornton, *The History of the British Empire in India,I,* London, 1841, p.73
4. Pamela Nightinghale, *Trade and Empire in Western India, 1784-1806,* Cambridge, 1970, p.33
5. T.I. Poonen, *Dutch Beginnings in India Proper 1580-1615,* Madras, 1933, p.1
6. K.N. Chaudhuri, *The English East India Company,* London, 1965, p.145
7. James Forbes, *Oriental Memoirs, I,* London, 1813, 1834, p.219
8. Francis Buchanan, *A Journey from Madras through the countries of Mysore, Canara and Malabar, II,* Madras, 1870, p.132
9. Letters to Fort St.George, 1703, Brabourne, Anjengo to Fort St.George, January 1703, p.99
10. Public Department, Despatches from England, 1687, Court of Directors, London to Bombay Castle, 3 August 1687
11. Anjengo Factory Records, 1704-1749, John Brabourne, Anjengo to Court of Directors, London, June 1704, p.7
12. *Ibid.,* p.8
13. A. Galletti, (tr.& ed.), *The Dutch in Malabar,* Madras, 1911, p.214
14. *Ibid.*
15. Despatches from England, 1705, Court of directors, London to Fort St.George, 12 January 1705, p.67; Anjengo Factory Records, 1704-1749, Alexander Orme, Anjengo to the Court of Directors, London, 20 April 1729, p.50
16. Anjengo Factory Records, 1704-1749, Alexander Orme, Anjengo to the Court of Directors, London, 20 April 1729, p.50
17. Anjengo Factory Records, 1704-1749, John Brabourne, Anjengo to the Court of Directors, London, September 1704, p.2
18. Anjengo Factory Records, 1704-1749, Gyfford, Anjengo to Fort St.George, 6 November 1719, p.99
19. Anjengo Factory Records, 1704-1749, Alexander Orme, Anjengo to Tellicherry, 13 November 1725, p.11

20. Anjengo Factory Records, 1704-1749, Nathaniel, Anjengo to the President and Council, Bombay, 22 February 1726, p.41
21. Anjengo factory Records, 1704-1749, Alexander Orme, Anjengo to the Court of Directors, London, 20 April 1727, p.49
22. Anjengo Factory Records, 1704-1749, Alexander Orme, Anjengo to the court of directos, London, 12 May 1727, p.62
23. Anjengo Factory Records, 1704-1749, William Wake, Anjengo to the Court of Directors, London, 15 December 1736, p.129
24. *Ibid.*
25. Anjengo Factory Records, 1704-1749, Salisbury, Anjengo to the Court of Directors, 5 February 1727, pp.131-132
26. Anjengo Factory Records, 1704-1749, Charles Whitehill, Anjengo to the Court of Directors, London, 18 February 1739, p.151
27. T.I. Poonen, *Dutch Hegemony in Malabar,* Trivandrum, 1978, p.98; K.M. Pannikar, *A History of Kerala, 1498-1801,* Annamalai, 1960, p.24; Ashin Das Gupta, *Malabar in Asian Trade, 1740-1800,* Cambridge, 1967, p.33
28. Letter from St.George, 1742, Rickards, fort St.George to Stephen Law, Governor, Bombay, 8 November 1742, p.76
29. Letter to Fort St.George, 1742, Stephen Law, Bombay Castle to Fort St.George, 26 April 1742, p.47
30. Letter from St.George, 1742, Rickards, fort St.George to Stephen Law, Governor, Bombay, 8 November 1742, p.76; Secretariat Inward Letter Book, 1742, Charles Whitehill, Anjengo to Bombay Castle, 12 December 1742, p.16
31. Secretariat Inward Letter Book, 1743, Whitehill, anjengo to Bombay Castle, 23 May 1743, p.165
32. Secretariat Inward Letter Book, 1743, Charles Whitehill, Anjengo to Bombay Castle, 22 October 1743, p.246; Anjengo Factory Records, 1704-1749, Charles Whitehill, Anjengo to Court of directors, 24 October 1743, p.222
33. Ashin Das Gupta *op.cit.,* p.34
34. *Ibid.*, p.35; Anjengo Factory Records and Diaries and Consultations, 1744, 12 March 1744, p.87
35. Anjengo Factory Records, 1704-1749, Anjengo to court of directors, 9 September 1747, p.241
36. Anjengo Factory Records and Diaries, 1750, 11 May 1750, p.160; Francis Day, *Land of Perumals,* Madras, 1863, 1909, p.63

37. Anjengo Factory Records and Diaries, 1746, Chief Anjengo to the Rajah of Travancore, 4 April 1746, p.90
38. Anjengo Factory Records and Diaries, 1746, Chief Anjengo to the Rajah of Travancore, 8 August 1746, p.124; Anjengo Factory Records, 1746, The Rajah of Travancore to Chief, Anjengo, 18 August 1746, p.126
39. Anjengo Factory Records, 1704-1749, Richard Bouchier, Chief, Anjengo to Court of directors, 9 September 1747, p.242
40. *Ibid.*
41. Secretariat Inward Letter Book, 1749, Chief, Anjengo to Bombay Castle, 23 May 1749, p.213; Secretariat Inward Letter Book, 1749, Chief, Anjengo to Bombay Castle, 14 September 1749, p.260
42. Secretariat Inward Letter Book, 1749, Chief, Anjengo to Bombay Castle, 16 November 1749, p.289; Anjengo Diary, 1808, Linguist, Fernandez, anjengo to Hnadley Commercial Resident, Anjengo, 10 May 1750, p.94
43. Secretariat Inward Letter Book, 1750, chief, Anjengo to Bombay Castle, 4 March 1750, p.94
44. Anjengo Factory Records and Diaries and Consultations, 1750, 16 February 1750, p.46
45. *Ibid.*, pp., pp.46-47
46. Anjengo Factory Records and Diaries and Consultations, 1750, 21 January 1750, p.49; Anjengo Factory Records and Diaries and Consultations, 1750, 9 June 1750, p.177; Anjengo Factory Records and Diaries and Consultations, 1750, 6 November 1750, p.86
47. Anjengo Factory Records and Diaries and Consultations, 1750, June 1750, p.179
48. Anjengo Factory Records and Diaries and Consultations, 1752, 27 September 1752, p.13
49. Anjengo Factory Records and Diaries, 1754, 1 February 1754, p.52
50. Anjengo Factory Records and Diaries, 1754, 9 February 1754, p.55; Anjengo Factory Records and Diaries, 1754, 10 February 1754, p.55
51. Anjengo Factory Records and Diaries, 1755, 5 September 1755, pp.10, 12
52. Anjengo Factory Records and Diaries, 1756, 29 March 1756, pp. 80-81,83; Paulin de Saint Barthélémy, *Voyages aux Indes Orientales,* vol.I, Paris, 1808, p.236
53. Anjengo Factory Records and Diaries, 1756, President and Council, Bombay Castle to Anjengo, 30 April 1756, p.104

54. Anjengo Factory Records and Diaries, 1757, 11 July 1757, p.134; Secret and Political Department Diary, 1757, John Spencer, Chief, Anjengo to John Cauillaud, Commander of the English forces, Tinnevelly, 13 April 1757, p.81

55. Anjengo Factory Records and Diaries, 1757, November 1757, p.131

56. Anjengo Factory Records and diaries, 1758, A contract made with the Rajah of Travancore and the Hon'ble Company, 5 July 1758, p.268; Anjengo Factory Records and Diaries, 1759, 31 October 1759, p.62

57. Anjengo Factory Records and Diaries, 1760, Rajah of Travancore to Thomas Whitehill, Anjengo, 24 October 1760, p.45

58. Anjengo Factory Diary, 1761, Anjengo to Rajah of Travancore, 21 May 1761, pp.187-188

59. Anjengo Diary, 1801, George Parry, Resident, Anjengo to Jonathan Duncan, governor, Bombay, 7 March 1801, p.69; Anjengo Factory Records and Diaries, 1764, 1 January 1764, p.75; Anjengo Factory Records and Diaries, 1765, 16 March 1765, p.206

60. Public Consultations, 1771, 25 February 1771, p.80; Anjengo Factory Records and Diaries, 1773, 22 March 1773, p.98

61. Anjengo Factory Records and Diaries, 1779, 2 August 1779, p.98; Anjengo Factory Records and Diaries, 1782, William Hornby, Bombay Castle to James Morley, Resident, Anjengo, 20 December 1781, p.11

62. Anjengo Factory Records Diaries and Consultations, 1783, Resident, Anjengo to Rawson Flart Boddom, Governor, Bombay, 8 March 1784, p.49; Anjengo Factory Records Diaries and Consultations, Hutchinson, Anjengo to Bombay Castle, 24 November 1785, p.180

63. Ashin Das Gupta, *op.cit.*, p.113; Anjengo Factory Records and Diaries, 1788, 14 December 1788, p.176

64. Anjengo Factory Records and Diaries, 1789, Hutchinson, Anjengo to William Medows, Governor, Bombay, 17 January 1789, p.37; Anjengo Factory Records and Diaries, 1790, Hutchinson, Anjengo to Rajah of Travancore, 27 October 1790, p.178

65. Anjengo Factory Records and Diaries, 1791, Rajah of Travancore to Hutchinson, Anjengo, 27 June 1791, p.85

66. Anjengo Factory Records and Diaries, 1792, John Hutchinson, Anjengo to Rajah of Travancore, 10 February 1792, p.87

67. Anjengo Factory Records and Diaries, 1794, Rajah of Travancore to Governor General, 14 February 1794, pp.26-27

68. Anjengo Factory General, 1795, John Hutchinson, Allepe to Hon'ble George Dick, governor, Bombay, 5 February 1795, p.12

69. Anjengo Factory General, 1797, Jonathan Duncan, Governor, Bombay to John Hutchinson, Resident, Anjengo, 26 February 1797, pp.38-39; Anjengo Diary, 1795, John Hutchinson to Raja Kesava Das, Dewan, Travancore, 15 April 1795, pp.50-51; Anjengo Diary, 1795, John Hutchinson to Raja Kesava Das, Dewan, Travancore, 15 April 1795, pp.50-51

70. Anjengo Factory General, 1797, John Hutchinson, Resident, Anjengo to the Rajah of Travancore, 14 March 1797, p.54

71. Anjengo Factory Records and diaries and consultation, 1795, John T. Dyne, Allepe to John Hutchinson, Anjengo, 26 April 1795, p.89

72. Anjengo Factory Records and diaries and consultation, 1795, John Hutchinson, Anjengo to Dyne, Alleppe, 27 April 1795, p.91; Anjengo Factory Records and diaries and consultations, 1795, Murdock Brown, Mahe to Hutchinson, Anjengo, 7 May 1795, p.130

73. Anjengo Factory Records and Diaries and Consultations, 1796, John Hutchinson, Anjengo to Jonathan Duncan, governor, Bombay, 13 September 1796, pp.23-24

74. Anjengo Factory Diaries and Consultations, 1797, Jonathan Duncan, Governor, Bombay to Rajah of Travancore, 30 April 1797, p.134; Pamela Nightinghale, *op.cit.,* p.112

75. Anjengo Factory Diary Secret and Political, 1797, Hutchinson, Anjengo to Jonathan Duncan, Governor, Bombay, 5 august 1797, pp.94-95; Anjengo Factory Diary Secret and Political, 1797, Rajah of Travancore to Governor, Bombay, 26 August 1797, pp.103-104

76. Anjengo Factory Diary Secret and Political, 1798, Hutchinson, Anjengo to Dewan, travancore, 28 June 1798, p.354

77. Anejngo Diary, 1799, George Parry, Anjengo to Jonathan Duncan, Governor, Bombay, 8 January, 1799, p.10; Anjengo Diary, 1799, Rajah of Travancore to Jonathan Duncan, Governor, Bombay, 29 July 1799, p.5543

78. Anjengo Diary, 1799, Rajah of Travancore to Jonathan Duncan, governor, Bombay, 24 August 1799, p.5550

79. Anjengo Factory General, 1800, Parry, Anjengo to Jonathan Duncan, Governor, Bombay, 8 June 1800, p.191; Anjengo Factory General, 1799, George Parry, Anjengo to Rajah of Travancore, 14 July 1800, p.231

80. Anjengo Factory General, 1799, George Parry, Anjengo to Rajah of Travancore, 18 July 1800, pp.238, 240

81. Anjengo Factory General, 1801, George Parry, Anjengo to Jonathan Duncan, Governor, Bombay, 5 March 1801, p.62

82. Anjengo Factory General, 1799, George Parry, Anjengo to Jonathan duncan, Governor, Bombay, 7 March 1801, p.65

83. Anjengo diary, 1803, Articles of Agreement between Macaulay, Resident, Travancore and Dewan, Travancore, 29 July, 1803, p.157

84. Anjengo Factory General, 1806, Extract of a letter from the Court of Directors in the Commercial Department, 30 April 1806, pp.640, 642

85. Anjengo Factory General, 1807, William Ramsay, Secretary, East India House, London to Bombay Castle, 5 February 1807, p.520

86. Anjengo Factory General, 1807, Handley, Anjengo to Duncan, Governor, Bombay, 31 October 1807, pp.803-804

87. Anjengo Diary, 1807, Handley, Anjengo to Bombay Castle, 31 October 1807, p.8010; Anjengo Diary, 1807, Rajah of Travancore to Bombay Castle, November 1807, p.8015

88. Anjengo diary, 1809, John Smee, Anjengo to Rajah of Travancore, 11 May 1809, p.5651; Anjengo Diary, 1809, John Smee, anjengo to Dewan of Travancore, 30 May 1809, p.6756

89. Commercial Department, Despatches from England, 1811, Court of Directors to Governor, Bombay, 10 July 1811, pp.293-294

90. See P.K. Leena, 'The History of the English East India Company's Settlement at Anjengo', Ph.D. dissertation, Calicut University, 1989, pp.273-276

91. Anjengo Factory Records, 1704-1749, John Brabourne, Anjengo to Court of directors, 9 September 1704, p.2

92. *Ibid.*

93. Anjengo Factory Records, 1704-1749, Alexander Orme, Chief, Anjengo to the Court of Directors, 13 December 1723, pp.35, 55

94. Anjengo Factory Records, 1704-1749, Salisbury, Anjengo to court of directors, 18 December 1736, p.119; Anjengo factory Records, 1704-1749, William Wake, Chief, Anjengo to the court of directors, 7 February 1738, p.139; Anjengo Factory Records, 1704-1749, James Salisbury, Anjengo to the Court of directors, 21 February 1738, p.144; Anjengo Factory Records, 1704-1749, Charles Whitehill, Anjengo to the Court of directors, 18 February 1739, p.146

95. Anjengo Factory Records, 1704-1749, Charles Whitehill, Anjengo to the Court of Directors, 28 april 1739, p.156; Anjengo Factory Records, 1704-1749, Charles Whitehill, Anjengo to the Court of Directors, 20 September 1740, p.156

96. Anjengo Factory Records, 1704-1749, Bouchier, Anjengo to Court of Directors, 23 December 1748, p.256

97. Anjengo Factory Records and diaries, 1749, Rajah of Travancore to Chief, Anjengo, 1 December 1749, p.33

98. Anjengo diary, 1761, Agreement for cloth between the merchants of Cotata and Thomas Whitehill, Anjengo, 3 January 1761, p.86; Anjengo diary, 1795, Extract from the Hon'ble Company's commands in their commercial letter, 28 April 1795, p.181

99. Anjengo diary, 1795, Extract from the Hon'ble Company's commands in their commercial letter, 28 April 1795, p.182

100. Anjengo Diary, 1795, Hutchinson, Anjengo to John Griffith, Acting governor, Bombay, 2 November 1795, p.198

101. Anjengo Diary, 1796, proposals from the Rajah of Travancore to John Hutchinson, Anjengo, 11 December 1796, pp.223-224; Anjengo Factory General, 1798, Rajah of Travancore to Acting Resident, Anjengo, 23 January 1798, p.9

102. Anjengo Factory General, 1798, George Parry, Anjengo to Dewan Raja Kesava Das, 10 August 1798, p.407

103. Anjengo Diary, 1799, George Parry, Anjengo to Rajah of Travancore, 16 September 1799, p.334; 29 July 1799, p.267; 16 september 1799, p.334

104. Anjengo Factory General, 1799, George Parry, Anjengo to Rajah of Travancore, 17 October 1799, p.382; Anjengo Factory General, 1799, Rajah of Travancore to the Resident, Anjengo, 22 November 1799, p.423; Anjengo Diary, 1800, Rajah of Travancore to Resident, Anjengo, 12 April 1800, p.133; Anjengo Diary, 1799, George Parry, Anjengo to Rajah of Travancore, 29 December 1799, p.5255

105. Anjengo Factory General, 1799, Dewan of Travancore to George Parry, Anjengo, 30 November 1799, p.432; Anjengo Factory General, 1800, George Parry, Anjengo to Rajah of Travancore, 25 January 1800, p.23

106. Anjengo Diary, 1800, George Parry, Anjengo to Jonathan Duncan, Governor, Bombay, 11 December 1799, p.436

107. Anjengo Factory General, 1800, George Parry, Resident to the Dewan of Travancore, 14 July 1800, p.231; Anjengo Factory General, 1800, George Pary, Resident, anjengo to Robert Rickards, 1 September 1800, p.279

108. Anjengo Diary, 1806, Handley, Resident, Anjengo to Henry Shank, Private Secretary to Hon'ble Governor, Bombay, 12 July 1806, p.408

Chapter 6

Confrontation in the East and North

The expansion of Travancore during the reign of Martanda Varma brought him and the later Rajahs of Travancore into contact and confrontation with the Nawabs of Carnatic and the Mysore sultans during the eighteenth century. As noted earlier, it was the Rajah of Travancore under the guidance of Martanda Varma who sought the help of the Nayaks of Madura in 1726 in their attempts to counter the *pillas*. They even accepted to pay tribute to the Mughals from this period onwards. In 1734, the Muslim chieftain, Safdar Ali Khan, son of Dost Ali Khan (1732-1740), the Nawab of Arcot, ravaged Travancore and the western coast. Two years later in 1736, the son-in-law of Dost Ali Khan, usurped the throne of Madura from the Queen (Regent) Meenakshi, who killed herself in despair. Very soon around February or March 1740, Chanda Sahib and his brother Bada Sahib attacked Travancore. Ramayyan Dalawa was ordered to defend Travancore territory and drive out the marauders.[1] Thus Travancore had to contend with new powers from the east. Later Travancore had also to contend with the Mysore sultans who came from the north. These two factors had a great impact on the history of Travancore. We shall deal with them presently one after the other.

Confrontation and Compromise in the East

In 1743, the Nizam of Hyderabad, a vassal of the Mughal Emperor, conquered Trichinopoly and Madura from the Marathas who had displaced the Muslims and carried away Chanda Saheb to Satara in 1741.The year 1744 saw the commencement of the rule of the Nawab of Arcot in the area held till then by the Nayaks of Trichinopoly, Madura and Tinnevely. In that year Anwar-ud-din was appointed Nawab of Arcot by the Nizam of Hyderabad. With the death of Anwar-ud-din there were two contenders for the throne of Arcot, backed by two European powers. Chanda Saheb was ackowledged the Nawab of Arcot by the French, whereas Muhammad Ali was espoused by the English. Both were related to each other. In 1749, Muhammad Ali duly succeeded his father Anwar-ud-din as Nawab of Arcot, with the help of the English. Chanda Saheb was defeated and killed.[2]

A little later about 1752, the Rajah of Travancore, Martanda Varma, acquired from Moodemiah, the Nawab's Pathan Officer-in-charge of the Tinnevely region (formerly in the service of Chanda Saheb), a range of districts extending 30 miles from Kalakadu to Cape Comorin lying at the foot of the mountains that separated Travancore from Tinnevely. Besides the above, the fort of Kalakadu with several others of less defence were purchased. The Rajah of Travancore claimed that these territories belonged to him previously and were annexed illegally by Moodemiah.[3]

On knowing about this transaction, Muhammad Ali dismissed Moodemiah and appointed his general Maphuz Khan, who was his own elder brother, as his representative in Tinnevely. The above tract of land purchased by the Rajah of Travancore was the bone of contention between both the parties for many years to come. Muhammad Ali, the Nawab of Carnatic considered Tinnevely as belonging to him, but on the other hand Martanda Varma contended that the part of country lying on the way from Madura to Tinnevely always belonged to him.[4] But the Nawab accused the Rajah of illegally obtaining the territory by bribing Moodemiah.[5]

The Nawab sent his army to Tinnevely to collect the revenue due to him.[6] On knowing this, Martanda Varma became worried. He believed that the Nawab had designs of entering his kingdom since to go to Tinnevely the army had to pass through part of his country.[7] The Rajah at once sent an appeal to Fort St.George. On receipt of the appeal, the English issued instructions to the Nawab's troops not to violate the territories of the Rajah.[8] The English at Madras were the allies of the Nawab and they were also friendly with the Rajah of Travancore. As a result they were caught unawares.

The Nawab claimed that he had sent his army to Tinnevely to retake the territory sold off illegally by Moodemiah. But it also appears that another reason for sending the army to Tinnevely was to suppress the *Poligar*, who held the estate of Tinnevely conferred to him earlier by the Nayaks and who was rebelling against the Nawab.[9] The Rajah of Travancore vigourously assisted the *Poligar,* Pulithevar against the Nawab and even gave refuge to the deserters of the Nawab's army. He even recovered Kalakadu and its dependencies. The Nawab reprimanded the Rajah for this act of defiance.[10]

But the Rajah did not persist with his defiance. Probably he knew that it was futile to confront the Nawab who was supported by the English, for it had the potential to lead to the interference of the Nawab in the affairs of Travancore. This he wanted to avoid at all cost. As a result, he conveyed his willingness to settle his disputes with the Nawab amicably.[11] Meanwhile, the English army under the command of Colonel Heron reached Tinnevely with the intention of helping Maphuz Khan in suppressing the *Poligars.* The Travancoreans finding that they were no match for the combined troops of the Nawab and the English fled from the scene abandoning the districts. Instead, the Rajah requested the Madras Governor to intervene and settle the differences between him and the Nawab. Subsequently the Rajah of Travancore seems to have even entered into a treaty with the Nawab of Arcot, by which the former agreed to pay a tribute of Rs.6000 annually, along with an elephant, obtaining in return the Nawab's help against his external and internal enemies.[12]

By 1757, the district of Tinnevely came under the management of the English East India company. They began to let these districts to the merchants and in return they collected rent from them.[13] But the rent could not be collected easily as Maphuz Khan, in his turn, had rebelled against his own master and brother and started attacking the eastern frontier of the territory of the Rajah of Travancore.[14] The Company at once despatched Captain Callaud with a party of Europeans and Sepoys for quelling the rebels. They also requested assistance from the English at Anjengo. Though Maphuz Khan was finally defeated, he still retained possession of Kalakadu and the eastern district of Travancore. The Nawab outrightly dismissed Maphuz Khan and appointed Yusuf Khan, a Tamil Hindu convert to Islam, as his successor.[15]

In June 1757, the English factors of Anjengo wrote to Fort St.George reporting the advantages the Company might derive through friendship with the Rajah of Travancore.[16] Martanda Varma once again expressed his willingness to have the differences between him and the Nawab settled amicably by the English. But in spite of all the letters exchanged, the Rajah's troops often made incursions not only into Tinnevely country, but also into the limits of the English.[17]

The very next year Martanda Varma, though only 53 years of age, passed away due to sickness. He was succeeded by his nephew Rama Varma. On his accession to the throne, the Company decided to present him with a pair of pistols, a pair of handsome looking glasses, two pairs of rich China damasks, two pieces of ordinary velvet,.scarlet, fine cloth and six pieces of taffeta. Besides these, 65 venetians, rose water, sandalwood and sugar were also given to the Rajah.[18]

In May 1759, Yusuf Khan was made the renter of Madura and Tinnevely districts. He was instructed by Fort St.George to preserve the friendship with the Rajah of Travancore. As a result he entered into an alliance with the Rajah of Travancore against Maphuz Khan.Thus came about the friendship between the English, the Nawab and the Rajah. Later, in acknowledgement of the readiness with which the Rajah lent his assistance in quelling the rebellious *Poligars*, Yusuf Khan granted him 12 districts of Kalakadu and this grant was confirmed by the English government in Madras.[19]

The Rajah of Travancore could not retain possession of Kalakadu for a long period, for Yusuf Khan too rebelled against his master and began to endeavour to shake off the Nawab's authority and establish himself as an independent chieftain. The Madras government felt this change in Yusuf Khan and was concerned about his desire of independence. They cautioned the Anjengo chief to prevent Yusuf Khan from acquiring fire-arms and war-like stores.[20] But Yusuf Khan, to accomplish his ambition, sought aid from the French and then from the Rajah of Travancore. The latter refused to help him as he did not want to go against his ally, the Nawab, and would not take up arms against the English. Yusuf Khan stood isolated against the combined might of the English, the Nawab and the Rajah of Travancore.

Yusuf Khan in resentment marched against Travancore. The Madras governement viewed the activities of Yusuf Khan with much concern. They sent a whole regiment and also a supply of three hundred barrels of gun-powder to Anjengo. Besides this, a small detachment of artillery and stores were sent to Anjengo with discretional directions to assist the Rajah of Travancore. The Chief of Anjengo was requested by the Madras government to prevail upon the Rajah of Travancore to join the English forces and enter Tinnevely, while they would march towards Madura. The Rajah complied to join forces with the English. Further a detachment of artillery consisting of 30 men including two officers arrived at Anjengo from Bombay to assist the Rajah of Travancore in his operations against Yusuf Khan.[21]

But in the meantime, Yusuf Khan soon made up matters with the Rajah of Travancore. Under the terms of the treaty concluded, Yusuf Khan and Rama Varma pledged to assist each other with their army, in case of attack on any one of them and not to interfere in the internal affairs of one another. But Yusuf Khan could not carry on his war with the Nawab and the English at the same time. He was caught and hanged by the English by the order of the Nawab.[22]

After the death of Yusuf Khan his successor thought it proper to assume possession of all the countries lying on the eastern side of the Ghats. In 1764, Nawab Muhammad Ali ordered the Rajah of Travancore to retire with his people from Tinnevely and, in case of non-compliance, he threatened to invade his districts of Kalakadu ceded to him by Yusuf Khan and ratified by the Company.[23]

The Rajah, however, asked the Chief of Anjengo to inform the Madras government that such measures were inconsistent with the ancient friendship subsisting between the Company and him and that he could not make a difference between the Company's agents at Madras and Anjengo, esteeming that both acted on common interest. But Muhammad Ali soon took possession of the twelve districts of Kalakadu. This time the Rajah did not bother to wage a war and delivered up all the districts of Kalakadu. He also surrendered the fort and everything in it and retired to Towala.[24]

The Chief at Anjengo, with whom the Rajah maintained direct correspondence, however, knew about the consequences that might follow if the 12 districts were not restored to the Rajah. They feared that the Rajah might not honour the pepper contracts. As a result, he wrote to Fort St. George requesting them not to take any decision which would be detrimental to their interests in Travancore.[25]

The Madras Government referred the matter to the Nawab. He sent an envoy, by the name of Vencatachillim, to confer with Travancore. Engineer Call, a servant of the Company, was deputed by the Madras Government to arbitrate. The Rajah of Travancore hoped that matters would be settled in such a way as to prevent any future disagreement between the Nawab and him and that he would gain possession of his land in Tinnevely. The Chief of Anjengo even assured the Rajah that he would use his ability and make the Nawab do him justice.[26]

After a good deal of discussion and correspondence with the Nawab, a settlement was effected. Contrary to all expectations, according to the provisions of the settlement, the Rajah was expected to relinquish all pretensions to the Kalakadu districts and to fulfil all the engagements made with the English. The annual tribute to be paid to the Rajah was increased to Rs.15000. Further he was bound to pay two lakh rupees to the Nawab in connection with Kalakadu district. They mutually agreed to help each other with an army against all enemies internal and external. It was stipulated further that the Rajah should never assist any of the *Poligars* against the Nawab. The Rajah, realising the futility of resisting the Nawab, who was a stronger ally of the English than the Rajah of Travancore himself at that critical period, agreed to honour the settlement. Though this was detrimental to his original claims, yet it proved to be a sagacious move as it established a lasting friendship between all the parties. This friendhip stood in good stead to the Rajah of Travancore in the future, for as late as 1784, the Nawab of Arcot demanded tribute from the Rajah of Travancore or face the consequences of the invasion of Travancore. The dexterous prime minister of Travancore, Kumaran Chempaka Raman Pillay deflected the pressure exerted by the Nawab by agreeing to pay Rs.200000 to the English.[27]

Confrontation in the north

In 1761, the Zamorin of Calicut once again invaded Cochin. The Rajah of Cochin sought aid from Rama Varma, the Rajah of Travancore. The latter immediately despatched a force under General de Lannoye.The Zamorin's troops were repulsed. Subsequently the Zamorin agreed to live in peace with Travancore thereafter. This was in conformity with the treaty of 1757 concluded between the Rajahs of Cochin and Travancore. However, Travancore obtained possession of Alangad and Parur, conquered during the war in accordance with the terms of the treaty of 1757. As a reward for this help, the Rajah of Cochin ceded a tract of land, extending about thirty miles from Vypin on the coast to the inaccessible Annamalai hills. About the year 1762, a strong fort and arsenal were built at Cariapalli on the coast, while a wall twenty feet thick and twelve feet high, with some stone batteries and bastions at intervals, was constructed all along the frontier, under the supervision of Eustache de Lannoye between 1761 and 1765. But Mohibbul Hasan claims on the basis of Dutch records that the lines were completed only in 1777 and Ravi Varma extended its length and breadth as and when he liked. It was further protected by a deep ditch twenty feet wide and sixteen feet deep, while bamboos and thorny shrubs were planted close to the wall on the side of the ditch. This defence came to be known as the 'Travancore Lines' and was intended to repulse all attacks from the north.The remaining frontier was surrounded by sea on one side and the mountains on the other.

While friendship between the Rajah of Travancore and the Rajah of Cochin on the one side and the English, the Nawab of Carnatic and the Rajah of Travancore on the other was in the process of being consolidated, Hyder Ali Naik, a son of the soil of Mysore, had captured power in Mysore. He had already established his reputation as a formidable soldier, when he was at the service of the Hindu Maharajah of Mysore as *faujdar* at Dindigul. It appears that when Hyder Ali was a mere *faujdar*, Martanda Varma had asked his assistance to quell the remaining refractory chiefs. Hyder had readily offered his assistance, but by then the chiefs had been subjugated.Nevertheless Hyder Ali demanded compensation, not only from Martanda Varma, but also from his successor Rama Varma. It appears that Rama Varma was prepared to pay the money, but he refused to become Hyder Ali's vassal, since he was already a vassal of Muhammad Ali, the Nawab of Carnatic. As a precaution, Rama Varma strengthened the Travancore Lines in anticipation of an attack by Hyder Ali. During the 1760s, Hyder Ali actually invaded and took possession of all the northern parts of Malabar. He occupied all the petty states as well as the whole of the Zamorin's dominions and thus became the master of Malabar between Cannanore and Ponnani. The Zamorin seems to have perished in the flames of his palace. The Cochin Rajah fearing an attack by Hyder offered his allegiance to the Mysore chief and paid a sum of two lakhs of rupees and eight elephants, binding himself at the same time to be a tributary to Hyder.[28]

As expected, Hyder next turned his attention towards Travancore. He demanded fifteen lakhs of rupees and thirty elephants from the Rajah. The Rajah refused to comply with his demands on the ground that he was a tributary of Muhammad Ali, the Nawab of Carnatic, and that he could not pay tribute to both the persons. Hyder then threatened to invade Travancore with dire consequences. The Rajah probably never expected an attack coming from the north. But as it had come, the Rajah once again turned towards his old friends, the English, and asked them to supply him with money and arms and also sought their assistance if necessity arose. He even placed his troops at the disposal of the English as far as Calicut and Tinnevely.[29]

The Madras government who viewed the activities of Hyder with apprehension and distaste, asked the English at Anjengo to use every means to harass and distress Hyder and his forces. They were even asked to spirit up the Nairs, who had fled while Hyder advanced into northern Malabar, so that they employed themselves in recovering their lost lands. The Madras Government sought also the help of Bombay Castle to equip their marine and land forces to attack Hyder's possessions. The Travancore Rajah on his part stirred up rebellions against Hyder Ali in the Malabar and gave refuge to rebels in Travancore.[30]

Besides, the chief of Anjengo was given instructions to induce the Rajah to make a diversion by attacking Hyder's possession near the frontiers of his territory. He was to be furnished with miltary stores and every means to enable him to defeat Hyder's forces.[31] While Hyder was attempting an entry into Travancore, his dominions were invaded by the Nizam of Hyderabad, the Marathas and the English. He was thus forced to abandon his attempt on Travancore and returned to Seringapatam, his capital city in Mysore. He sued for peace and a treaty was concluded at Madras with the East India Company in 1769, in which special provisions were made for the future safety of the Rajah of Travancore.[32]

Nathaniel Stackhouse had taken charge of Anjengo in March 1774. During his chiefship orders came from Bombay Castle to reduce the Chiefship of Anjengo to a Residency.[33] In the meantime, Hyder Ali entered northern Malabar once again. The Rajah of Travancore became apprehensive of Hyder's inroads into Travancore. So he took the initiative of requesting the English at Anjengo to acquaint Bombay Castle of the whole affair and in case Hyder invaded his dominions, he wanted the English to help him, keeping in view the long friendship existing between them. But Fort St.George convinced the Rajah that there was no cause of anxiety as due to the friendship subsisting between Hyder and the English, the former would not take up arms against any power included in an alliance with the English.[34]

However, contrary to the expectations of the English, Hyder did attack and the whole of the territory of the Rajah of Cranganore succumbed to Hyder's general Sardar Khan. He desecrated and destroyed the temples. But in 1777, Hyder had entered into a treaty with the Dutch and had even released the officers of the garrison taken prisoner by him, when he overran the territory of the Rajah of Cranganore, and had even decided to deliver the Dutch fort in the area back to the Dutch.[35]

Meanwhile war broke out between the English and the French in Europe in 1778. In India too, the two powers were hostile towards one another. Pondicherry, a French territory, lying south of Madras, was captured by the English in 1778. The French governor of Pondicherry wrote a frantic letter to Hyder to take the French settlement of Mahe in northern Malabar under his protection. But Hyder was not in the least interested in the struggle of the Europeans. The English after their victory over Pondicherry wanted to attack Mahe, but for a time fear of Hyder deterred them from attacking it. However, forces comprising of three battalions of sepoys were sent overland to Anjengo with the objective of capturing Mahé and the Rajah of Travancore was asked to assist them with provision and other conveniences.[36]

In the same month another letter was written to the Rajah to inform about the arrival of Pringle as a pilot party to examine the roads leading from Pallamcotah in Tinnevely to Anjengo, through which the contingent would march towards Mahe. In January 1779, the Madras government sent another letter to the Rajah, stating that they had meant to send six hundred soldiers by sea to Mahe, but owing to lack of conveyances, they were being sent overland. Further the Resident of Anjengo was asked to procure vessels for transporting the troops to Mahe.[37] Mahe was captured in the month of March 1779. This capture estranged Hyder's relations with the English.

In fact, a few years later, the Dutch at Negapatam on the Coromandel coast and Cochin had united with Hyder to break up the friendship between the English and the Rajah of Travancore.[38] The Rajah was, however, asked to lose no time in preparing the troops and sending such provisions to the neighbourhood of Cochin as the troops from Britain would stand in need of.[39] Colonel Humberston commanding at Calicut was not sure whether he must remain at Calicut or proceed overland to Palamcotah. But orders went from Anjengo for the detachment to land at Colachel, a sea-port about 15 leagues to the southward of Anjengo, from where Palamcotah was nearby. According to secret information from Anjengo, the Dutch at Cochin had gathered 300 Europeans, 200 Malays and 1500 sepoys and topasses. But the English were confident of defeating them. Bekel Rajah of Malabar had sent horses for the assistance of the English. Further even the Nizam of Hyderabad supported the English in their fight against the Dutch and Hyder.[40]

However, confident the English were about defeating Hyder, on 27 July 1782, Colonel Humberston received a very disturbing news from Anjengo. Hyder's forces consisting of one thousand horses, two battalions of sepoys, 1000 peons with two guns were between Dindigul and Madura on their way to Calicut. Fierce fighting broke out between these forces and the English, assisted by the Rajah of Travancore. But before any decisive result could be achieved Hyder Ali passed away on 7 December 1782.[41]

Hyder Ali was succeeded by his son Tipu Sultan to the throne of Mysore. Rumours were soon afloat of a treaty of peace pending between the British and Tipu. The Rajah of Travancore insisted that in case of a treaty, his name should be nominally inserted as an ally of the English. He seems to have feared Tipu so much. In the meantime, the English and the Marathas had concluded a treaty of perpetual peace and friendship to counter Tipu.[42]

In October 1783 information reached Travancore that Tipu along with a great part of his army and also a detachment of French troops, had recommenced hostilities at Mangalore and had captured the English general Mcloed and several officers.[43] This time the English decided to annihilate Tipu Sultan altogether. Captain Fullerton captured Paliacachery and prepared to attack Seringapatam. But this plan was thwarted by Fort St.George who asked him to suspend all operations. It was felt in Travancore that the Madras government committed a great folly in asking Fullerton to withdraw his troops.[44]

Meanwhile England and France concluded a peace treaty in September 1783. But Tipu who until then had the support of the French was unwilling to stop hostilities. He accused the French of deserting an ally who had begun war for their sake. But he realised that he could never succeed without assistance from the French. The latter on their part never trusted Tipu. Finally an agreement for the cessation of hostilities was arrived at between Tipu and Major Campbell, commander of the English forces on the Malabar coast. The treaty of Mangalore was signed on 11March 1784 which established peace between the English Company and Tipu Sultan. The Rajah of Travancore was named and included in the treaty as a friend and ally of the English.But there was no reference to the Travancore Lines in the treaty.[45]

However, the treaty of Mangalore provided peace only for a brief period. Tipu continued to nurse grievance against the state of Travancore, which had not only defied him by allying with the English, but had also given refuge to the rebel rulers of Chirakkal, Calicut and Kolathunad of northern Malabar, who, Tipu wished, should be returned to him. The English were well aware of the acute dislike that Tipu nursed against the Rajah of Travancore and it was in fact to avert a crisis in future that they had included the Rajah's name as an ally of the English in the treaty of Mangalore. But Tipu refused to abide by the above treaty and according to secret information, in December 1785, Tipu's army marched towards Malabar.[46] It was known to the English at Anjengo that in the event of an attack on Travancore, the Rajah's forces were incapabale of opposing Tipu's troops, owing to lack of arms. The English settlement at Anjengo was also not fully equipped for any emergency. Their military forces consisted of four battalions of sepoys, irregulars carrying muskets were about 12000 and the rest were bow and spear men.[47] But both the Rajah and the English had time, for they knew there were less chances of an immediate attack on Travancore as only after Tellicherry, Tipu would turn towards Travancore.

On 23 April 1787, the Rajah obtained information that Tipu intended to capture the fort of Kodungalloor (Cranganore) belonging to the Dutch which was adjacent to his country from where he could commence hostilities towards Travancore. The Rajah in spite of raising an army of 100000 men, including some mercenaries from Madras, once again appealed to the English in Madras for assistance. The latter assured him of protection and support, but cautioned him not to give unnecessary reason for Tipu to attack his dominion and asked him to keep clear of all disputes prevailing in the neighbourhood. It appears that in 1788, Major Bannerman was appointed as a representative of the British government in Travancore and the Rajah resolved to see no messenger from Tipu or receive any communication from him, except in the presence of the British representative.[48]

According to the English records hostilities actually commenced between Tipu and the Rajah of Travancore by 22 July 1788. This was at a time when Tipu despatched an embassy to France seeking French help in his struggle against the English. Tipu created havoc in the conquered territories. The Rajah wrote to the English at Anjengo about the cruelties committed by Tipu against the kings and Brahmins of Calicut, Coteyat and Calinad. It appears that thirty thousand Brahmins had fled to Calicut, along with many Nayar overlords and chieftains. The English records maintain that Tipu unleashed terror everywhere he went. The entire country was laid waste. Christian churches and Hindu temples were equally desecrated by him. Towers of pagodas, palaces, houses of the nobles, of the rich and even the huts of the poor were committed to flames by this ferocious leader. Also, vast areas of pepper vines were destroyed by him. It appears that Tipu targetted Christian churches because he equated them with British Christians and therefore traitors in his eyes. Similarly he seems to have targetted the Hindu temples, and the houses, palaces and lands of the nobles for they were generally under the control of the Brahmins and Nayars, his sworn enemies, who had sided with the British, unlike the Rajah of Cochin.[49]

Fort St.George resolved to send two battalions of sepoys to the Rajah of Travancore and for this, the 10th battalion from Tanjore and the 43rd from Trichinopoly were ordered to move.[50] The Rajah was asked to provide quarters for these troops and to make payments to them. For the purpose of settling the accounts between the Rajah and the Company, it was planned to appoint a civil servant as paymaster to the detachment and to act as a Resident of Travancore. Accordingly George Powney who was Collector of Tinnevely was appointed Resident and paymaster in Travancore, with instructions that the Company's troops were to be employed only in the defence of the Rajah's own country.[51] That Powney was not subject to the control of the Resident of Anjengo and was directly answerable only to Fort St.George clearly brings out the diminishing importance of Anjengo settlement in its relation with the Rajah of Travancore.

Cornwallis, the Governor General of British India, took keen interest in the happenings of Travancore. He wrote to John Holland, Governor-in-Council of Fort St.George, that if authentic information was obtained of Tipu invading any part of the dominion of the Nawab of Arcot or the Rajah of Travancore, then he was to consider him from that moment as at war with the English, because in that case Tipu violated the treaty of Mangalore without any provocation.[52] On the other hand, if Tipu was being provoked by the Rajah of Travancore by collusive purchases of forts or places in the territory of one of his tributaries, then the English should refrain from interfering in his favour and the Rajah could no longer count on their friendship.[53]

It so happened that the towns of Cranganore and Ayacottah were in the possession of the Dutch for the past 150 years. But of late the Rajah of Travancore had made frequent offers to purchase them. Tipu demanded these towns, along with the tract on which the Travancore Lines stood, on the ground that they belonged to the Rajah of Cochin who was his tributary and that the Dutch had no right to sell them and the Rajah of Travancore had no right to purchase. Tipu even seems to have contended at one stage that the Dutch held them only on lease. But the Dutch, alarmed by the threats of Tipu, concluded a hasty bargain with the Rajah of Travancore on 31 July 1789. The later sent in his troops to occupy them. A deal was clinched at a price of 300000 Surat silver rupees to be paid in instalments, with the Dutch commander, Van Angelbeek, without the consent of the Madras Government. The Rajah of Travancore used various arguments like that the Dutch never paid any tribute to the Rajah of Cochin and so had an independent right to dispose of them. Mohibbul Hasan maintains that the Rajah of Travancore did not purchase them because he regarded them strategically important for the defence of his kingdom, rather he acquired them for self-aggrandisement and in order to abet the Dutch in their schemes. As this was increasingly becoming a bone of contention, the Rajah was asked by the English to restore both Cranganore and Aycottah, separated only by two and half miles, to their former owner and leave them to their fate. Besides, the Rajah seems to have laid claim to the territory of one Kolut Nair, a tributary of Tipu. He was once again asked to observe strict neutrality in all the disputes of his neighbours and even advised to return a number of refugee rulers from Malabar, some of whom were in exile for more than twenty years. Tipu was in fact never happy that the Travancore Rajah had offered protection to rebellious fugitives consisting of Nayars and Nambudiris of Malabar.[54] This showed the extent to which the English were willing to go to avoid any war with Tipu.

On 15 December 1789, Tipu sent a *vakil* with an ultimatum to Rama Varma, known by then as Dharma Raja. His principal demands were the withdrawal of Travancore troops from Cranganore and Ayacottah, the demolition of the Travancore Lines in the Cochin state and the return of Malabar refugees like the rulers of Calicut, Chirakkal and Kolathanad. But the Rajah would not comply satisfactorily to any of these demands. He continued to harbour the rebels. Tipu too was trying his level best to arrive at a settlement with Rama Varma and wean him away to his side, through letters and intermediaries. In June 1789, he seems to have written the following letter to Rama Varma with the objective of befriending him :

> I understand from what the Rajah of Cochin said of you that you are a good man and a great ruler who wants to be friendly with our Sircar. Since you are prudent and wise, you can presume the benefit that may accrue from allying with you.... I am sending my vakeels with the presents of some jewels, a horse and a dress for your kind acceptance.

But all such overtures seem to have been of no avail. The Rajah of Travancore was as suspicious as ever about the intentions of Tipu.

On 29 December 1789, Tipu declared war against the Rajah of Travancore and marched against Cranganore, after a skirmish in which his troops were attacked. began attacking his territory. This pushed Lord Cornwallis, probably prodded by the Rajah of

Travancore to declare war officially against Tipu Sultan for attacking the territories of the Rajah in direct violation of the treaty of Mangalore.[55] In spite of some initial successes, in which Tipu was rumoured to have escaped narrowly, and his palanquin, sword and other articles were taken as trophies to Travancore, the prospect of Travancore's troops in the war seemed bleak. As a result, George Powney, the Resident of Travancore, came up with an idea. He thought of creating dissension in Tipu's forces. So, the Rajah was advised to encourage the Muslim Mappilas and the Nairs to revolt against the authority of Tipu, assuring them of the Company's protection. Powney further wrote to all the petty Rajahs of Malabar and the Rajah of Cochin to cooperate with the English in the war against Tipu.[56]

Though we do not know for sure whether Tipu really intended to invade Travancore, Mohibbul Hasan claims that the Travancore troops were continuously harassing and provoking Tipu's forces. Whatever might be the truth in this contention, nothing could deter Tipu from executing his designs. Very soon in the month of April 1790, he broke through the Travancore Lines and the Travancore troops fled in panic. Tipu directed the immediate demolition of the fortifications sending off as spoil to his capital 200 pieces of canon and a vast quantity of ammunition. The Christian community was a special target of Tipu's troops. Cranganore was destroyed during Tipu's invasion by the French commander, Henri de la Salle Lally.

It is curious to note that at the time when Tipu attacked, there were two English regiments of native troops belonging to the Madras establishment at Ayacottah, as well as one European regiment and two of sepoys, which had been despatched from Bombay to the same place. But never did they cooperate with the Travancore army to the great advantage of Tipu.

Tipu's troops laid waste the entire country (of northern Travancore), while the inhabitants fled to the hills. The Christians again were a special target of Tipu. Tipu marched as far as Alwaye, a famous watering place of the Travancore raja. Diwan Kesava Pillay did what he could to stop or delay Tipu's advance. It now appeared that the whole of Travancore might well be overrun. The Rajah had slipped away to the far south with his remaining forces (some 10000 of them huddled into Vypin under English protection).

In the meantime, the south-west monsoon broke out with severity impeding further the progress of Tipu's troops. Tipu had no idea of the Malabar rains. His arms and ammuntions were washed away. Thus the progress of his troops was blocked finally at Verapoly. At Alwaye Tipu received intelligence that the British had declared war on Mysore and were marching towards Seringapatam, his capital. This compelled him to withdraw his forces from Malabar and return to Mysore. This he did after a ceremonial destruction of the famous Travancore Lines in which he himself was supposed to have wielded the inaugural pick.Soon peace was called for.[57] Tipu's forces left Malabar never to return again. Ultimately he was forced by circumstances to sign the treaty of Seringapatam in 1792. This time the name of Travancore was not even mentioned in the Treaty. The Rajah himself got nothing out of the treaty, though it was for his sake that the English and their allies have gone for war.

According to the treaty of Seringapatam, Tipu formally ceded the whole of Malabar country as possesed by him before the war and included in the Calicut district. He was forced to cede half of his dominions to the English. Besides the cession of territories, he had to pay an indemnity of more than three million pounds and to send two of his sons as hostage to the English Company.[58] In his schedule of the ceded districts he included the Travancore districts of Alangad, Parur and Kunathnaud as belonging to him. But when the Malabar Commissioners were appointed by the Company, Dewan Kesava Pillay, the first minister of Travancore, informed them that these districts belonged to Travancore. Powney was appointed by Lord Cornwallis to investigate into the state of the three districts and to confer on this subject with the advocates of Tipu Sultan.[59]

When the Commissioners arrived to investigate into the affairs of the three districts, the Rajah refused to cooperate with them, as by then, enmity had arisen between the Rajah and Powney owing to the misunderstanding generated by the Dewan Kesava Pillay. The Rajah refused to have any discussion on this issue with Powney as he considered him insincere and asked his replacement by a trustworthy person. The Board finally acquiesced to his wish and appointed Boddam to enquire into the facts and report.[60] The enquiry began and it was found by the Commissioners that Tipu had no right to include the territories in question to his dominions. Thus it was only in 1796 that the Governor General gave a final decision confirming Travancore's undisputed claim to the districts of Alangad, Parur and Kunathnaud.[61]

Thus success of the British military power and the conclusion of peace with Tipu afforded immense satisfaction to the Rajah who was for the moment free from the menace of Tipu Sultan. The English company then demanded the defrayal of the entire war expenses from the Rajah. They convinced him that it was only owing to the help rendered by them, that his dominions were saved from the hands of Tipu Sultan.[62] The Rajah who hoped to have a peaceful atmosphere during the rest of his life was rudely shocked by the repeated request for money by the Company. It is to be noted that it was not the Resident of Anjengo but the Resident of Travancore, who on behalf of the Madras Government, persistently pestered the Rajah to pay more and more war expenses. In 1793, it was decided to appoint an English political resident at Travancore on a permanant basis, which reduced the power, role and importance of the Resident at Anjengo in Travancore.[63]

After the defeat of Tipu, the Rajah of Travancore became too much dependent on the English. He truly believed that but for the English saviours, his dominion would have passed into Tipu's hands. He began to rely more and more on the English, thereby getting profoundly entangled into the intricacies of treaties, subsidies, etc.

Rama Varma wanted to conclude a permanent treaty with the English for the defence of his country against enemies. This treaty was duly ratified by the Court of directors in 1797.[64] The Court of Directors and the Governor General were exceedingly pleased with the Rajah and his Dewan Kesava Pillay. Though an enhancement in the amount of tribute had been obtained by the English through this treaty, yet the English expected to derive still greater advantages in due course in return for undertaking the responsibility for the permanent protection of the Rajah. The King and the Dewan were also happy over the success of their negotiations. Reputation of the Rajah spread throughout his kingdom. He was popularly known as *Dharma Rajah* or even *Kilavan Rajah* (old King). His Dewan Kesava Pillay was held in high esteem by both the English and the Rajah.[65]

In 1798, Rama Varma passed away and was succeeded by his nephew, Bala Rama Varma. He was only sixteen years of age on his succession to the throne. Dewan Kesava Pillay continued to serve the young Rajah in his ministerial capacity.[66] However, it appears that the young Rajah did not reciprocate the Dewan's feelings. Shortly afterwards, the Dewan was found dead in his bedroom. In fact, English records maintain that he was foully disposed off by poison by the adherents of the Rajah. The death of the Dewan cast a gloom over the land. The English regretted the death of the Dewan.[67]

The usual procedure after the death of a Dewan was to consult the Company officials before making any appointment. It was in the interest of the Company to appoint such a person who was inclined towards them, as the entire pepper contract was to be conducted between the Dewan in the name of the Rajah and the Company. A wrong choice could result in considerable trouble to the Company. However, they found that the Rajah had already appointed his friend Jayanthan Sankaran Nambudiri as the Dewan and invested him with all powers to direct and supervise the subordinate officers. This action of the new Rajah which bore the stamp of a certain independence, dismayed the Company officials as they knew that he had not heeded to the advise of the English higher ups who had asked the Rajah to make the selection in consultation with Major Bannerman.[68]

The action of the Rajah proved beyond any doubt that he was disgusted with the Company's interference in the internal affairs of Travancore, which was tolerated by the former Rajahs. But he soon realised his folly of appointing Sankaran Nambudiri to the high office. The new *Dewan* acted in an irresponsible manner and was unscrupulously corrupt. He appointed his favourites as subordinate officers. Corruption started creeping into the administration. In order to tide over the financial stringency he decided to raise a general contribution from the public. He prepared a list of people who could afford to pay and summoned them demanding immediate payment inflicting corporal punishment in case of refusal.[69]

This was resented by large sections of the people who rose in revolt under the leadership of Velu Thampi, a nephew of the former Dewan Kesava Das, demanding the dismissal of the corrupt *Dewan* and the abolition of all arbitrary impositions on the people. Finding no other way, the *Dewan* even took out the crown jewels from the strong room of the Padmanabhapuram palace and pledged them. In fact in 1798-99, the Rajah of Travancore had even forced his subjects to deliver the full quantity of pepper contracted with the Company without paying a single rupee to them. As a result merchants and local farmers refused to deliver any further quantity of pepper without advance payment.[70] Matters reached such a state that the Rajah himself was obliged to sell his private jewels to raise sufficient money to fulfil his engagements with the Company. The Rajah was thus forced to dismiss Jayanthan Nambudiri. This time he chose to inform the Madras Government about the dismissal.[71] The Rajah like the former Rajahs had fallen in line.

After the dismissal of the *Dewan*, the Rajah consulted Major Bannerman and appointed Ayyappa Chempaka Ramen Pillai as *Dewan*. The Rajah seems to have held the new *Dewan* in high esteem.[72] Jonathan Duncan, Governor of Bombay approved of the selection of Ayyappa Pillai as the Dewan.[73] But the former *Dewan* had left the finances of the State in doldrums. The treasury was empty. It was left to the new *Dewan* to stabilise the finances of the State. It was quite obvious to everyone that the English hands had gained in strength in the course of time that they were able to impose their wishes on the *Dewan* with relative ease.

Their hands were further stengthened in the course of 1799, when they defeated Tipu Sultan. But Tipu, in spite of some of his excesses, shines almost all alone in the firmament of Indian rulers of the eighteenth century, who never entered into any form of alliance or treaty or accepted any subsidy from the English, which could possibly compromise the independence of Mysore.[74] He preferred to die defending his capital and country single handedly against a coalition of the Marathas, the Nizam of Hyderabad, the Nawab of Carnatic and the Rajah of Travancore, led by the English, rather than compromise with the English. This left the English unchallenged in the Carnatic. The Mysorean wars had administered a shock treatment to the Travancore society. The Rajah of Travancore probably realised that the English were equally dangerous as allies or foes. But this realisation seems to have come too late. There was no one to stop the English any more in their quest for supremacy in south India.

Notes and References

1. Robert Sewell, (ed.), *A Sketch of the Dynasties of Southern India,* Madras, 1883, p.65; R.Bishop Caldwell, *A History of Tinnevelly,* New Delhi, 1982, pp.65,87,256; Shungoony Menon, *A History of Travancore,* Delhi, 1878, 1984, p.138; Levin Bowring, *Haider Ali and Tipu Sultan and the Struggle with the Mussalman Powers of the South,* Oxford, 1893, p.22
2. R.Bishop Caldwell, *A History of Tinnevelly,* New Delhi, 1982, pp.85-87. Chanda Saheb was actually the relative of Nawab of Arcot, who had earlier occupied Trichinopoly and Madura but who was defeated by the Marathas and sent prisoner in 1741. Muhammad Ali was the son of the Nawab of Arcot Anwaruddin who was appointed Nawab of Arcot by the Nizam. John Keay, *The Honourable company. A History of the English East India Company,* New York, 1991, p.290; Robert Sewell, *op.cit.,* pp.63-64
3. *Ibid.,* pp.91, 97. Moodemiah was the Pathan officer of Alam Khan, a soldier of fortune, formerly in the service of Chanda Sahib. Caldwell, *op.cit.,* pp.97, 256
4. Military Consultation, 1755, Fort St.George to Chief, Anjengo, 21 April 1755, p. 148; Caldwell, *op.cit.,* p.92. Maphuz Khan was the elder brother of Muhammad Ali.
5. Records of Fort St.George, Country Correspondence, Military Department, 1755, Nawab Annaverdy Khan Bahadur to Fort St. George, 16 April 1755, p.34
6. Military Consultation, 1755, Fort St.George to Alexander Heron, Major Company's forces of Coromandel, 5 April 1755, p.133
7. Military Consultation, 1755, Fort St.George to George Scott, Chief, Anjengo, 5 April, 1755, p.133; Military Consultation, 1755, Fort St.George to George Scott, Chief, Anjengo, 5 April, Military Consultation, 1755, Fort St.George to George Scott, Chief, Anjengo, 4 April 1755, p.131
8. Military Consultation, 1755, Fort St.George to George Scott, Chief, Anjengo, 5 April, 1755, p.133
9. *Ibid.,* 7 August 1755, p.57. Poligar was the holder of a palaiyam or estate held on service tenure
10. *Ibid;* Caldwell, *op.cit.,* p.257; Menon, Shungoony, *op.cit.,* p.162
11. *Ibid.*

12. Records of Fort St.George, Military Consultation, 1757, Rajah of travancore to Fort St.George, 28 June 1757, p.557; Caldwell, *op.cit.*, pp.257-258

13. Military Consultation, 1757, Fort St.George to George Scott, Chief, Anjengo, 9 February 1757, p.79

14. *Ibid.*

15. *Ibid.*

16. Military Consultation, 1757, John Spencer, Chief, Anjengo to George Pigot, Fort St.George, 31 May 1757, p.556

17. Military Consultation, 1757, George Pigot, fort St.George to John Spencer, Chief, Anjengo, 8 September 1757, p.898; Military Consultation, 1758, Fort St.George to John Spencer, Chief, Anjengo, 9 January 1758, p.20

18. Military Consultation, 1758, John Spencer, Chief of Anjengo to George Pigot, Fort St.George, 4 September 1758, p.443. Also see Shungoony Menon, *A History of Travancore,I,* Delhi, 1887, 1984, p.174; Anjengo Diary, 1758, 20 August 1758, p.12

19. Military Consultation, 1759, Fort St.George to Thomas Whitehill, chief, Anjengo, 23 October 1759, p.801; Military Consultation, 1764, Chief, Anjengo to Robert Falk, President and Governor-in-Council, fort St.George, 20 November 1764, p.827; Caldwell, *op.cit.,* p.258

20. Military Consultation, 1762, George Pigot, Fort St.George to Thomas Whitehill, Chief, Anjengo, 22 October 1762, p.401

21. Military Consultation, 1763, Bombay Castle to George Pigot, Fort St.George, 23 March 1763, p.223; Military Consultation, 1763, George Pigot, Fort St.George to Thomas Whitehill, Chief, anjengo, 22 April 1763, p.224; Military consultation, 1763, Thomas Whitehill, Chief, Anjengo to George Pigot, Fort St.George, 25 May 1763, p.363; Military Consultation, 1763, Thomas Whitehill, Chief, Anjengo to George Pigot, Fort St. George, 2 May 1763, p.345

22. Military Department, Country Corresspondence, 1764, copy of an agreement given by the King of Travancore to Yusuf Khan, 16 February 1764, p.369; Caldwell, R., *op.cit.,* pp.129-130

23. Military consultation, 1764, Thomas Whitehill, Chief, Anjengo to Charles Campbell, Major and Commander of the Company's forces, 26 October 1764, p.796

24. *Ibid*; Military Department, country Correspondence, 1764, Rajah of Travancore to the Governor, Fort St.George, 1 November 1764, p.401

25. Military Department, country Correspondence, 1764, Rajah of Travancore to the Governor, Fort St.George, 26 October 1764, p.797

26. Military Department, country Correspondence, 1764, Translation of a Portuguese copy of an Ola from the Rajah of Travancore to Governor, Madras, 2 December 1764, p.856; Military Consultation, 1765, Thomas Whitehill, Chief, Anjengo to Robert Palk, fort St.George, 25 May 1765, p.568

27. Military Consultation, 1767, Thomas Whitehill, Chief, Anjengo to Robert Palk, fort St.George, Bouchier, Fort St.George to Thomas Whitehill, Chief, Anjengo, 18 July 1767, p.582; Shungoony Menon, *op.cit.*, p.197; Paulin de Saint Barthélémy, *Voyagès aux Indes Orientales*, vol.I, Paris, 1808, p.46

28. Denys Forrest, *Tiger of Mysore*, London, 1970, pp.22, 24-25; Shungoony Menon, *op.cit.*, p.200; Paulin de Saint Barthélémy, *op.cit.*, p.225; Sreedhara Menon, *A Survey of Kerala History*, Kottayam, 1967, p.285; Mohibbul Hasan, *History of Tipu Sultan*, Calcutta, 1951, p.156; Francis Day, *The Land of Perumals*, Madras, 1863, p.144; Levin Bowring, *Haider Ali and Tipu Sultan and the Struggle with the Mussalman Powers of the south*, Oxford, 1893, p.139; A. Martineau, *Les Origines de Mahé*, Paris, 1917, p.xii

29. T.I. Poonen, *Dutch Hegemony in Malabar*, Trivandrum, 1978, p.160; Galletti, *The Dutch in Malabar*, Madras, 1911, p.154; Shungoony Menon, *op.cit.*, pp.200,205; Secretariat Inward Letter Book, 1766, Chief, Anjengo to Bombay Castle, 13 March 1766, p.225

30. Military Consultation, 1767, Fort St.George to Thomas Whitehill, Anjengo, 5 September 1767, p.843; Mohibbul Hasan, *op.cit.*, p.154

31. *Ibid.*

32. T.I. Poonen, *op.cit.*, p.161; Shungoony Menon, *op.cit.*, p.203

33. Anjengo diary, 1776, Bombay Castle to Nathaniel Stackhouse, 11 February 1776, p.13

34. Military Consultation, 1776, George Bigger, Chief, Anjengo to Lord Pigot, Fort St.George, 26 October 1776, pp.1314-1315; Military Department, Country Correspondence, 1776, Fort St.George to the Rajah of Travancore, 6 December 1776, p.199

35. A. Galletti, *op.cit.*, p.173; Military Consultation, 1777, John Torpess, Resident, Anjengo to Lord Pigot, fort St.George, 18 March 1777, p.670

36. S.P. Sen, *The French in India*, Delhi, 1971, p.102; Military Department, Country Correspondence, 1778, Fort St.George to the Rajah of Travancore, 23 December 1778, p.367

37. Military Department, Country Correspondence, 1779, Fort St.George to the Rajah of Travancore, 20 January 1779, p.15

38. P.K. Leena, 'A History of the English East India Company's Settlement at Anjengo', Ph.D.dissertation, Calicut University, 1989, p.341

39. Anjengo Residency Diary, 1782, Colonel Humbertson to the Rajah of Travancore, 10 February 1782, p.2

40. Anjengo Residency Diary, 1782, John Hutchinson, Resident, Anjengo to Lord Macartney, Fort St.George, 22 February 1782, p.9; Anjengo Residency Diary, 1782, John Hutchinson, Resident, Anjengo to Colonel Humberstone, Calicut, 3 April 1782, p.23

41. S.P. Sen, *op.cit.*, p.289

42. Anjengo Diary, 1783, Hutchinson, Resident, Anjengo to Bombay Castle, 14 September 1783, p.775

43. Military Consultation, 1783, John Hutchinson, Resident, Anjengo to I. Cox., Hippesley, Acting Resident, Tanjore, 9 October 1783, p.4632; A. Martineau, *Bussy et l'Inde Française, 1720-1785,* Paris, 1935, p.341

44. Military Consultation, 1783, Hutchinson, Resident, Anjengo to Fort St. George, 27 November 1783, p.5424

45. S.P. Sen, *op.cit.*, pp.380-381; Military Consultation, 1784, John Hutchinson, Anjengo to the Rajah of Travancore, 22 March 1784, p.1291; A. Martineau, *op.cit.*, p.424; Maistre de la Tour, *The History of Hyder Shah and Hyder Ali Khan Bahadur and of his son Tippoo Sultan,* London, 1855, p.293

46. Anjengo Diary, 1785, R.H.Boddam, Bombay Castle to John Macpherson, fort William, 25 November 1785, p.480; Kate Brittlebank, *Tipu Sultan's search for legitimacy,* Delhi, 1997, p.25

47. Anjengo Diary, 1786, John Hutchinson, Resident, anjengo to Alexander Davison, Governor, Fort St.George, 23 January 1786, p.269; Military Department, Country Correspondence, 1787, Rajah of Travancore to the Governor, Fort St.George, 2 September 1787, p.151

48. Anjengo Diary, 1788, Rajah of Travancore to John Hutchinson, Resident, Anjengo, 23 april 1788, p.1131; Shungoony Menon, *op.cit.*, p.214; Caldwell, *op.cit.*, p.211; Denys Forrest, *op.cit.*, p.131

49. Military consultation, 1788, Rajah of Travancore to John Hutchinson, Resident, Anjengo, 1788, p.3248; Military Consultation, 1789, George Powney, Parvour to John Holland, Governor in Council, 14 December 1789, p.3344

50. Military Consultation, 1789, Campbell, Fort St.George to Resident, Anjengo, 30 January 1789, p.351

51. Military Consultation, 1789, Fort St.George to George Powney, Resident, Travancore, February 1789, p.377; Military Consultation, 1789, Fort St.George to George Powney, Resident, Travancore, 26 May 1789, p.1479

52. Military Consultation, 1789, Cornwallis, fort William to John Holland, Fort St. George, 29 August 1789, p.2627; Military Consultation, 1789, Cornwallis, Fort William to John Holland, Fort St. George, 9 September 1789, pp.2660-2661; see also Denys Forrest, *Tiger of Mysore,* London, 1970, p.123

53. Military Consultation, 1789, Cornwallis, Fort William to John Holland, Fort St. George, 9 September 1789, p.2660-61

54. *Ibid.*, p.2661; Mohibbul Hasan, *op.cit.*, pp.154-162; Maistre de la Tour, *op.cit.*, p.273; Bowring, *op.cit.*, p.140; Denys Forrest, *op.cit.*, p.123

55. Anjengo Diary, 1790, Sober, Lieut. 10th battalion commanding the detachment to John Hutchinson, Resident, anjengo, 1 January 1790, p.2; Anjengo Diary, 1790, Cornawallis, Fort St.William to Fort St.George, 28 January 1790, p.2; Mohibbul Hasan, *op.cit.*, pp.163,165; Forrest, Denys, *op.cit.*, p.123; Maistre de la Tour, *op.cit.*, p.273 ; C.K. Kareem, *Kerala under Haider and Tipu,* Cochin, 1973, p.91; Kate Brittlebank, *Tipu Sultan's search for legitimacy,* Delhi, 1997, pp.25,94

56. Military Consultation, 1790, Powney, Resident, Travancore to Fort St.George, 19 March 1790, p.748; Military Consultation, 1790, Powney, Resident, Travancore to Fort St.George, April 1790, p.1013; Bowring, *op.cit.*, p.141; Mohibbul Hasan, *op.cit.*,pp.164-165

57. Denys Forrest, *op.cit.*, p.132; Military Consultation, 1791, George Powney, Resident, Travancore to Charles Oakley, Acting President in Council, Fort St.George, 28 May 1791, p.2880; Bowring, *op.cit.*, pp.143-44, 145-146; Denys Forrest, *op.cit.*, p.131; Mohibbul Hasan, *op.cit.*, pp.164-167; Robert Sewell, *op.cit.*, p.68fn; Paulin de Saint Barthélémy, *Voyage aux Indes Orientales,* vol..I, Paris, 1808, p.224

58. Military consultation, 1792, R.Abercomby, Campnear Pareapatam to George Powney, Resident, Travancore, 29 March 1792, p.1716; Ramakrishna Mukherjee, *The Rise and the Fall of the East India Company,* Berlin, 1955, 1957, p.271; William Logan, *Malabar,* I, New Delhi, 1989, p.473; Mohibbul Hasan, *op.cit.*, pp.208-209

59. Military Consultation, 1792, Rajah of Travancore to Sir Charles Oakley, Fort St.George, 23 November 1792, p.6231

60. Military Consultation, 1792, Rajah of Travancore to Sir Charles Oakley, Fort St.George, 23 November 1792, p.6231; Military Consultation, 1792, Fort St.George to Rajah of Travancore, 4 February 1793, p.604

61. Shungoony Menon, *op.cit.*, pp.246-247; Mohibbul Hasan, *op.cit.*, pp.208-9

62. Military Consultation, 1791, Powney, Resident, Travancore to the Rajah of Travancore, February 1791, p.355

63. Military Consultation, 1791, Powney, Resident of Travancore to Fort St.George, 7 January 1791, p.587; Fort St.George to Powney, Resident, Travancore, 20 May 1791, 2488; Fort St.George to George Powney, Resident, Travancore, June 1791, p.3116; Military Consultation, 1792, Fort St.George to Powney, Resident, Travancore, 15 January 1792, p.535; Anjengo Diary, 1793, An extract from the Minutes of council in the Political Department, 26 April 1793, p.73; Anjengo Diary, 1786, 16 April 1786, p.81

64. Anjengo Factory Diaries, Political, 1797, Copies of the proposed terms of permanent treaty, 14 March 1797, pp.57, 64; Anjengo Diary, 1797, Jonathan Duncan, Governor, Bombay to John Shore, Governor General in Council, 31 August 1797, p.1827

65. Anjengo Diary, 1798, Kesava Das, Dewan to Jonathan Duncan, governor, Bombay, 16 February 1798, p.845

66. Anejngo Diary, 1798, John Taddy Dyne, Resident, Anjengo to Jonathan Duncan, Governor, Bombay, 19 February 1798, p.843; Anjengo diary, 1798, Kesava Das, Dewan to Jonathan Duncan, Governor, Bombay, 16 February 1798, p.846

67. Foreign Department, Secret Consultation, 1804, Colonel Macaulay, Resident, Travancore to Lieut.Colonel Kirkpatrick, 20 July 1800, p.15305; Anjengo Diary, 1799, George Parry, Resident, Anjengo to Jonathan Duncan, Governor, 20 April 1799, p.159

68. Anjengo Diary, 1799, Lord Mornington to Rajah of Travancore, 25 April 1799, p.5544

69. Nagam Aiya, *The Travancore State Manual, I,* Trivandrum, p.418

70. Anjengo Diary, 1801, George Parry, Resident, Anjengo to Jonathan Duncan, Governor, Bombay, 7 March 1801, p.64

71. *Ibid;* Anjengo Diary, 1799, Rajah of Travancore to Lord Mornington, 9 July 1799, p.5547

72. Anjengo Diary, 1799, Rajah of Travancore to Lord Mornington, 9 July 1799, p.5547

73. Anjengo Factory General, 1799, Jonathan Duncan, Governor, Bombay to Rajah of Travancore, 27 September 1799, p.325

74. Forrest, *op.cit.,* p.27

Chapter 7

The Last Phase: Subordination and Revolt

The new *Dewan*, Chempaka Ramen Pillai, who was appointed on the advice and the approval of the English never seems to have realised the debt trap in which the Rajah and the State were entangled. Nor did he realise the constant pressure exerted by the English on the Rajah. Instead, he seems to have busied himself in indulging in corruption that within a span of six months, he had accumulated six lakhs of rupees through dishonest and fraudulent means.[1] Fortunately for the Rajah, the *Dewan* passed away very soon. On his death, the Rajah appointed a new *Dewan* by the name of Thampi Padmanabha Chempakaram Pillai, once again without consulting the English.[2] This only showed the desire of the Rajah to steer clear of the English somehow, though he could not really do anything to disentangle himself from the dictates of the English. The English were not happy about the appointment of the new *Dewan* and made their displeasure known.[3] But they did not stretch the matter any more.

But the Rajah knowing fully well his weaknesses seems to have not really wanted to displease the English. Consequently, he asked the new *Dewan* to be vigilant in the regular fulfilment of the obligation in the treaty of ever lasting friendship with the English. Besides, he wanted him to be prompt in the service of the Sri Padmanabha Swamy temple, which seems to have been built way back in the twelfth century according to some sources.[4] Contrary to the Rajah's expectations, he too was found weak and inefficient and highly corrupt. He was even accused of complicity in certain crimes. The *Dewan* so ill-managed even the most trivial affairs that the Rajah felt compelled to dismiss him just eight months after his appointment.[5]

All these events detrimental to his authority did not prevent him to request the English in November 1800, for the annual presents from the Company which were in arrears for the previous six years. George Parry, the Resident at Anjengo made the calculations for six years and the total amount came to about Rs.4884, which were duly presented to the Rajah.[6] It appears at this juncture that neither the Rajah nor the English really wanted to do anything that would jeopardise the smooth relations between them.

During 1800, the *Tiyya* community, whose traditional occupation was toddy-tapping, was extremely displeased and agitated by the additional tax imposed by the *Dewan* on coconut trees, to improve the finances of the state. Though the Rajah promised to relinquish this tax, nothing concrete seems to have been done in that direction. This pushed the *Tiyyas* to rise in revolt against the *Dewan* and the state. The *Sepoys* of Anjengo consisting of Nairs, *Tiyyas*, *Mappilas* and *Topasses* seem to have rendered some help to put down the revolt.[7] There were casualities on both sides. Ultimately the revolt of the *Tiyyas* was suppressed by the new *Dewan* Velu Thampi, with the help of the *Sepoys*, but not before the demands of the *Tiyyas* were not conceded.[8]

In fact, in place of Padmanabha Pillai, the Rajah had appointed Velu Thampi, the nephew of the late Dewan Raja Kesava Das as the *Dewan* in 1801.[9] On assuming charge Velu Thampi immediately wrote to Jonathan Duncan, the Govenor at Bombay about his appointment and gave his assurance of continuing the existing relationship between the Company and the Rajah of Travancore.[10] It seems that Velu Thampi wanted to sincerely foster and strengthen the alliance with the English.

In 1800, when the Travancore government entered into the Subsidiary Alliance introduced by Lord Wellesley, the activities of the Company could not be carried on alone by the Resident of Anjengo. In fact the chiefship of Anjengo had been reduced to a residency in 1776 itself. As a result, Major Macaulay was appointed as the Political Resident at Travancore by the Bombay government.[11] The main idea behind this appointment was to secure the revision of the existing treaty with Travancore incorporating the provisions of the subsidiary alliance and thereby bring the Travancore government under the Company's effective control. He was the first to hold this important office, though previously as we know, the Bombay government used to have an official appointed to transact all business with the Rajah concerning the welfare of the Company.[12] But Major Macaulay had wider powers than his predecessors. He was requested to give the Bombay government the amplest support in all its dealings with the state of Travancore. He was also requested to correspond with George Parry, the Resident at Anjengo, who was henceforth known as the Commercial Resident of Anjengo and to give him full support in the concerns and transactions with Travancore.[13] It seems at this juncture that there was a certain pre-meditation at the higher levels of authority to promote the importance of the Resident of Travancore, at the expense of the Anjengo settlement, which on the whole would have been viewed as a liability to the Company due to its diminishing importance in trade during this period, as we have seen in the previous chapter.

On his part, George Parry was always on good terms with the Rajah. In 1801, when the Rajah made an official visit to Anjengo, Parry presented him with a fine grey horse and in return the Rajah presented Parry with a *Chawdee* and *Mop Balemalla* and a *Padakam*, along with one beer sapkler.[14] As it was against the rules of the Company to accept presents from anyone since 1796, Parry accounted for all the gifts to the Bombay government.[15]

Thus there came to be two Company authorities in Travancore viz., the Commercial Resident of Anjengo and the

Political Resident of Travancore. The Commercial Resident was under the control of the Bombay Government whereas the Political Resident was answerable to the Madras government.[16] Of the two, the Political Resident had greater power. He had access to all the records of the Anjengo Presidency. The Commercial Resident was to furnish him with all the information that he required.[17] Besides, previously the Commercial Resident directly corresponded with the Rajah of Travancore. As a result, the Political Resident was unaware of the transactions taking place between the Commercial Resident and the Rajah of Travancore. This often ended in accusations and counter-accusations between the two. To avoid such unpleasant situations in the future, an order was issued in 1803 prohibiting irregular intercourse of all Europeans with the Rajah of Travancore or with his minister or with any public officers of the Rajah except through the official channel of the Political Resident.[18] This order had momentous consequences in the history of Travancore. It made the Political Resident very powerful. Thereafter, the Commercial Resident who had till then been very close to the Rajah could correspond only through the Political Resident. This sounded the death-knell of the Commercial Residency at Anjengo. It was but a logical consequence of the amalgamation of Attingal Queendom with Travancore way back in 1743. The Rajah of Travancore would have naturally disliked this new development because it obliged him to direct all his relationhip towards the Political Resident alone.

From the time of his elevation to the office of the *Dewan*, Velu Thampi was guided by the advice of Major Macaulay. He favoured the strengthening of alliance with the English as desired by Macaulay. But the Rajah, as we know, was always wary about the intentions of the English, though he was not in a position to do anything about it. As a result he seems to have been quite reluctant to fall in line with the wishes of his Dewan Velu Thampi, favourably disposed towards the English. In fact there seems to have been hostile factions in the court of the Rajah itself against the pro-English policy of the *Dewan.*

In the year 1803, Major Macaulay, though he was only a Political Resident, began to take interest in the commercial transactions of the Company with the Rajah also. Thus, he directly entered into an agreement with the Dewan Velu Thampi on behalf of the English East India Company for the supply of pepper, without the prior concurrence of the Resident at Anjengo.[19] This had for consequence the strengthening of the hands of Velu Thampi by Macaulay, at the expense of not only the Commercial Resident at Anjengo, but also the Rajah. In fact, the Rajah was reluctant to allow any change or modification in the existing relations with the Company. But the English who seem to have decided upon strengthening the hands of Velu Thampi as a counter-balance to the Rajah's power invested the former with an honorary *Khelaut* or dress in the name of Governor General Wellesley. The ceremony of investiture was carried out with a 15 gun salute and with all respect and honours on 14 August 1803.[20]

However, Macaulay's intrusion into the commercial concerns of the Company was detested by William Handley, the new commercial resident at Anjengo.[21] He was of the view that Macaulay had no business to enter into pepper contract with the *Dewan* as such contracts were under the jurisdiction of the Commercial Resident. But Macaulay justified his action on the ground that the pepper contract embraced some subjects of a political nature.[22] When matters were thus between Macaulay and Handley, the Rajah of Travancore in his turn refused to fulfil the contract. Handley informed Macaulay about the same and asked him to take steps for the speedy delivery of pepper into the Company's warehouse.[23]

Moreover, the Travancore forests and its timber resources for the purpose of naval construction had acquired a great national importance for the British government and the Company.[24] Earlier in 1802, the Bombay government had given special powers to George Parry of Anjengo and Torin of Tellicherry to obtain timber and planks for making 74 gunships at Colaba and Mazagon docks of Bombay for making keel pieces and beams of the ships.[25] The Dewan Velu Thampi, who, as we know, was very close to Macaulay, however failed to fulfil the contract though he had given his assurance to Parry. It was found subsequently that the *Dewan* had sold off the timber and planks to other European merchants. It is worth noting also that during this period there were many private Malabar merchants like Chacooty who was the most affluent dealer of timber in the entire coast.[26] Handley asked Macaulay to remonstrate the *Dewan* for the breach of the timber contract. But Macaulay did not evince interest in this affair.[27] Finally in December 1803, Velu Thampi himself visited Handley at Anjengo fort with the sanction of Macaulay and assured him of delivering the whole of timber and plank without fail.[28]

Further in 1804, Macaulay objected to the clandestine purchase and sale of pepper by individuals living under the protection of the English, for it was injurious to the Company's interests. He pointed out that Fort St. George had prohibited such purchase and sale from all the British ports in Malabar.[29] Handley retorted that he had permission to indulge in such methods from the Bombay government, for otherwise the pepper would have been sold to private merchants and foreigners to the detriment of the Company's interests.[30] While such wrangling continued between Macaulay and Handley with regard to the pepper and timber trade, without any solution in sight, the attention of the Company and its officials was suddenly attracted by what was known as the Nair revolt in Travancore.

Nair Insurrection-1804

We had seen the close relationship that existed between Dewan Velu thampi and Macaulay, the Political Resident in Travancore, which was resented by some factions in the court of

Travancore itself. Even the Rajah was not very happy about Velu Thampi's intimate relationship with Macaulay over and above his head. He resented particularly his pro-English policy. The *Dewan* actually sought the advice of Colonel Macaulay on every issue. It seems that the *Dewan* had supported any idea of Macualay irrespective of its adverse effects.

One such matter was the idea of modification of the Nair brigade of the Rajah of Travancore. Macaulay probably sensing that the officers and soldiers of the Nair brigade were not completely dependable and were liable to revolt against the English at any time, wanted to bring the Nair Brigade under the control of the Company. This was to be done with the consent and concurrence of Dewan Velu Thampi. Naturally the Nairs became extremely restless.

The English were conscious of this restlessness. According to information obtained by the Company officials, the Nairs intended to revolt and their prime target was the Anjengo settlement. As a result additional troops were sent for the protection of Anjengo.[31] Likewise another detachment was sent to Quilon for the protection of the Company's properties there.[32]

It appears that the Nairs also conspired to eliminate Velu Thampi, the faithful ally of the English. English records maintain that this was planned and piloted by high officers of the Travancore state with the consent of the Maharajah of Travancore.[33] Velu Thampi with the help of Colonel Macaulay unearthed the conspiracy on time and imprisoned the conspirators. The Rajah did not oppose this move. Instead it was by his orders that they were arrested. The list of the rebels arrested at Travancore were :

1. Papoo Thamby, an officer of the palace in charge of the ladies' department
2. Mootoo Pillay, Accountant
3. Palavan Pillay, Commander of the Nair Brigade

4. Conjee Neelam Pillay, late Sumbrady
5. Neelacanden Pillay, in charge of the southern division
6. Huvadanum Pillay, Treasury
7. Cochie Narayan Pillay, Paymaster general
8. Gosseyn Gamadegeree, a foreign merchant[34]

In November 1804, the Nair militia rebelled once again. It appears that this time also they conspired with the Rajah of Cochin to murder both Macaulay and Velu Thampi. Macaulay cautioned Handley and asked him to take refuge elsewhere as he felt that the Nair fury was directed against the entire English nation. But Handley refused to quit Anjengo for safety. According to confidential news he obtained from spies, Anjengo settlement was not in danger.[35] He felt that however violent the Nair troops might be, both the subjects from the highest to the lowest have respected the fort of Anjengo as they did one of their own temples and the property of the Company remained sacred to them.[36] Consequently for Handley there was no cause for worry. He further felt that if he were to desert the Anjengo fort at the first alarm it would generate a suspicion that hostile measures were being resorted against them and it might throw the entire country in a greater state of agitation.[37]

But very soon another plot to murder Handley and his family seems to have been discovered. Macaulay asked Handley to leave the place immediately and take refuge elsewhere with his family.[38] But Handley was adamant in his decision to stay back at Anjengo for he believed that it was against the dictates of prudence to abandon the property of the Company entrusted to his care. The warehouse contained valuable pepper and piece goods amounting to more than four lakhs of rupees and deserting it would alarm the people.[39]

But Macaulay confirmed that the attempt on Handley's life was true. It was the Nair troops, sent to Anjengo for protection against the rebels, who had planned to murder Handley and his family. Macaulay, however, assured that orders were sent for their arrest. They were to be disarmed, stripped and dismissed from the service of the Rajah of Travancore with every mark of disgrace.[40] Handley was shocked at the revelation. Nevertheless, he wanted to know from Macaulay whether the Nairs had intended to wipe out all the officials of Anjengo fort or whether their fury was directed only towards him. Macaulay did not offer any explanation and this led Handley to think that Macaulay's intention was to instil scare in him.[41] Thereafter, Handley firmly believed that the intended assasination was a figment of Macaulay's imagination devoid of any truth. He believed therefore that no such crime was ever meditated or resolved to be undertaken by the Nair officer or by any of the Nairs.[42]

But Handley's doubts did not prevent the English from coming down heavily and brutally on the Nairs who partcipated in the rebellion or conspired to overthrow British supremacy in the region. Some rebels were hanged, some were beheaded and others were blown off the canon's mouth. One of them, Krishna Pillai had his legs tied to two elephants and the animals were driven in opposite directions tearing the victim to pieces.[43]

Velu Thampi's Revolt

While the Nair revolt was crushed ruthlessly by the Rajah of Travancore in alliance with Macaulay and the concurrence of Velu Thampi, there was mounting tension once again in Travancore, with regard to the subsidiary treaty of 1805 imposed on the Rajah of Travancore much against his wish. In fact a force was assembled at Tinnevely in 1805 under General MacDowell for the purpose of compelling the Rajah to sign the treaty. This treaty proclaimed the virtual British paramountancy over Travancore. By this treaty the British government became entitled to advise the Rajah on every issue connected with the administration of the affairs of Travancore.[44] The Rajah could hold no communication with any foreign state and could not allow any European into his service or allow them to remain within his territories without previous sanction of the British government.[45] Thus the Rajah was reduced to a virtual puppet in the hands of the English.

According to the treaty the subsidy that the Rajh had to pay the Company was fixed at Rs.800000 per annum out of which an amount of Rs.401655 was subsidy under the treaty of 1795.[46] However hard Velu Thampi tried, that much amount could not be raised from the revenues of the State, especially when things were not at all bright in the trade front. As a result, the Rajah was forced to seek remission from the supreme authority of the Company in Calcutta. The Governor General authorised remission of payment of one half of this additional subsidy for a period of two years commencing from the date of the signature of the treaty of 1805.[47]

But this did not improve matters. Velu Thampi who was always friendly with Macaulay and had earlier assisted him in imposing the treaty on the Rajah, had developed in course of time a grave suspicion about the policy of the English who kept on harping for the payment of subsidies knowing fully well the Rajah's inability to make the payment.

By 1808, Velu Thampi had definitely turned against the English and their objectives. He wrote several letters to the higher Company authorities in Bengal, Madras and Bombay indicating the disapprobation of the Rajah to the new treaty. Macaulay was furious. He used strong language against the *Dewan* regardless of the meritorious service and severe trials that he had faced for promoting British paramountancy in Travancore.[48] The *Dewan* was even ordered either to expedite payment or relieve the finances of the state by the speedy discharge of the Carnatic Brigade. It was calculated that by disbanding this brigade, the Rajah could gain one and a half lakh rupees.[49] But the Rajah refused to disband the Brigade for he had an emotional attachment to it. These soldiers were indispensable for collecting the finances of the state and they were regarded as an essential part of his dignity and personal safety.[50]

The *Dewan* was bent upon taking the cudgels on behalf of the Rajah. The arrears amounted to Rs.800000. The *Dewan* promised to pay only two lakhs within one month and three more lakhs by next year. Macaulay was in a rage. He ordered the dismissal of the *Dewan* and his replacement by someone more amenable to the interests of the Company.[51] This led to open rupture between them.

Velu Thampi began to prepare for a general uprising to evict the English from Travancore. He sought the help of the French and the Zamorin of Calicut.[52] It was believed that even the Rajah of Cochin sided with him.[53] He ordered the people of every district within Travancore to train themselves in the use of bows and arrows. The Nairs were ordered to drill constantly and to fire ball cartridges.[54] The Rajah of Cochin was also asked to arm and train Nairs and *Tiyyas* in a similar manner as was being done in Travancore.[55] Besides this, written orders issued by the *Dewan* were circulated to public officers instigating the people to turn against the English. Announcements written in cyphers to annihilate British influence in Travancore were also circulated.[56]

Fort St.George ordered Macaulay to immediately arrest the *Dewan* and his accomplices and to keep them under arrest till peace prevailed in Travancore.[57] When matters stood thus, the *Dewan* professed his willingness to resign. Macaulay thought this to be the best solution. He promised him an honourable treatment and a large allowance.[58] However, English records maintain that this was only a ploy on the part of the *Dewan*. He was accused of actually conspiring to murder Macaulay at his residence, with the help of his confidential friend Padmanabhan Pillay and a minister of the Rajah of Cochin, at the head of thousand Nayars.[59] Macaulay seems to have managed to escape in a boat with the help of a

Portuguese clerk. But his house was ransacked and some sepoys and domestic servants were killed. There was also a simultaneous attack on the subsidiary force at Quilon on 29 December 1808. Though Velu Thampi had not personally taken part in the operation, the English held that he was the brain behind the attempt to kill Macaulay. Velu Thambi, in his turn, issued a momentous proclamation from Kundera in Central Travancore inviting the people to overthrow the foreign yoke.[60]

The Company swung all their forces into action to capture the *Dewan*. On his side the *Dewan* also gathered a huge force.[61] The Company took measures to convince the inhabitants of Travancore of what they termed as the rash and unprovoked aggression of Dewan Velu Thampi and of the fatal consequences that would follow if anyone opposed the English.[62]

On 15 January 1809 and on 17 January 1809, proclamations were issued by the Madras government warning the inhabitants of Tinnevely and Travancore not to take part in the rebellion organised by Velu Thampi. The troops under Velu Thampi, Paliathu Menon and others were no match to the English troops. By this time, the Rajah thoroughly alarmed at the state of affairs disclaimed any knowledge of Velu Thampi and his activities. Velu Thampi realising that the Rajah had forsaken him fled towards the northern frontiers of the province. The English accused him of perpetrating a wholesale massacre of Europeans before fleeing.[63] It was held that three European military officers including Surgeon Hume, twelve European soldiers and thirty three sepoys were seized by the troops under Velu Thampi at Allepey as per orders from Velu Thampi himself and were murdered, some on the beach at Porcad, probably by Velu thampi's brother, while some others were drowned in the Pallathurthi river. Besides, with the collusion of Paliathu Menon, the Cochin minister, the British resident's home at Cochin was attacked and the resident seems to have escaped with difficulty.[64]

It was then feared that the *Dewan's* fury would then be directed against the Anjengo settlement, where John Smee had taken over as the new commercial resident on the death of Handley.[65] The Rajah gave him assurance that Anjengo settlement was not in danger and that there was no cause for any worry. But Smee received orders from Bombay not to rely on the promises of the Rajah. They authorised him to use his own discretion and leave the factory and to transport the most valuable things on board the ship 'Upton Castle'.[66] But they placed a condition on his departure. He was expected to address a letter to the Rajah apprising him of the Company's property that was being left behind. The Rajah would be held responsible for any damage to the said property. As per instructions, Smee left Anjengo and retired to Calicut.[67] But before that he had obtained an assurance from Velu Thampi's deputies that the settlement would not be atacked and had handed over the charge of the fort to the linguist, Sebastian Diaz Fernandez, the next in command of the Anjengo fort, whose ancestors had served the Company faithfully for about a hundred years.[68] In the Anjengo settlement the post of Linguist had become almost hereditary since four generations. The family of Fernandez occupied this post.[69]

Further, the Rajah in order to be in the good books of the English, had officially dismissed the *Dewan* on 12 February 1809.[70] He had appointed one Comara Pillay to the post under pressure from the Company.[71] He even undertook the responsibility of capturing Velu Thampi and his associates and thus ensure the prosperity of his dominion and maintain the rights which were granted by the treaty of 1805. Again at the instigation of Macaulay, Comara Pillay was dismissed and Womana Thampi alias Martanden Eravy was appointed as the *Dewan* on 18 March 1809. Womana Thampi disliked Velu Thampi and he launched a massive man-hunt for the fleeing *Dewan*, disowned by the Rajah of

Travancore. An award of Rs.50000 was offered for the apprehension of Velu Thampi.

Besides, when Handley was away in Calicut, Macaulay imprisoned the linguist on the suspicion that he had helped the *Dewan* to escape.[72] The linguist admitted meeting Velu Thampi on 20 February 1809 at Cherringha near Anjengo, fearing that he might target Anjengo fort and its inhabitants. But he never played any role in the escape of Velu Thampi and had actually kept the British flag flying aloft at Anjengo.[73] On the other hand, neither Velu Thampi nor his forces seems to have had any intention to dishonour or bring down the British flag at Anejngo.[74] This might have been occasioned by the linguist's meeting with Velu Thampi at Cherringa.

Finally due to the relentless drive of the new Dewan, and the help rendered by the Sepoys of Anjengo who were thorough with the geography of the country, Velu Thampi was spotted at a Bhagawati temple in the deep animal infested jungles of Travancore where he had taken shelter. But when he was finally caught, Velu Thampi was breathing his last from the stabs which was said to have been inflicted by himself with a poniard and his brother standing over him with sword drawn.[75] It appears that Velu Thampi's brother and six accomplices were captured alive and hanged at Quilon, Porcad and Pallathurthi, the spots where the Europeans were massacred previously. Macaulay returned to Trivandrum, the capital of Travancore from a ship where he had found shelter during the uprising. Velu Thampi's body was removed to Trivandrum where it was exposed at Kunnammalay, for public execration. Womana Thampi literally wiped out Velu Thampi's relatives. With the death of Velu Thampi, the revolt was completely suppressed and all the ensuing expenses were borne by the Rajah of Travancore. After the suppression of the revolt, the Rajah, in order to express his joy, presented Colonel Macaulay with a ring, Colonel Saint Leger who was in charge of a brigade with two shawls and the other officers with two shawls each.[76]

Velu Thampi's revolt was destined to fail mainly because the Rajah of Travancore had decided not to break off his ties with the English. In fact in 1783, the Madura kingdom on which the Travancore Rajahs were dependent earlier passed into British administration. In 1792, northern Malabar had become British territory. In 1799, the kingdom of Tanjore had been handed over to the English by King Sarfoji in exchange for a pension and the neighbouring district of Tinnevely to which the Travancore Rajah laid claim at least partly, had been ceded to the English in 1801 by the Nawab of Carnatic.[77] The Rajah of Travancore was no doubt conscious of these developments in his neighbourhood, where the English had become the most important power to be reckoned with. This seems to have pushed him to become subservient to the English and save at least his position nominally, rather than throw in his lot with Velu Thampi who, like Tipu Sultan earlier, was largely isolated in his struggle against the English.

Notes and References

1. Foreign Secret Consultation Proceedings, 17 May 1804, pp.15346-47
2. Anjengo Diary, 1801, Rajah of Travancore to Jonathan Duncan, Governor, Bombay, 7 April 1801, p.2088
3. Anjengo Diary General, 1880, George Parry, Resident Anjengo to Thampi Padmanabha Chempakaraman, Valiasarvadhikariakkar, Travancore, 14 July 1800, p.230
4. M.J. Koshy, *Encyclopaedia of Kerala,* vol.XX, New Delhi, 1994, p.37
5. Anjengo Factory General, 1801, Rajah of Travancore to George Parry, Resident, Anjengo, 6 April 1801, p.86
6. Anjengo Diary, 1800, George Parry, Resident, Anjengo to Jonathan Duncan, Governor, Bombay, 10 November 1800, p.325
7. Foreign Secret Department Consultations, 17 May 1804, Colonel Macaulay, Resident, travancore to Lt.Colonel Kirkpatrick, Secretary to Government in Foreign Secret and Political branch, September 1800,

p.15350. Curiously even in a biography of Velu Thampi Dalawa, there is no mention about the Tiyya revolt, see G.Parameswaran Pillai, *Velu Thampi Dalawa,* Quilon, 1964; Anjengo Diary, 1798, George Parry, Resident, Anjengo to Rajah of Travancore, 26 May 1798, p.250

8. *Ibid.*

9. Anjengo Diary, 1801, Rajah of Travancore to Jonathan Duncan, governor, Bombay, 7 april 1801, p.2088; Anejngo Factory General, 1801, Rajah of Travancore to George Parry, Resident, Anjengo, 6 April 1801, p.86

10. Anjengo Diary, 1801, Velu Thampi, dewan, Travancore to Jonathan Duncan, governor, Bombay, 7 April 1801, p.2089

11. Anjengo diary, 1800, Bombay Castle to Major Macaulay, Resident, Travancore, 16 April 1800, p.139; Anjengo Diary, 1776, Bombay Castle to Nathaniel Stackhouse, Chief, Anjengo, 11 February 1776, p.13

12. Anjengo Diary, 1793, Bombay Castle to the Rajah of travancore, 1 May 1793, p.80

13. Anjengo Diary, 1800, Jonathan Duncan, governor, Bombay to Major Macaulay, 16 April 1800, pp.5291-92

14. Anjengo Diary, 1801, George Parry, Resident, Anjengo to Jonathan Duncan, Governor, Bombay, 23 January 1801, p.18

15. Ibid; Anjengo Diary, 1757, Rajah of Travancore to chief, Anjengo, 5 September 1757, p.28; Secret Sundries Travancore, 1809, Macaulay, Travancore to Falconar, fort St.George, 27 March 1807, p.1796; Anjengo Diary, 1796, Notice put up by John Hutchinson, Resident Anjengo, 24 February 1796, p.48

16. Anjengo Diary, 1801, Clive, Fort St.George to John spencer, Commissioner of Malabar, 5 September 1801, p.5986; Anjengo Diary, 1802, 29 July 1802, p.4353

17. Anjengo Diary, 1802, James Augustus Grant, Bombay Castle to Fort St.George, 11 September 1802, p.314

18. Anjengo Diary, 1803, Fort St.George to Jonathan Duncan, Governor, Bombay, 17 February 1803, p.75

19. *Ibid.*, p.76

20. Anjengo Factory General, 1803, Colonel Macaulay Political Resident, Travancore to the Commercial Resident, Anjengo, 13 August 1803, p.164; Anjengo Factory General, 1803, Colonel Macaulay, Resident, to Handley, Resident, Anjengo, 13 August 1803, p.164

21. Anejngo Factory General, 1803, colonel Macaulay Political Resident, Travancore to the Commercial Resident, Anjengo, 12 August 1803, p.163

22. Anjengo diary, 1803, Appointment of a political Resident in Travancore in 1800, the correspondence that then ensued with the officer upto 1803, p.5208

23. Anjengo Factory General, 1803, Handley, Commercial Resident, Anjengo to Macaulay, Political Resident, Travancore, 25 September 1803, p.19

24. Anjengo Diary, 1809, Francis Warden, Chief Secretary, Bombay to Edmonstone, Fort William, 24 June 1809, p.6389

25. Anjengo Diary, 1802, Bombay Castle to Resident, Anjengo, November 1802, p.6789; Anjengo Factory General, 1802, Court of directors, London, to Governor in Council, Bombay, 5 May 1802, p.417

26. Anjengo Factory General, 1803, Factor, Mahe to Jonathan Duncan, governor, Bombay, 20 April 1803, p.27

27. Anjengo Factory General, 1803, Handley, Commercial Resident, Anjengo to Lt.Colonel Macaulay, Political Resident, Travancore, 1 December 1803, p.79

28. Anjengo diary, 1803, Handley, Commercial Resident, Anjengo to Jonathan duncan, governor, Bombay, 21 December 1803, p.11

29. Anjengo diary, 1804, Macaulay, Political Resident, Travancore to Handley, commercial Resident, Anjengo, 16 February 1804, p.76

30. Anjengo diary, 1804, Handley, Commercial Resident, Anjengo to Macaulay, Political Resident, Travancore, 17 February 1804, p.77

31. Anjengo Diary, 1804, Handley, Commercial Resident, Anjengo to Jonathan Duncan, Governor, Bombay, 9 March 1804, p.135

32. *Ibid.*

33. Foreign Department Secret Consultation, 1804, Macaulay, Political Resident, travancore to Lord William Bentinck, Governor, Fort St.George, 25 April 1804, p.6

34. Foreign Secret Department Consultation, 1804, Macaulay, Political Resident, Travancore to Wellesley, 27 March 1804, p.6315

35. Anjengo Diary, 1804, Handley, Commercial Resident, anjengo to Jonathan Duncan, Governor, Bombay, 23 November 1804, p.796

36. *Ibid.*

37. *Ibid.*

38. Anjengo Diary, 1804, Macaulay, Political Resident, Travancore to Handley, Commercial Resident, Anjengo, 25 November 1804, p.798

39. Anjengo Diary, 1804, Macaulay, Political Resident, Travancore to Handley, Commercial Resident, Anjengo, 27 November 1804, p.799

40. Anjengo Diary 1804, Macaulay, Political Resident, Travancore to Handley, Commercial Resident, Anjengo, 11 December 1804, p.835

41. Anjengo Diary, 1804, Handley, Commercial Resident, Anjengo to Macaulay, Political Resident, Travancore, 12 December 1804, p.838; Anjengo Diary, 1804, Handley, Commercial Resident, Anjengo to Jonathan Duncan, governor, Bombay, 12 December 1804, p.840

42. Anjengo Diary, 1804, Handley, Commercial Resident, Anjengo to Jonathan Duncan, Governor, Bombay, 16 December 1804, p.856

43. V. Nagam Aiya, *The Travancore State Manual, I,* Trivandrum, 1906, p.418

44. Secret Sundries Travancore, 1808, A memorandum by Colonel Macaulay, 10 March 1808, p.49; Shungoonny Menon *A History of Travancore,* Delhi, 1878, 1984

45. Maclean's *Manual of Administration of the Madras Presidency, I,* Madras, 1938, p.36

46. Political Despatches from England, 29 September 1809, p.139

47. Political Consultation, 1806, Macaulay, surgeon, travancore to Colonel Macaulay, Political Resident, Travancore, 31 October 1806, p.1480

48. Secret Sundries Travancore, 1808, Copy of a declaration from Macaulay to the Dewan of travancore, 9 July 1808, p.22

49. *Ibid;* Political consultation, 1807, Handley, Commercial Resident, Anjengo to N.B.Edmonstone, fort William, 20 January 1807, p.87

50. Secret Sundries Travancore, 1807, Dewan, Travancore to Macaulay, Political resident, Travancore, 10 July 1808, p.24

51. Secret Sundries Travancore, 1807, Macaulay, Political Resident, Travancore to G.Buchan, Chief Secretary to Government, 3 November 1808, pp.92-93

52. Secret Sundries Travancore, 1808, John Tady Dyne, Commercial Resident, Anjengo to Colonel Macaulay, Political Resident, travancore, 24 October 1808, p.107; R. Bishop Caldwell, *A History of Tinnevelly-*Reprint, New Delhi, 1982, p.263

53. Secret Sundries Travancore, 1808, Macaulay, Political Resident, Travancore to Buchan, Fort St.George, 2 December 1808, p.103; Caldwell, *op.cit.,* p.262

54. *Ibid.,* p.104

55. Secret Sundries Travancore, 1808, Colonel, Political Resident to Colonel Charlmers, Commanding Officer, Travancore, 1 December 1808, p.113

56. *Ibid.*

57. Secret Sundries Travancore, 1808, Buchan, Fort St.George to Macaulay, Political Resident, Travancore, 15 December 1808, p.118

58. Secret Sundries Travancore, 1808, Macaulay, Political Resident to Dewan, Travancore, 26 December 1808, p.562

59. Secret Sundries Travancore, Macaulay, Political Resident, Travancore to G.Buchan, Fort St.George, 28 December 1808, p.225; Caldwell, *op.cit.*, pp.263-264

60. Secret Sundries Travancore, 1809, Grorn Bart, Cochin to George William Gillo, Judge and magistrate, 29 December 1809, p.229; Secret Sundries Travancore, 1809, Dr.Macaulay, Travancore to Colonel Macaulay, Political Resident, Travancore, 6 January 1809, p.315; Caldwell, *op.cit.*, 263-264; Menon, Shungoony,*op.cit.*, pp.335, 339; P.K. Parameswaran Nair, *History of the Malayalam Literature,* (translated from Malayalam by E.M.J.Venniyoor) New Delhi, 1967, p.79

61. Secret Sundries Travancore, 1809, George Buchan, Fort St.George to Lt.Colonel chalmers, 2 February 1809, pp.780-781

62. Secret Sundries Travancore, 1809, Buchan, Fort St.George to Lt.Colonel Sentleger, 26 January 1809, p.685

63. Anjengo Diaries General, 1809, John Smee, Commercial Resident, anjengo to Jonathan Duncan, Governor, Bombay, 11 april 1809, p.113

64. *Ibid;* Caldwell, *op.cit.*, pp.263-64, 269

65. Anjengo Diary, 1808, Dyne, Anjengo to the Rajah of Travancore, 2 July 1808, p.119

66. Anjengo Diary General, 1809, F.Warden, Bombay to John Smee, commercial Resident, anjengo, 17 February 1809, p.63

67. *Ibid* ; Anjengo Diary General, 1809, John Smee, Commercial Resident, Anjengo to Jonathan Duncan, governor, Bombay, 9 March 1809, p.69

68. Anjengo Diary General, 1809, John Smee, commercial Resident, Anjengo to Jonathan Duncan, governor, Bombay, 28 March 1809, p.105; Anjengo Diaries General, 1809, E.D.Fernandez, Anjengo to Jonathan Duncan, governor, Bombay, 8 april 1809, p.124

69. Anjengo Diary General, 1809, S. Diaz Fernandez, Linguist, anjengo to Jonathan Duncan, governor, Bombay, 8 april 1809, p.124

70. Anjengo Diaries General, Macaulay, Political Resident, Travancore to Buchan, Fort St.George, 26 February 1809, p.1406

71. *Ibid.*

72. Anjengo Diary General, 1809, John Smee, Commercial Resident, Anjengo, to George Barlow, Fort St.George, 22 March 1809, p.3493; Caldwell, *op.cit.,* p.269

73. Anjengo Diaries General, 1809, Smee, Commercial Resident, Anjengo to Jonathan Duncan, governor, Bombay, 28 March 1809, p.105; Anjengo Diary, 1809, John Smee, Commercial Resident, Anjengo to colonel Macaulay, Political Resident, Travancore, 16 March 1809, pp.82-83; Anjengo Diary General, 1809, John Smee, commercial Resident, anjengo to Jonathan Duncan, Governor, Bombay, 28 March 1809, pp.104-105 139(fn), leena, 392, 402

74. Anjengo Diary, 1809, Francis Warden, Chief Secretary, Bombay to Edmonstone, Fort William, 24 June 1809, p.6391

75. Secret Sundries Travancore, 1809, Macaulay, Political Resident, Travancore to Falconer, chief Secretary to Government, Fort St.George, 2 April 1809, p.1878(leena p311)

76. Secret Sundries Travancore, 1809, Macaulay, Travancore to Falconar, fort St.George, 27 March 1807, p.1796; Caldwell, *op.cit.,* pp.268-270; Shungoony Menon, *op.cit.,* p.349

77. Caldwell, *op.cit.,* p.270; Robert Sewell(ed.), *A Sketch of the Dynasties of Southern India,* Madras, 1883, pp.53, 64

Conclusions and Observations

The west Europeans had established themselves in Malabar mainly in pursuit of the lucrative trade in pepper, the 'black gold' which Europe could not produce. At the time of their arrival, Malabar was split into different independent kingdoms and principalities, of which the three most important were Calicut, Cochin and Quilon. There were several other minor principalities in south Malabar like Attingal, Travancore, Porcad and Peritally. The rulers of these kingdoms and principalities were generally related to one another.

Attingal and Travancore seem to have come into existence during the fourteenth or rather the fifteenth century. The attempt by historians like Sreedhara Menon to trace the origin of the Travancore(Venad) rajas to the Cheras is not supported by any authentic evidence. The Queen of Attingal, in fact, was related to the Rajah of Travancore and the other neighbouring rulers. There is also no evidence to the contention that she was subordinate to the Rajah of Travancore or any other kingdom until the Rajah of Travancore, Martanda Varma, forcibly annexed it in 1743 in pursuit of his expansionist aims. Both the Rajah of Travancore and the Queen of Attingal were time and again under the influence of the local chiefs the *pillas* and the *madambees*, who had become an authority to be reckoned with in all affairs of the country.

The English chose to settle in Attingal which was governed by the Queen. They fortified themselves at a place called Anjengo with the permission of the Queen. Their initial objectives seem to have been straightforward trade. But the Malabaris including the Queen and the *pillas* very soon became suspicious about the real motives of the English. As a result they rose in revolt in 1721 to put an end to the English in the area, in which more than 150 Englishmen were killed. Though the English were shocked to the core by the revolt, they did not take any measures to personally apprehend the rebels. Instead they appealed to the Queen of Attingal for justice. After the amalgamation of Attingal with the Travancore kingdom, they made similar appeals to the Rajah of Travancore.

But the revolt and its aftermath brought about the diminution in the power of the Queen of Attingal and the interference of Travancore in Attingal's affairs. Martanda Varma who ascended the throne of Travancore in 1728, decided to assert his power not only against the local chiefs, but also against the neighbouring independent principalities and kingdoms. He conquered and annexed several territories like Quilon, Kayamkulam and Porcad upto the borders of Cochin. Attingal also was annexed. Even the kingdom of Quilon, which had pre-existed both Travancore and Attingal and had even gone to war against Travancore as early as 1517 and had always an independent existence, though its rulers were related to those of the other kingdoms including Travancore and Attingal, was annexed.

The English did not oppose these conquests and annexations. They took care to see that the Rajah's policy towards them was beneficial. In fact they hoped that the establishment of the Rajah of Travancore's supremacy in the region would create the necessary conditions for them in the trade as well as in the political fronts, given that the English had become a military power to be reckoned with in south India during this period and the Rajah sought regularly arms and ammunitions from them to wage his numerous wars.

In course of time Maratanda Varma had assumed a monopoly in the pepper trade of the region, contrary to the expectations of the English. On many occasions, the English swallowed their pride and tried their best to keep Martanda Varma in good humour. When Martanda Varma sought their help against the local chiefs it was more or less readily given. As a result Martanda Varma eradicated the menace of the *pillas* to his authority ruthlessly. Later the English came to the help of Travancore in their problems with the Nawab of Carnatic and also the Mysore sultans. Northern Malabar came under the direct control of the English in 1792.

These developments made the Rajah of Travancore more and more dependent on the English, which the latter exploited to the fullest extent and got an English Political Resident appointed at Travancore itself. It was also a time when the demand for pepper had fallen drastically in Europe and its price also had tumbled down consequently. The Rajah had never foreseen this eventuality, which struck at the principal revenue of his kingdom. As a result the Rajah became more and more indebted. In fact he lost his economic independence. Very soon, economic dependence led to political dependence. As a result, the English Political Resident came to wield a great power in the region and the Rajah finally succumbed to his pressure and subordinated his state to the English according to the treaty of 1805.

This subordination led the Rajah's *Dewan,* Velu Thampi to rise in revolt. The Rajah of Travancore thought it to be more prudent to ally with the English and maintain his authority at least nominally rather than risk his throne once for all. The Travancore kingdom thereafter became a princely state under the paramountancy of the British, until it chose to join the Indian Union reluctantly in August 1947, when the British finally left India. Nevertheless, the kingdom of Travancore will remain a classic example of how the loss of economic independence could also contribute to the loss of political independence ultimately.

Copy of the original Contract concluded between the Queen of Attingal and the English on 29th June 1694

(12)

Translate of a Contract, concluded with the Queen of Attinga
Dated June 29th Ano. 1694 *

Because the English if I called hither, have allways bin obedient to mee, I do hereby grant unto them the following priveledges; I give unto them the hill of the Sougey that is at Anjengo, to fortefy with Stone, & to abide there for ever; And I will send thither my officers, to set forth & appoint with Stone Land-marks the limitts of Land that belongs unto mee that on each side the said hill the Compa may build warehouses for their goods, And houses for their people to dwell in, within which limitts they shall rule, without any impediment, being obedient to Mee; I give unto the Engl Compa all the pepper in my Country, that they may contract, & pay for it, at the price Currant; And if any other do buy Pepper, and carry it forth by Sea, then shall the Compa use diligence & take the vessells & goods, And one half that is taken they shall give unto Mee, & the other half the Compa shall have; — For every candy of pepper that the Compa buy, they shall pay me 5 Cajar; & for other goods that they embarque, or disembarque, they shall pay Custome to me 2½ p Cent; Once every year before they weigh pepper, they shall visitt me at [illegible] Chequeery; and they shall take my people to be present at the weighing of Pepper; and for the Pepper weighed they shall pay Custome to my officers; And the pepper that is weighed they may ship off when they please; Any English Vessells that shall be ship-wreckd in my dominions shall be devided, half for me, & half for the Compa. They shall give passports to the Merchants of my [illegible] & if because of those passports the Dutch take the vessells, the English shall satisfy [illegible] boats & goods to the Merchants; And so I ordered this Contract to be made in conformity to the English Compa at Quiloan this 29th of June, 1694

* Anjengo Factory Records - 1704-1749, June 29, 1694, p.12. - National Archives, Delhi, Microfilm.

Copy of the Original letter from the Queen of Attingal Amutumbaran to the Honourable Governor of Fort Saint George after the Attingal Massacre dated June 1721

APPENDIX - II

A translate of a Malabar Letter from the
(Queen of Antanquall nam'd Amutumbaran to)
(the Hon.ble Gov.r of Fort St. George."

At first when I invited Merchants to trade here amongst the rest was the English to whom I gave a large spot of ground to buil a Fort on and also gave them assurances of not being molested. Notwithstanding which the English shelter'd one Comadevormur who had acted contrary to their Cast, after the arrivall of Mr. Gifford at Anjengo the Inhabitants of the Villages round the Fort rose in arm against the English and some of them was kill'd in the Villages. The beginning of this trouble was in August 1720 which occasion'd the Pepper trade to stand still. In January last there arriv'd four ships from Cochin with soldiers, which so terrify'd the Inhabitants that they quitted the place and came to me. I then sent my head man named Vanga Mutapilla to make up the differences between the English and the Inhabitants, and order'd them to return and live there as usuall, and on the 6th of Aprill last I sent for Co-Codervompilla, who is one of the head men, with some more Inhabitants and order'd them to make peace with the English and make satisfaction for all damages done them which they accordingly did. On the 14th. Aprill the Governour with severall other Gentlemen came with 150 soldiers to see me, when they arriv'd at my house the above nam'd Codervompilla with some Inhabitants combin'd together and fell upon them and cut them all off, which was unknown to me or any of my attendants. As soon as I heard what a treacherous thing the Inhabitants had been guilty of to the English especially at such a time, I with my Family and my Chief man Venga Mutapilla fled into another dominions and have since wrote the Inhabitants that if the English will come and live there as usuall I would return, otherwise continue where I was. I therefore desire you will send some people with forces with all speed and when you arrive I will come with my force and give you all the assistance I can and comply with anything that you shall require, and desire you'll consider it well and send me an answer per the Bearer Kisna Braminy with all speed.

Fort Saint George Records – 1721, June 1721, p. 92, The Tamil Nadu Archives, Madras.

Appendix I

Translatation of a Cantract, concluded with the Queen of Attinga Dated June 29th : An° 1694.

Because the English if I called hither, have always been obedient to mee, I do hereby grant unto them the following privileges; I give unto them the hill of the jouges that is at Argengo to fortify with stone & to abide there for ever. And I will send thither my officers, to set forth & appoint with stone Land marks the limits of Land that belong unto me, that on each side of the said hill the Company may build ware houses for their goods, and houses for their people to dwell in, within which limits they shall rule, without any impediment, being obedient to me. I give unto the English Company all the pepper in my Country that they may contract & pay for it, at the price currant. And if any other do buy Pepper, and carry it forth by sea. Then shall the Company diligence & take the Vesselles & goods, and one half that is taken they shall give unto me & the other half the Company shall have, For every candy of pepper that the Company buy, they hall pay me 5 pugas & for other goods that they embarque or disembarque, they shall pay Custom to me 2. Once every year before they weigh pepper, They shall visit me at: and they shall take my people to be present at the weighing of pepper; and for the pepper weighed they shall pay customs to my officers; and the pepper that is weighed they may hip of when they please, Any English vessels that shall be shrip-wrecked in my dominions shall be devided, half for me & half for the Company. They shall give passports to the Merchant of my dominions and if because of the passports the Dutch take the vessels, the English shall at if for the boats & goods to the merchants. And so I ordered this Contract to be made in writing to the English Company at Quiloan this 29 of June 1694.

Appendix II

Translation of a Malabar Letter from the (Queen of Antanquall nam'd Amutumbaran to the Honble Govr of Fort St. George.)

At first when I invited Merchants to trade here amongest the rest was the English to whom I gave a large spot of ground to build a Fort on and also gave them assurances of not being molested. Not withstanding which the English shelter's one Comadevormur who had acted contraty to their Cast, after the arrivall of Mr. Gifford at Anjengo the Inhabitants of the Villages round the Fort rose in arme against the English and some of them was kill'd in the Villages.

The beginning of this trouble was in August 1720 which occasion'd the Pepper trade to stand from Cochin with soldiers, which so terrify'd the Inhabitants that they quitted the place and came to me. I then sent my head man named Vanga Mutapilla to make up the differences between the English and the Inhabitants, and order'd them to return and live there as usuall, and on the 6th of April last I sent for Codervompilla, who is one of the head men, with some more Inhabitants and order'd them to make peace with the English and make satisfaction for all damages done them which they accordingly did. On the 14th April the Governour with severall other Gentlemen came with 150 soldiers to see me, when they arriv'd at my house the above named Codervompilla with some Inhabitants combin'd together and fell upon them and out them all off, which was unknown to me or my of my attendants. As soon as I heard what a treacherous thing the Inhabitants had been guilty of to the English especially at such a time, I with my Family and my Chief man Venga Mutapilla fled into another dominion and have since wrote the Inhabitants that if the English will come and live there as usuall I would return, otherwise continue where I was, I therefore desire you will send some people with forces with all speed and when you arrive I will come with my force and give you all the assistance I can and comply with anything that you shall require and deisre you'll consider it well and send me an answer per the Bearer Kisna Braminy with all speed.

Appendix III

Translation of an agreement written in a silver Ola into by the princess of Attingal and Ezachiel king ESQ 5 April 1729.*

"On the 25th Medam 904 has been wrote this. This is the term agreed for the continuation of Union of the English Company with the Duties, Customs and all other things agreeable to a writing passed between the princess mother who had born in the planet called Ashwedy and the chief John Brabourne are to be continued and from the year next ensying of 905 (1750) the Company will present yearly with 75 venetians to the princess as soon after they can begin to receive pepper in the assistance of my writers-to each candy they will give me the custom of five rajees/50 Chakrams from which I allow 20 percent to the Company. The chief must have good-will and deligence to make the trade more augmented that by which means the estate may have more augmented that by which means the estate may have more profits. All pepper that may have in my country I will cause to be transported to the Fort of Anjengo free of any embarrassment whatever in these territories-and the Company must not give to any other person but to the English Company-In witness I Tevan Changaran writer to the Princess by her royal order have wrote this olla of agreement with my own hand in the govern of Chief Ezachiel King-Shri Tullam"

* Anjengo Diary-1803. Translate of an agreement written in a silver *ola* into by the Princess of Attingal and Ezachiel King Esq. Anjengo, 5 April 1729. 20 January 1803, pp.15-16. Tamilnadu Archives, Madras.

Annexe

Table of Pepper exported from Anjengo from
1696 to 1808

Year	*Candies* exported	Rate per *Candy*
1696	200	
1697-1742	(No definite quantity was exported it ranged betwen 300 to 500 *Candies)*	
1725	1000	Rs.65/- per *candy*
1727	500	Rs.65/- per *candy*
1728	300	Rs.65/- per *candy*
1729	200	Rs.65/- per *candy*
1730	320	Rs.65/- per *candy*
1731	328	Rs.65/- per *candy*
1732	708	Rs.65/- per *candy*
1733	612	Rs.65/- per *candy*
1734	607	Rs.65/- per *candy*
1736	761	Rs.65/- per *candy*
1738	394	Rs.65/- per candy
1739	677	Rs.65/- per *candy*
1740	677	Rs.65/- per *candy*

1741	700	Rs.65/- per *candy*
1742	400	Rs.65/- per *candy*
1743	135	Rs.65/- per *candy*
1744- 1748	(Prohibition was enforced so no purchases were made	
1749	500	Rs. 75/- per *candy*
1750	1500	Rs. 75/- per *candy*
1751	1500	Rs. 75/- per *candy*
1754	1600	Rs. 75/- per *candy*
1758	1500	Rs. 75/- per *candy*
1759	2000	Rs. 75/- per *candy*
1760	2000	Rs. 75/- per *candy*
1761	600	Rs. 75/- per *candy*
1763	1000	Rs. 75/- per *candy*
1764	2000	Rs. 75/- per *candy*
1765	2000	Rs. 75/- per *candy*
1770	2000	Rs. 75/- per *candy*
1779	2000	Rs. 75/- per *candy*
1782	1000	Rs. 75/- per *candy*
1783	1000	Rs. 75/- per *candy*
1788	1400	Rs. 75/- per *candy*
1789	600	Rs. 75/- per *candy*
1791	2000	Rs. 75/- per *candy*

1793	1000	Rs. 75/- per *candy*
1794	4000	Rs. 75/- per *candy*
1795	1000	Rs. 117/- per *candy*
1796	3000	Rs. 117/- per *candy*
1798	500	Rs. 117/- per *candy*
1799	3000	Rs. 117/- per *candy*
1800	3000	Rs. 115/- per *candy*
1801	2573	Rs. 115/- per *candy*
1803	3000	Rs. 115/- per *candy*
1804	3000	Rs. 115/- per *candy*
1805	3000	Rs. 115/- per *candy*
1806	3000	Rs. 115/- per *candy*
1807	3000	Rs. 115/- per *candy*
1808	3000	Rs. 115/- per *candy*

* Compiled from Anjengo Factory Records- 1696- 1808

GLOSSARY

Ashure	Aswati Umayamma Rani
Banksaul	warehouse, godown
Cadjan	Palm Leaf
Calliel Vidill	the name of a house
Candy	a weight used in south India varying much in different parts from 640 lbs to 500 lbs
Chequeen	an ancient gold coin
Chetties	Tamil-speaking merchant class
Conicopoly/Concoply	Accountant
Couche Mauden Pilla	Cuddamon Pilla
Dalawa/Tollawa/Dalavay	Minister of the Rajah of Travancore
Dhanam	gift
Dewan/Diwan	prime minister
Fanam	a silver coin, seven of which are equal to a rupee
Faujdar	commander
Karanavan	uncle and manager of a hereditary estate/ Senior male member of a matriarchal family
Kariakkar/Carriacar	An executive agent, manager or supervisor
Kilavan Raja	Old King
Madembee	nobles of Travancore
Mappillas/ Moplahs	Malabar Muslims
Mudaliar	a Tamil caste title

Moors	Muslims
Mootha Thampuran	the old or senior Queen of Attingal
Ola	Palm leaf/ palm leaf manuscripts
Pagoda	temple/ a type of gold coin
Pillas	Pillamars or nobles
Rajee-Raja	a coin used in Travancore kingdom
Rajah	king
Rani	Queen
Rejadore	a word signifying governor or magistrate of the King
Sudra	the lowest category of people in the Indian caste system
Swaroopam	dynasty
Tamburatti/Thumbratte	a female member of the royal family
Thampuran	a king
Tharavad	a joint family in Kerala
Topasses	Christians of Portuguese-Indian origin
Vakil	advocate
Yogam	Congregation or council
Yogakkar	Members of the Yogam

Bibliography

Archives and Libraries

India Office Library Records, London

Anjengo Factory Records

A short treatise by way of Essay on Attinga on the Malabar coast, John Wallis, 1727

Bombay Letter copy book outwards

Bombay Letters Received

Copies of Letters sent by Commissary sir John Goldesborough

Factory Records Miscellaneous

Maharashtra State Archives, Mumbai :

Secret and Political Department Diaries

Secretariat Inward Letter Book/Secretariat Inward

Secretariat Outward Letter Book/Secretariat Outward

Selections :
a) Collection of papers received from the India Office for Bombay Gazette work, 1681-85
b) Extract of the linguists conference with the King of Travancore at Quilon, 18 March 1756
c) Foreign powers extract selections 48/1796 Surat Factory Records, 1678-1680

Tamilnadu Archives, Chennai :

Anjengo Accounts – Journals

Anjengo Diary

Anjengo Factory diaries – Secret and Political

Anjengo Factory Records – Accounts : Stores

Anjengo Factory Records and Diaries

Anjengo Factory Records – General

Anjengo Factory Records : Political

Country Correspondence

Despatches from England : Commercial Department

Despatches from England : Political Department

Despatches from England : Public Department

Despatches from England : Secret Department

Despatches to England : Commercial Department

Despatches to England : Political Department

Despatches to England : Secret Department

Letters from Fort St. George

Letters to Fort St. George

Military Department Consultations

Military Department : country correspondence

Political Consultation

Political and Secret correspondence

Public Consultation : Fort St. George

Public Department

Secret Sundries, Travancore

Treasury

National Archives of India, New Delhi

Anjengo Factory Records : Microfilm, 1704-1769 : A translate of contract with the Queen of Attinga, dated June 29, Anno 1694

Anjengo Factory Records

Anjengo Factory Records : diaries and consultation Book

Anjengo Factory Records – Political Diary

Foreign Department Secret Proceedings

Foreign Department Political Consultation

Foreign Secret Department Consultation

Foreign Political Proceedings

Fort St. George Records – Microfilm

Libraries :

Bibliotheque Nationale, Paris

Centre d'études de l'Inde, Paris

Connemara Library, Chennai

Madras Unversity Library, Chennai

Secretariat Library, Chennai

Theosophical Society Library, Adyar, Chennai

Royal Asiatic Society, Bombay

Bombay University Library, Bombay

Nehru Memorial Museum Library.

Books :

Acton , Lord, *The Cambridge Modern History-III,* Cambridge, 1907, 1969

Aiya Nagam, V, *The Travancore State Manual- 1,* Trivandrum, 1906

Aiyangar, Krishnaswami, S, *Comemoration Volume,* Madras, 1936

Aiyer, Sathianada, R. & Aiyangar, Krishnaswami, S., *History of the Nayaks of Madura,* Oxford, 1924

Alexander, P.C, *The Dutch in Malabar,* Annamalai, 1946

Ali Sheikh, B., *British Relations with Haider Ali,* Mysore, 1963

Aquarone, J.B.(tr.), *D.João De Castro, Gouverneur et Vice-Roi des Indes Orientales (1500-1548),* vols. I & II, Paris, 1968

Arasaratnam, S., *Islamic Merchant Communities of the Indian Subcontinent in southeast Asia,* Kuala Lumpur, 1989

Arnold, T.W., *The Preaching of Islam,* London, 1935

Auber, Peter, *An Analysis of the Constitution of the East India Company and of the Laws Passed by Parliament,* London, 1826

Augur, C.M, *Church History of Travancore,* Madras, 1903

Ayyar, Krishna, K.V, A History of Kerala, Coimbatore, 1965

Baden-Powell, *The Land Systems of British India,* 3 vols., Oxford, 1982 (reprint)

Badger, Perry, George, (ed.), Jones, Winter, John, (tr.), *The Travels of Ludovico Di Varthema in Egypt, Syria, Arabia Deserta and Arabia Felix, in Persia, India and Ethiopia, A.D.1503 to 1508, New York, n.d.*

Barbosa, Duarte, *A Description of the coasts of East Africa and Malabar,* Trans.,Henry E.J.Stanley, London,1767

Barros, João de, *Decadas de Asia,* vol.1, Lisboa, 1778

Bartolomeo, Paolia Da San, *A Voyage to the East Indies,* London, trans.William Johnston 1800

Bayly, C.A., *The Raj : India and the British, 1600-1947,* London, 1990

_________, *Indian Society and the Making of the British Empire,* Cambridge, 1998

Bayly, Susan, *Saints, Goddesses and Kings : Muslims and Christians in south Indian society, 1700-1900,* Cambridge, 1989

Biddulph, John, *The Pirates of Malabar and an English Woman in India Two Hundred Years Ago,* London, 1907

Birdwood, George, Sir, *Report on the Old Records of the India Office,* London, 1891 (second reprint)

Bouchon, Geneviève, *Les Musulmans de Kérala à l'époque de la découverte Portugaise,* Genève, 1973

_________, *Mamale de Cananor – Un adversaire de l'Inde Portugaise* (1507-1528), Paris, 1975

_________, *L'Asie du Sud à l'époque des Grandes Découvertes,* London, 1987

Bowring, Levin, Sir, *Haider Ali and Tipu Sultan and the struggle with the Mussalman Powers of the South,* Oxford, 1893

Bristow, Robert, Sir, *Cochin Saga,* London, 1959

Brittlebank, Kate, *Tipu Sultan's search for legitimacy,* Delhi, 1997

Bruce, John, *Annals of the English East India Company-I and II,* London, 1810

Bruce, John, *Plans for the Government and Trade of Great British in the East Indies,* London, 1813

Buchanan Francis, *A Journey from Madras through the Countries of Mysore, Canara and Malabar,* Madras, 1870

Burn, Richard, ed, *The Cambridge History of India –IV,* London, 1937

Burnell, A.C.(ed.), *The Voyage of John Huygen Van Lischoten to the East Indies,* vol.I, London, 1885

Burton Francis, *Goa and the Blue Mountains,* London , 1851

Caldwell, Bishop, R, *A History of Tinnevelly*-Reprint, New Delhi, 1982

Chand, Tara, *Influence of Islam on Indian Culture,* Allahabad, 1963

Chatterton, Keble, E, *The Old East Indiamen,* London, 1914

Chaudhuri, K.N, *The English East India Company,* London, 1965

Chaudhuri, K.N, *The Trading World of Asia and the English East India Company 1660 – 1760,* Cambridge, 1978

Collins, Maurice, *British Merchant Adventures,* London, 1942

Connar and Ward, *Geographical and Statisical Memoir of the Survey of Travancore and Cochin State* Travancore, 1863

Courtier, John, Le, *Letter Chiefly from India Containing , «An Account of the Militiary Transactions of the* Coast of Malabar During the late War together with a short Description of the Religion, Manners *and Customs of the Inhabitants of Hindustan »,* London, 1790

Dahmen, Pierre, *Robert de Nobili, Apôtre des Brames,* III, Paris, 1931

Dale, Stephen, *Islamic Society in south Asian Frontier : The Mappillas of Malabar : 1498-1922,* Oxford, 1967

D'Albuquerque, Afonso, *Commentaries,* (tr.& ed. by Walter de Grey Birch, four volumes, London, 1875-1884

Dames, M.L.(tr. & ed.), *Book of Duarte Barbosa,* vols. I & II, London, MCMXXI 1621, 1989 (reprint)

Danver, F.C., *Report to the Secretary for India in Council on the Portuguese records relating to the East India contained in the Archivo Da Torre Do Tombo and the public libraries at Lisboa and Erora,* London, 1891

_________, *The Portuguese in India,* vols.I & II, London, 1894

Das Gupta, A, *Malabar in Asian Trade- 1740 – 1800,* London, 1914

Day, Francis, *The Land of Perumals,* Madras, 1863

Delacroix, S.(ed.), *Histoires Unverselles des Missions Catholiques – Les Missions Modernes,* II, Paris, 1957, p.44

Dellon, *Nouvelle Relation d'un Voyage fait aux Indes Orientales,* Amsterdam, M.DC.XCIX

Dodwell & Price, J.F. (trs.), *The Private Diary of Ananda Ranga Pillai, 1736-1761,* Madras, 1904-1908

Dowson, John (ed.), *The History of India as told by its own historians, The Muhammadan period.* eight volumes, London, 1867

Dumont, Louis, *Homo Hierarchicus.* Chicago, 1970

Du Val (ed.), *Voyage de Francis Pyrard de Laval,* trois parties, Paris, 1679

Duperron, Anquetil, *Voyage en Inde, 1754-1762,* Paris, 1997

Fawcett, Charles, *The English Factories in India : Bombay, Surat and Malabar Coast-III,* London, 1954

Forbes, James, *Oriental Memoires-I and II,* London, 1813

Forrest, Denys, *Tiger of Mysore,* London, 1970

Foster, William, *The Embassy of Sir Thomas Roe to the Court of the Great Mogul-1615-1619,* Nandeln, 1877, 1967

Fryer, John, *A New Account of East Indies and Persia bieng Nine Year's travels, 1672-1681,* vol.I, London, 1909

Galletti, A.(tr. & ed.), *The Dutch in Malabar,* Madras, 1911

Gardner, Brian, *The East India Company,* London, 1971

Ghurye, *Caste and Class in India,* Bombay, 1950

Gopalan, A.K., *Kerala – Past and Present,* London, 1959

Goulard, Simon, (tr.), *Histoire de Portugal contenant des Entreprises, Navigations et gestes mémorables des* Portugallois, tant en la conquête des Indes Orientales,par eux déscouvertes, qu'ès guerres *d'Afrique et autres exploits depuis l'an 1496 sous Emmanuel I, Jean III et Sébastien I,* Paris, 1587

Gray, Albert (tr.), *The Voyage of Francis Pyrard of Laval,* I, London, 1887

Grose, Henry, John, *A Voyage to East Indies,* (London, 1757)

________, *Voyages aux Indes Orientales* (tr. By G.Hernandez), London, 1758

Gundert, H., *Keralopatti,* Trivandrum, 1961

Guyon, Abbé, *Histoire des Indes Orientales, Anciennes et Modernes,* 3 volumes, Paris, 1699

Hamilton, Alexander, *A New Account of East Indies,* London, 1728

Hasan, Mohibbul, *History of Tipu Sultan,* Calcutta, 1951

Hirth Friedrich & Rockhill, W.W. (tr.), *Chau Ju-Kua: His work on the Cinese and Arab trade in the 12th and 13th centuries, entitled Chu-fan-chi,* St.Petersburg, 1911

Hough, James, *The History of Christianity in India- II,* London, 1839.

Hunter, W.W, A History of British India-I, London, 1899

Husain, Mahdi, *The Rehla of Ibn Batuta,* translation and commentary, Baroda, 1976

Ives, Edward, *A Voyage from England to India,* London, 1773

Irschick, Eugene, *Dialogue and History-Constructing, south India, 1795-1895,* Berkeley, 1994

Irvine, William (tr.), *Storia Do Mogor or Mogul India, 1653-1708,* by Niccoloa Manucci, four volumes, London, 1906-7

Iyengar, Srinivasa, P.T., *History of the Tamils,* Madras, 1929

Jeffrey, Robin, *The Decline of Nayar Dominance : Society and Politics in Travancore, 1847-1908,* New York, 1976

Keay, John, *The Honourable Company. A History of the English East India Company,* New York, 1991

Karashima, Noboru, *South Indian History and Society: Studies from Inscriptions A.D. 850-1800,* New Delhi, 1991

Kareem, C.K., *Kerala under Haidar and Tipu,* Cochin, 1973

Keith A.B, *A Constitutional History of India-1600-1935,* London, 1841

Khan, Shaffat, Ahmad, *The East India Trade in the XVIII Century,* London, 1923

Kincaud, Dennie, *British Social Life in India-1608- 1937,* London, 1938

Kosambi, D.D, *The Culture and Civilisation of Ancient India* in *Historical Outline,* London, 1965

Koshy, M.J., *Encyclopaedia of Kerala,* vol.XX, New Delhi, 1994

Kulke, H., Rothermund, D., *A History of India,* London, 1992 (reprint)

Kumar, Dharma, *Land and Caste in South India. Agricultural Labour in the Madras Presidency during the 19th century.* Cambridge, 1965

Kunju, Ibrahim, A.P, *Medieval Kerala History,* Trivandrum, 1975

Kunju, Ibrahim, A.P, *Rise of Travancore: A Study of the Life and Times of Martanda Varma,* Trivandrum, 1976

Latourette, K.S., *A History of the Expansion of Christianity,* III, New York, 1971

Legge, James (tr.), *Fa Hien, A Record of Buddhistic Kingdoms,* New York, 1965

Logan, William, *Malabar,* I, Madras, 1951

_________, *Malabar,* 2 vols., New Delhi, 1989 (reprint)

Logan, William, ed ., *A Collection of Treaties Engagements and Other papers of Importance Relating to British Affairs in Malabar-III,* Madras, 1891

Love Davison, Henry, Indian Record Series : Vesiges of Old Madras-II, London, 1913

Maclean, *Maclean's Manual of the Administration of the Madras Presidency,* Madras, 1938

Maistre de la Tour, *The History of Hyder Shah and Hyder Ali Khan Bahadur and of his son, Tippoo Sultan,* (revised and corrected by Gholam Mohamed, son of Tippoo Sultan), London, 1855

Major, R.H.(ed.), *India in the fifteenth Century,* New York, n.d.

Malgonkar, Manohar, *Kanhoji Angrey,* Bombay, 1959

Martineau, A., *Dupleix et l'Inde Française,* vol.II, Paris, 1923

_________, *Les Origines de Mahé,* Paris, 1917

_________, *Bussy et l'Inde Française, 1720-1785,* Paris, 1935

Mateer, Samuel, *Land of Charity,* London, 1871

Mateer, Samuel, *Native Life in Travancore,* London, 1883

Mathew, K.S., *Portuguese Trade with India in the 16th century,* Delhi, 1983

Mathew, K.S.(ed.), *Indian Ocean and Cultural Interaction, A.D.1400-1800,* Pondicherry, 1996

________, *French in India and Indian Nationalism (1700 A.D.-1963 A.D.),* vols. 1 & 2, New Delhi, 1999

Mayer, Adrian, C., *Land and Society in Malabar,* Oxford, 1952

Menon, Dilip, M., *Caste, Nationalism and Communism in south India : Malabar 1900-1948,* Cambridge, 1994

Menon, K.N., *Portuguese Pockets in India,* New Delhi, 1953

Menon, Padmanabha, *History of Kerala-I,* Ernakulam, 1924

Menon Shungoonny, *A History of Travancore,* Delhi, 1878, 1984

Menon, Sreedhara, A., *Kerala District Gazetteers,* Trivandrum, 1962-5

Menon, Sreedhara, A, *A Survey of Kerala History,* Kottayam, 1967, Madras, 1984

Mill, James, *History of India-I,* Delhi, 1817, 1972

Miller Roland, E, *Mappila Muslims of Kerala, A Study in Islamic Trends,* Madras, 1976

More, J.B.P., *The Political Evolution of Muslims in Tamilnadu and Madras, 1930-1947,* Hyderabad, 1997

________, *Freedom Movement in French India, The Mahe Revolt of 1948,* Thalessary, 2001

Moreland, W.H, *Akbar to Aurangzeb,* Delhi, 1972

Morelet, Arthur (tr.), *Journal du Voyage de Vasco da Gama,* Lyon, 1864

Mukherjee, Ramakrishna, *The Rise and Fall of the East India Company,* Berlin, 1955, 1957

Nainar, M.H., *Arab Geographer's Knowledge of Southern India,* Madras, 1942

Nair, Parameswaran, P.K., *History of the Malayalam Literature,* (translated from Malayalam by E.M.J.Venniyoor) New Delhi, 1967

Nair, Ramachandran, Adoor, *Slavery in Kerala,* Delhi, 1986

Nightingale Pamela, *Trade and Empire in Western India-1784-1806*, London, 1970

Narayanan, M.G.S., *Perumals of Kerala: Political and Social conditions of Kerala under the Cera Perumals of Makotai (A.D.800-1124)*, Calicut, 1996

__________, *Re-interpretations in South India History*, Trivandrum, 1977

Nolan E.H, *The Illustrated History of the British Empire in India and the East from the earliest times to the suppresssion of the Sepoy Mutiny in 1857 –I and II*, London, n.d.

Pannikkar, K.M, *Malabar and the Portuguese*, Bombay, 1929

Panikkar, K.M, *Asia and Western Dominance*, London, 1953, 1972

Pannikar, K.N., *Against Lord and State – Religion and Peasant Uprisings in Malabar, 1836-1921*, Delhi, 1989

Parry, J.H, *Trade and Dominion : The European Overseas Empire in the Eighteenth Century*, London, 1971

Philips, *An Account of the Religion, Manners and Learning of the People of Malabar in the East Indies*, London, 1717

Pillai, Velu, T.K, *A History of Travancore*, Trivandrum, 1935

Pillai, Velu, T.K, *The Travancore State Manual-I, II, III, IV*, Trivandrum, 1940

Pirès, Tomé, *The Suma Oriental, 1512-1515*, (tr.from Portuguese by Armanda Cortesao), 2 volumes, Nendeln, 1944, 1967 (reprint)

Podipara, J., Placid, (tr.from Malayalam), *The Vathamana-ppustakam* by Cathanar T.Paremmakal, Roma, 1971

Poonen, T.I, *Dutch Beginning in India Proper –1580- 1615*, Madras, 1933

Poonen T.I, *Dutch Hegemony in Malabar and its Collapse A.D-1663- 1795*, Trivandrum, 1978

Powell, Baden, *Land Systems of British India-I*, Oxford, 1892

Prasad, Ishwari, *India in the Eighteenth Century,* Allahabad, 1973

Prasad, R.C, *Early English Travellers in India,* Delhi, 1965

Raynal Abbe, *A Philosophical and Political History of the Settlement and Trade of the Europeans in the East and West Indies-II,* London, 1783

Reinaud, *Relation des Voyages faite par les arabes et persans,* 2 volumes, Paris, 1845

Renneville, R.C., *Recueil des Voyages de Schouten de la Compagnie des Indes Orientales,* vols.VI & VII, Amsterdam, 1725 (second edition)

Roberts, P.E, *History of British India,* London, 1938

Rockhill, W.W., Chau Ju Kua (Notes on the Relation and Trade of China), *T'oung-Pao,* Leiden, vols.XV,XVI, 1914-15

Romein, Jan, *The Asian Century,* London , 1962

Rowlandson, M.J.(tr.), *Tuhfat al Mujahideen,* London, 1833

Ruthnaswamy, M, *Some Influence that made the British Administrative System in India,* London, 1939

Saint Barthélémy, Paulin de, *Voyage aux Indes Orientales,* trois volumes, Paris, 1808

Sastri, Nilakanta, *The Colas,* Madras, 1975 (reprint)

_________, *A History of south India,* Madras, 1966

Sekhar, A.C., *Evolution of Malayalam,* Poona, 1953

Sen, Surendranath, *Indian Travels of Thevenot and Careri,* New Delhi, 1949

Sen, S.P, *The French in India, 1763-1816,* Calcutta, 1951, Delhi, 1971

Sewell, Robert (compiler), *A Sketch of the Dynasties of Southern India,* Madras, 1883

Sinha, Krishna , Narendra, *Haider Ali,* Calcutta, 1941

Smith, George, *The Student Geography of India,* London, 1882

Stanley, Henry, J.,(tr.), *The Three Voyages of Vasco Da Gama and his Viveroyalty from the Lendas da India of Gaspar Correa*, New York, MDCCCLXIX

Stein, Burton, *Peasant State and Society in Medieval South India*, Delhi, 1980

Subrahmanyam, S., *The Political Economy of Commerce, Southern India, 1500-1650*, Cambridge, 1990

Temple, R.C., Sir, (ed.), *The Papers of Thomas Bowrey, 1669-1713*, London, 1927

Tennent, J.E., *Ceylon*, volumes I & II, London, 1860

Thapar, Romila, *From Lineage to State*, Bombay, 1984

Thomas, P, *Christians and Christianity in India and Pakistan*, London, 1954

Thorton, Edmond, *History of British Empire in India-I*, London, 1841

Thurston, Edgar, *History of the Coinage of the Territories of the East India Company in the Indian Peninsula-II*, Madras, 1890

_________, *Castes and Tribes of southern India*, vols.II & VII, Madras, 1909

Van Rheede, Henrick, Adriaan, *Memoir written in the year 1677 A.D.*, Madras, 1911

Varmaraja K.Rama, *A Contribution to the History of Cochin*, Trichur, 1914

Veluthat, Kesavan, *Brahman Settlements in Kerala*, Calicut, 1978

_________, The Political Structure of Early Medieval South India, New Delhi, 1993

Visscher, Jacob, Canter, *Letters from Malabar*, Madras, 1862

Watson, Bruce, Ian, *Foundations for Empire* : English Private Trade in India 1659-1760, Delhi, 1980

Weber, Max, *The Religion of India : The Sociology of Hinduism and Buddhism*, New York, 1958

Welsh, James, *Military Reminiscence-II*, London, 1830

Wheeler, Talboys, J, *A History of English Settlements in India*, Calcutta, 1878

Wicquefort, A. De (tr.), *Voyages célèbres et remarquables faits de Perse aux Indes Orientales*, by Jean-Bebert de Mandelso, 2 volumes, Amsterdam, M.DCCC.XXVII, 1727

Yule, Henry ed., *The Book of Marcopolo-II*, London, 1903

________, (tr.&ed.), *Cathay and the Way Thither*, 2 volumes, London, 1866

________, *Hobson-Jobson, A Glossary of Colloquail Anglo-Indian Words and Phrases, and of kindred terms, Etymological, Historical, Geogrphical and Discursive*, London, 1903

MALAYALAM

Pillai, Parameshwaran, G, *Velu Thampi Dalawa*, Quilon, 1964

Pillai, Kunjan, Elamkulam, P.N, *Kerala Charithrathile Iruladanja Edukal*, Kottayam, 1967

________, *Unnunilisandesam Caritradristiyilkuti*, Trivandrum, 1953

Moothathu, Pachu, Vaikathu, *Thiruvithamkoor Charithram*, Cochin, 1867, 1986

ARTICLES :

Aiyar, L.V.R., 'A fifteenth Century Malayalam Prose Text', *The Maharaja's College Magazine*, Ernakulam, 21, 1, Sept.1938

Ayyangar, Srinivas, Tamil Studies, Journal of Annamalai University, 21, 1957

Bayly, C.A., 'The Pre-History of Communalism? Religious Conflict in India, 1700-1860', *Modern Asian Studies*, vol.19, No.2, 1985, pp.177-203

Dale, Stephen, F., 'The Islamic Frontier in south-west India. The Shahid, a cultural ideal among the Mappilas of Malabar', *Modern Asian Studies*, II, I, February, 1977

Gurukkal, Rajan, 'From Clan and lineage to Hereditary Occupations and caste in Early South India, (in), Dev Nathan(ed.), *From Tribe to Caste*, 1997

_________, 'Charecterising Ancient Society: The Case of South India', Indian History Congress, 59th Session: Ancient India Section Presidential Address, Panjabi University, Patiala, 28-30 Dec, 1998

Hardgrave, Robert, L., jr., 'The Mappilla Rebellion, 1921 : Peasant Revolt in Malabar', *Modern Asian Studies*, II, 1, 1977,. pp.57-99

Kieniewwiez, Jan, The Portuguese Factory and Trade in Pepper in Malabar during the 16th Century-Indian Economic and Social History Reiew- Vol. VI, No.I, (March, 1969).

Kunju, Ibrahim, « Umayamma Rani » Journal of Kerala Studies- 11 March, 1975

More, J.B.P., 'Some maritime aspects of the Indian Ocean region, 1660-1760', K.S.Mathew (ed.), *Indian Ocean and Cultural Interaction (A.D.1400-1800)*, Pondicherry, 1996

_________, 'West European and Mughal Interaction during the reign of Aurangzeb', Pius Malekandathil & T.Jamal Mohammad, *The Portuguese, Indian Ocean and European Bridgeheads*, Tellicherry, 2001

Veluthat, Kesavan, 'Into the « Medieval » - and out of it: Early South India in Transition', Presidential Address, Section II: Medieval History Congress. Indian History Congress, 58th session, Bangalore, Nov.14-16, 1997

Wood, Conrad, 'The first Moplah Rebellion against British rule in Malabar', *Modern Asian Studies*, vol.10, 4, Oct.1976, pp.543-556

Miscellaneous :

The Calcutta Review-Volume CVII July 1898

Leena, P.K., 'The History of the English East India company's Settlement at Anjengo', Ph.D. Dissertation, University of Calicut, 1989

Livros das Monções, Lisboa, 1889

Travancore Archaelogical Series, Trivandrum

Wallis, John, 'A short Treatise by way of essay of Attinga on the Malabar coast', 1721

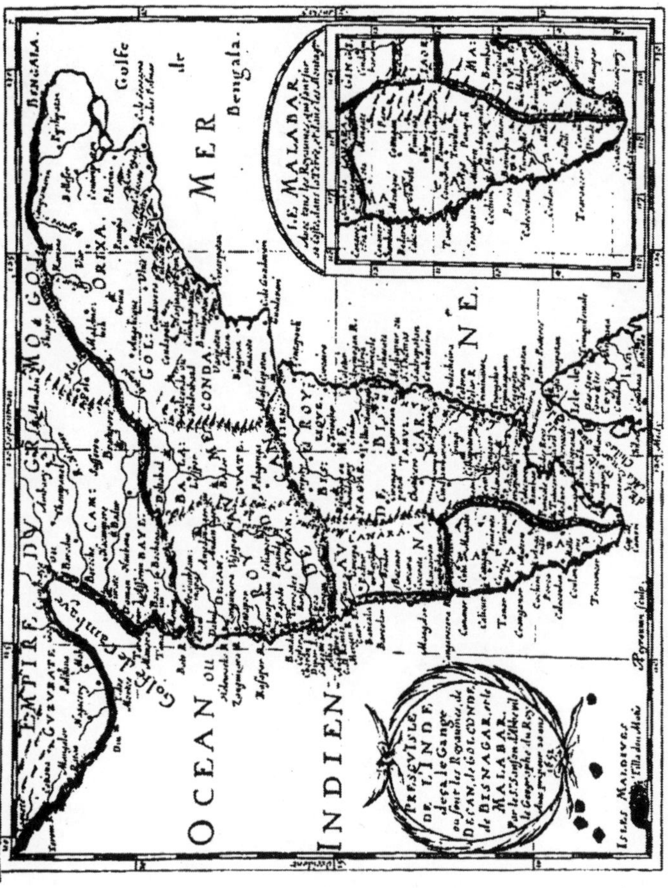

MAP OF THE PENINSULA OF INDIA. (DANVER, 1894)

From "L'Asie," par le Sieur Sanson d' Abbeville, Geographe d'ordinaire du Roy-Paris, 1652.

INDEX